Wellington the Beau

Wellington the Beau

THE LIFE AND LOVES OF THE DUKE OF WELLINGTON

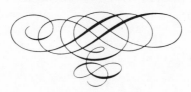

PATRICK DELAFORCE

THE WINDRUSH PRESS · GLOUCESTERSHIRE

To Jill

First published in Great Britain by
The Windrush Press,
Windrush House,
Adlestrop,
Moreton-in-Marsh,
Gloucestershire
1990

British Library Cataloguing in Publication Data
Delaforce, Patrick 1923–
    Wellington the beau: the life and loves of the Duke of Wellington.
    1. Great Britain. Wellington, Arthur Wellesley, Duke of
    1769–1852
    I. Title
    941.07002

    ISBN 0–900075–76–7

Typeset by DP Photosetting, Aylesbury, Bucks
Printed and bound by Biddles Ltd, Guildford

CONTENTS

AUTUMN

INDIAN SUMMER

INTRODUCTION

The day after he had been gazetted Duke of Wellington, Arthur Wellesley rode on a white horse into Paris, dressed modestly in a plain blue frock-coat and wearing a round top hat.

By May 1814 his fame as the conqueror of all the French armies in Portugal, Spain and southern France had made him a hero to the British public. Admired and envied by one sex, he was shortly to be courted and loved by the other.

During his long life he earned many nicknames. His veterans referred to him as 'Arty' or 'Atty', even 'Nosey' for obvious reasons. His Iberian officers called him the 'Peer' and sometimes 'Old Douro' after his audacious crossing of that river. To the Spaniards he was known as the 'Eagle', and later on his favourite niece's children would call him 'Dukey'. His two closest women friends were later to refer to him as the 'Magician'. The public, for a variety of reasons, would eventually name him the 'Iron Duke'. But many of his close friends in the army and in the 'bon ton' had already christened him 'Beau'. During the Peninsular campaign an excited Guards officer early one morning rushed into army HQ asking 'Has anyone seen Beau Douro?' A recumbent figure on the ground swathed in a black boat-cloak rose quickly and replied, 'Well! by God, I never knew I was a Beau before!'

The definition of a beau is that of a man who is either a fop, a ladies' man or a lover. Wellington certainly was not a fop.

His mother, Anne Hill, the Countess of Mornington, was mainly instrumental in forming his attitudes to the opposite sex. She was a lady of strong character with high principles and a very strict sense of duty. She treated her younger son Arthur (Richard was the more brilliant eldest son) as dunce of the family. According to Sir Herbert Maxwell, the Duke's earliest biographer, Arthur annoyed his mother with 'his slow thick speech and dull manner which gave him an air of stupidity'.

His father Garret Wesley, 1st Earl of Mornington, died when the boy was aged twelve, and a few years later his mother is reported (by Sir

Herbert Maxwell again) as having said 'I vow to God I don't know what I shall do with my awkward son Arthur, he was food for powder and nothing more.' Not content with this, she wrote of him in 1787 when, aged 18, he had proudly shown her his first scarlet army jacket, 'Arthur has put on his red coat for the first time today. Anyone can see he has not the cut of a soldier!'

No wonder he grew up with very distinct views on women!

What did the Beau look like? Many portraits have been painted of him by John Hoppner, Robert Home, Francisco Goya, by Lady Burghersh (his niece), Sir Thomas Lawrence and others. In addition there are several very detailed descriptions of his physique. He had a robust frame with broad shoulders, strong chest, long arms and a height of 5 foot, 10 inches. He rode considerable distances, hunted into his seventies and walked in the parks and countryside, often with an elegant lady on his arm. His long-sighted eyes were a dark violet blue-grey colour and were often described as 'piercing'. He had a long grave face in repose, with a not very high forehead, straight and prominent eyebrows, a long Roman nose (responsible for one nickname), a broad underjaw and a strongly marked chin. His hair was plentiful, curly and black in his youth, cropped short for his campaign, and went white as silver in his old age without a trace of baldness. He had a loud booming distinct laugh and was always quick to take or exchange a joke or anecdote.

On campaign he wore a blue or grey frock-coat, a cocked hat covered with oilskin and grey 'trowsers'. He had several cloaks; grey, for nightwork and sleeping rough. His low cocked hat rarely had a plume. The boots known as 'Wellingtons' were his own invention: outside his trousers he wore gaiters of strong leather which overlapped and were fastened with straps and buckles. He rarely wore a sash except on the occasions of reviews and balls when he wore his full red uniform with decorations. He preferred to wear the Order of the Garter under his left knee, the Golden Fleece suspended round his neck, and seldom wore his full collection of ribbons, medals and orders.

He kept to simple and severe habits; rising early, retiring late, eating very little and drinking still less, which was quite remarkable in his time and age. Arthur Wellesley spent most of the years of his youth from 27 to 36 campaigning in India, and in the Iberian Peninsula, aged 39 to 45, so that it was as a middle-aged man that he took the hearts of the beautiful ladies in London and Paris by storm. The magnetism of this handsome conqueror even affected Bonaparte's mistresses, although all remarked on his simple modesty, at odds with his military fame. No matter where he went – to India, to Portugal, to Spain, to France and

Belgium and back in England – it was the young, beautiful, *married* ladies who succumbed.

'Colonel Wellesley had at that time a very susceptible heart particularly towards . . . married ladies.' After his romantic conquest of Brussels and Paris he was asked if he had received much female adulation and he answered honestly 'Oh yes! Plenty of that! Plenty of that!'

Throughout his life he kept portraits of his '*inamorata*' in his office or study wherever that happened to be. In Apsley House a portrait of pretty Mrs Freese once had pride of place. In Paris Wellington kept portraits of Napoleon's ladies (now *his* ladies) on view: the singer La Grassini as well as a print of Pauline Borghese (Napoleon's youngest and most beautiful sister), with ironically the Pope in the centre, presumably keeping the peace. Portraits of the American Mrs Patterson and the lovely Lady Charlotte Greville were also to be seen by those privileged to penetrate into the Duke's private sanctuary at Stratfield Saye – but pride of place was later given to Harriet Fane, Mrs Arbuthnot, with whom the Duke had his longest and most steadfast relationship of all. It is clear that the Wellesley family marital relationships were usually, if not always, disastrous!

Richard Wellesley, later Lord Wellesley and the Earl of Mornington, lived for many years with a beautiful French actress-courtesan named Gabrielle Rolland who bore him five children. He eventually married her and then commenced a series of notorious affairs with the courtesans, Harriette Wilson and Moll (also known as Sally Douglas). His second and final marriage in 1825 to his brother's early and long-lasting flame Marianne Patterson née Caton, infuriated the Duke beyond measure.

The other brothers fared little better. Henry and Gerald Wellesley had each married daughters of Lord Cadogan who were, in turn to desert them.

When Wellington was in Paris at the height of his fame as the conqueror of Waterloo, the whole city was at his feet but Madame de Staël, who in the last three years of her life came to know the Duke very well, wrote 'Never has God created a great man with less expenditure . . . he has "*pas de coeur pour l'amour*".' Lady Granville wrote in June 1817:

> The Duke of Wellington in Paris with neither love nor hatred to display, his wife being at Cambray and his loves dispersed over the earth so '*il se laisse admirer*' as a great hero with very simple unaffected manners.

Spring

Chapter One

A YOUNG MAN
IN IRELAND

1769 was a vintage year for heroes.

The most famous pair of protagonists the world has ever seen were born in that year: a Corsican called Napoleon Bonaparte, and in the Anglo-Irish society of Dublin, young Arthur Wesley. The former shot like a meteor to fame, to immense power, and finally fell to ignominious defeat, captivity and isolation on a small Atlantic island. The latter, a very slow starter indeed, climbed steadily and tenaciously to middle-aged military fame. But, unlike Napoleon, the future Prince of Waterloo, went on climbing until he was entrenched in British folklore as the Iron Duke, the Peer, the Dandy, Nosey, Old Douro and the Beau. To the end of his long distinguished life the Duke of Wellington was loved by many beautiful ladies, by dozens of small children and, after Waterloo, was respected throughout Europe as a professional politician and diplomat.

Arthur Wesley was born on May Day at No. 5 Merrion Street, Dublin. He was the sixth child (the first Arthur and the first William had already died) of cultured and distinctly non-military parents. His father was the eccentric Garret Wesley, Lord Mornington, who, for a gentleman, was a remarkably good musician and amateur architect. Mornington had married Anne Hill in 1759, the strong-minded eldest daughter of the future Lord Dungannon.

Young Arthur was born and bred an aristocrat among the essentially frivolous Anglo-Irish society. The young sprigs of gentry and nobility raced their horses, drank their claret, hunted, danced and gambled. They went to balls, concerts and genteel picnics against a background of rural poverty, impoverished tenant farmers and a great deal of urban misery. The barons, privy councillors, bishops, members of the Irish parliament, and the untrained non-military young captains, majors and colonels lived off rents, mortgaged their Palladian-style mansions, follies and temples in their estates – and lived for the morrow. It was a thoroughly irresponsible and amusing life.

One aspect of this cheerful upbringing was that young Arthur, when he grew out of his moody introspective adolescence, became the boisterous centre of social activity wherever he went, whether he was campaigning in India or the Peninsular, or taking part in the sophisticated lifestyle of society in Paris, Brussels, Vienna, Madrid and later in London. Although he had but one sister and an unfriendly mother his formative years in Dublin society taught him how to behave with the Fair Sex. He was able to talk to them, to flirt, to dance with them, and to behave in a courteous, civilised manner. Many contemporary diarists noted how frequently he was 'in good spirits' and how his loud characteristic laugh boomed above the jollity and the chit-chat of society.

The Wesley family had a town house in Dublin and a sumptuous mansion known as Dangan Castle set in an estate with lakes, ponds, trees and follies. So although money flowed for the Wesley parents and for their beloved first-born Richard it was less plentiful further down the line – and became even more so – on Lord Mornington's death when Arthur was twelve. To the fourth surviving child, the 'dunce' of the family, came curtailment of his time at public school, no prospects of university, only second-rate tutoring, temporary exile (with his mother in Brussels), a rather time-wasting year in France and, above all, little money for purchase of army rankings. Young officers were rarely promoted on account of efficiency or by luck – progress depended on deployment of capital. No capital meant no promotion. Of course, once above a certain rank battles won meant promotion, honours, grants of money and often loot.

Arthur's education had been undistinguished. The Diocesan School at Trim near Dublin which was known as Talbot's Castle, was followed by a short spell at a preparatory school called Brown's establishment in Chelsea. He entered Eton in 1781, the year his eccentric father died and Richard succeeded to the title as Lord Mornington. Outshone by all his brothers, including the two young ones, Arthur was removed in 1784 from Nayler's house to allow the scanty family funds to be deployed on Gerald and Henry. A few months followed with a tutor in Brighton, before the impoverished Lady Mornington whisked him away to Brussels for a year. Arthur had learned little at any of his schools, and he learned nothing in Brussels apart from a little French language and some violin playing. He made few friends at any of his schools – perhaps he was not at any one of them long enough to nourish friendships. He played no games – no cricket, no fives. This sad, lonely and forlorn child was seen to observe but never to participate. Derided as 'awkward and backward' by his family, his mother and eldest brother decided arbitrarily that he was not worth spending money on to keep him at school. In class Wesley major (Arthur) was classified in 53rd place, and Wesley minor (Gerald) a year or so younger sat in 54th place (out of 79).

Trivial anecdotes abound about Arthur's schooldays. He was seen to be 'lounging and watching'. He engaged in fisticuffs with 'Bobus' Smith at Eton (and won) and with a young blacksmith (and lost). He was seen jumping over a wide black, boggy ditch. He played childlike tricks in various gardens. Later he reminisced about the maids at Eton, and was quoted as making up a laborious jape about a mythical elopement. Nothing of consequence emerged from his schooldays.

In later life he admitted to his biographer Glieg, that he had been a 'dreamy, idle and shy lad' who refused to take part in any games and he was observed as being 'quiet, dejected and observant.' His inertia was partly due to ill-health, throughout his life he was subject to heavy colds, and in his campaigning days in India and the Peninsula he suffered from rheumatism, lumbago and ague. As his frame grew in height and weight, he remained spare and lean. He dismissed his frequent illness as 'something to be got the better of.' The subject of health was to become of great importance to him, because without healthy soldiers in his armies, he would lose battles. The care and cleanliness of his soldiers' feet and legs was vital – no marching soldiers, no campaigns.

Once he laboured through the difficult stages of adolescence his energy grew apace. Soon he was able to ride up to a hundred miles a day and was to hunt all his life. His shooting was haphazard although his eyesight was superb until his late seventies but his hearing suffered in later life due to a remarkably stupid ear-surgeons's treatment. He ate sparingly and in a hard drinking era, drank relatively little. He believed in unusual medicaments such as vinegar rubbing to stimulate the limbs. In short he took as much care of himself and his troops as was compatible with the everyday risks (riding in the rain for five hours, bivouacing in the open on a windswept slope). His tall strong figure on his horse 'Copenhagen' looming on the horizon was worth ten thousand, twenty thousand, or more, troops in a tight-run battle. In the field his stamina and tenacity became proverbial. He needed but a few hours sleep each night and his energy taxed the resources of officers and men half his age.

After a year of inactivity at Brussels with his mother chez M. Louis

Goubert, it was decided '*faute de mieux*' that her awkward son 'food for powder and nothing more' should be speeded on his way to a military career. In the late nineteenth century there were no military colleges such as Sandhurst. Provided a gentleman could ride and occasionally charge, then he was thought to be perfectly suited to become an officer. So in 1786, to Angers on the Loire went 'Young Arthur' to attend the Royal Academy of Equitation. With a Scots governor by his side (later to become General Sir A. Mackenzie), with several boon companions (Messrs Walsh, Fortescue and Wingfield), and under a degree of supervision from the director, Marquis Marcel de Pignerolle, the seventeen-year-old youth was set to work. His riding skills were polished up. He became a hard-riding, practical and ungraceful horse-man, which was to stand him in great stead in the next twenty years. He took lessons in fencing, basic mathematics and dancing. But he was still ill and listless much of the time, playing rather defensively with his small dog Vick. His allowance must have been very small but he and his friends gambled for small stakes under the eye of Madame de Pignerolle. The 'groupe des lords', as the Wesley group were called (there were 116 British students out of the 334 youths at the Academy), were encouraged to meet the local society. In their pretty uniforms of scarlet coats, sky-blue facings and yellow buttons, the cadets were an amusing *divertissement* for the Dukes of Praslin and Brissac and their ladies. Arthur met and liked the Duchesse of Sabran (and greeted her most warmly in Paris no less than twenty-eight years later). The storming of the barricades at the Bastille was three years ahead and some of the Angers gentry, including the Duc de Brissac and M. de Pignerolle went to the guillotine.

There are conflicting views on Arthur's performance at Angers during 1786. M. de Pignerolle claimed that his Irish '*pensionnaire*' had promise. His governor Mr Mackenzie remembered him as lacking in physical endurance. Later as general he ventured to ask Arthur, after Waterloo, to explain the great change that had occurred in that period. 'Ah, that is India' was the answer, referring to the hundreds of miles ridden and marched on dusty plains under hot skies fighting not only Indian armies but also constant disease, illness and alcoholic hospitality.

The Beau was growing up although he had made few friends at Angers and learned nothing of military techniques. Later he was described as speaking the language '*bravement*', the way he fought the French.

On his return to London at the end of 1786 his mother noticed him at the Haymarket Theatre. 'I do believe there is my ugly boy Arthur,' she is quoted as saying of him. Richard promptly solicited a commission for him from the Duke of Rutland, then Lord Lieutenant of Ireland. Richard described his young brother as 'perfectly idle . . . it is a *matter of indifference* to me what commission he gets, provided he gets it soon.' The relationship between the two brothers is perfectly illustrated by this request. The Wesley family managed to purchase for his eighteenth birthday the first step in what was destined to be a famous career. Not that the position of ensign in the 73rd Highland Regiment, then serving in India, was much to boast of! Richard had previously declined for him a commission in the artillery, possibly because mathematics were known not to be one of Arthur's strong points. Wellington's formidable rival to-be across the Channel was coincidentally being commissioned into the French artillery.

Richard was now twenty-seven and had been given a seat on the English Board of Treasury. He and Lady Mornington had persuaded his temporary patron Lord Buckingham, the new Lord Lieutenant of Ireland, to take young Arthur on as one of his ADCs for ten shillings a day. Arthur was thus gazetted lieutenant in the 76th Regiment (the Highlanders in India were forgotten) on Christmas Day 1787. By now his total income was £300 per annum, just sufficient for a young blade to support himself. There is no doubt that Richard as head of the family was taking his duties towards the younger children seriously. Sister Anne was being 'finished' for society and groomed for marriage in two years' time. The younger boys were still at Eton and Richard, despite his French mistress and children, found the money for their school fees. And yet another military transfer took place in the New Year to the 41st Foot to enable Arthur *not* to go on service to the East Indies. *Mirabile dictu* Lady Mornington had decided that her eighteen-year-old son was now presentable.

> I must do everything for him . . . as he is really a very charming young man, never did I see such a change for the better in any body, he is wonderfully lucky, in six months he has got two steps in the army and appointed Aid de Camp to Lord Buckingham which is ten shillings a day.

Moreover his mother's eccentric friends at Llangollen described him as 'a charming young man. Handsome, fashioned, tall and elegant.'

The viceregal court in Dublin taught Arthur all he needed to know about Society. He fetched and carried for Lord Buckingham and the vicereine; ordered their supper and tidied up after their guests. He attended many parties, rode, danced at St Patrick's Hall, gambled, and predictably was soon in debt. There was some time for reading, which enabled him to catch up with part of his lost education. He had time to play the violin. Richard's patronage was repaid by some estate business and management in Ireland. He exchanged yet again into the Twelfth Dragoons – a rather smarter regiment.

Several anecdotes survive from this period. One young lady refused to go on a picnic if Arthur 'that mischievous boy' was also included. Not listless now! Another beauty, Lady Aldborough, was bored with him at a ball, abandoned him to the musicians and went home with another beau called Cradock. Arthur was living on Lower Ormond Quay and was probably behind with his rent since his landlord, a friendly bootmaker, kept his more pressing creditors at bay.

Mrs St George, a notable journal-keeper, was loaned Dangan Castle for her honeymoon and wrote of Arthur that he was 'extremely good humoured,' and the object of much attention from the female part of what was called 'a very gay society'. He was fined for brawling with a Frenchman. Colonel George Napier thought he had the makings of a great general but other Napiers disagreed and thought him a 'shallow saucy stripling'. A visitor to Dangan Castle found him reading 'an Essay Concerning Human Understanding' by Locke. Arthur became a freemason of the Trim Lodge No. 494, County Meath and thought and talked about local politics. Richard had been an MP since 1784 and younger brother William, now aged twenty-six, was found an English seat. Mr Henry Grattan, the great Irish orator, praised Dublin's first *independent* parliament and criticised the British aristocracy entrenched at the castle who fought to keep the *status quo*. In March 1790 Arthur made his first political speech in Trim and lambasted Mr Grattan before an audience of eighty. Richard wrote approvingly from Westminster and when the Irish parliament dissolved that spring Arthur was returned for Trim which was a good safe Westminster-sponsored seat. Next year he was promoted to command a company in the 58th Foot in the Irish establishment but soon exchanged into the 18th Light Dragoons. His life was very much of a pattern. On duty at the castle, living in Grafton Street, rare speeches in the House of Commons, managing the mortgaged Dangan Castle estates to provide part of Richard's income. Music and concerts (he still played the violin), riding, walks for wagers, occasional hunting, dances and balls and picnics. An ideal life for a young man without a care in the world and little thought for the morrow. One doubts whether the French Revolution conjured up possible thoughts of war. Arthur just changed one handsome scarlet uniform for another.

In 1792 France was in turmoil and had become a republic. The family mansion at Dangan Castle was for sale. Richard was spreading his wings in Westminster, making his way under William Pitt. The young ADC was now twenty-three and had just met a pretty young woman called Kitty Pakenham.

Chapter Two

COURTING KITTY

Pakenham Hall on the outskirts of Castlepollard is sixty miles due west of Dublin. It had been the home of the Longford family for over three centuries. 'Lady Longford's Lily' was the sobriquet for the Hon. Catherine Dorothea Sarah Pakenham, one of the belles of Dublin in 1792. She was the second child of the 2nd Baron Longford, an Anglo-Irish Royal Naval landowner. Her mother was born Catherine Rowley, a strong-willed Protestant lady related to the Edgeworths, so that young Catherine, or Kitty, grew up with young Maria Edgeworth, destined to become an author of repute. The Longfords were a family of substance and they expected, indeed demanded, that their daughters married men of equal substance.

Kitty was born in 1772 and was three years younger than Arthur Wesley, she was an attractive girl: small, slim, with grey eyes and a lovely rosy complexion, who soon became one of the Dublin beauties. Maria Edgeworth, her closest friend, was also small, but darker, perhaps more intellectual and less attractive. Both girls were lively and gossipy and enjoyed reading and painting, but Kitty was more religious, wrote poems in a romantic style, and her generosity to the needy was praiseworthy. Like most Anglo-Irish families the Pakenhams and the Wesleys were connected by marriage. The two families owned town houses in Dublin and Dangan Castle was halfway between Pakenham Hall and Dublin so that it was inevitable that the 'Longford Lily' would meet Arthur Wesley, the dashing young ADC to the Lord Lieutenant of Ireland. Indeed they probably met, and possibly played together as children at Summerhill, home of her cousins the Langfords, adjacent to Dangan Castle.

Although Arthur Wesley and Kitty Pakenham met and soon fell in love the auspices were unfavourable. The young man now a captain in the 58th Foot and local member of parliament for Trim, was on the face of it a reasonable match. They had at that stage many friends, family and interests in common, including music, and perhaps even books and literature. She was certainly one of the most attractive young women at the Dublin Castle revelries. Unfortunately her brother Tom was dead set against any understanding. On Tom's grandmother's death he was due to become an earl, and he made it clear that a debt-ridden captain of the Foot with no prospects was no match for his sister. Nevertheless, Arthur persisted and made an official proposal for Kitty's hand in the spring of 1793. The penniless captain was soon refused by the family and he was given a homily by Kitty's father. In those days the girl's feelings were rarely considered and Lord Longford and his son Tom next turned down Arthur as a captain in the 18th Light Dragoons, then as a major and finally as a lieutenant-colonel in the 33rd Foot. Richard had been quite easily persuaded to pay for these new promotions during the year. Kitty's brother was a major at seventeen and friends of Arthur's were colonels at twenty-one since no military skill was needed, just money and influence.

In January 1793 Arthur made a speech in the Dublin parliament in which he defended Lord Westmorland the viceroy, deplored the imprisonment of Louis XVI and the invasion of the Netherlands by the French. Prime Minister Pitt said there would be peace for fifteen years. The next month the French king was dead and France declared war on England, and Arthur rather half-heartedly started his military career in earnest. He burned his violin and vowed to give up or reduce his gambling at cards, he even set aside a couple of hours a day for study. News of the Terror in France swept England. His future friend Madame de Staël was one of the refugees from Paris to escape the 'September massacres', but his French acquaintances in Angers perished. Danton rallied, Marat died and Captain Bonaparte soldiered with his battery of guns at Avignon.

The young man of twenty-four was described by Sir Jonah Barrington the lawyer and wit as being of 'juvenile appearance and unpolished address but frank, open-hearted and popular'. His occasional speeches in parliament were not successful and rarely on important subjects. Rejected by the Pakenham family Arthur drifted along. He drilled his men of the 33rd Foot and made an efficient job of the regimental accounts. He asked brother Richard to request Prime Minister Pitt and Lord Westmorland to put him in the flank corps (to see some action) for the proposed military campaign to Flanders.

The protocol of the day insisted that the suitor, once rejected, could not continue to make visits to Pakenham Hall and pay court, so as to leave the coast clear for other possible swains. Tom Pakenham and his mother bullied timid little Kitty in this way. Letters between the two were officially proscribed! Arthur was still ADC at the castle and continued to meet Kitty, almost certainly chaperoned, at balls and other festivities. The viceroy, Lord Westmorland, rather approved of Arthur's attempted match.

For Kitty the year of 1793 must have been the most traumatic in her life. The horrors in Paris and the awful final chapter for the French royal family must have been the first shock. Shortly after Lord Longford's refusal to allow her courtship by Arthur to continue, her father died. Despite the parties and balls for her twenty-first birthday another tragedy loomed. She was a great favourite of her grandmother Elizabeth, Countess of Longford, who died in January 1794, and the countess had favoured a match between the two young lovers and with her death, Arthur's hopes receded. Just before the Duke of York took his famous 30,000 men to climb a hill in the flat Low Countries, Arthur wrote a despairing and final letter to Kitty. With his new rank and commanding an annual income of about £500 he made a second unsuccessful proposal to the implacable Tom Pakenham, now the earl, and his widowed mother.

> If this letter should reach you I hope you will impute my troubling you this second time to the fear I have that my first letter may have offended. It never was intended to offend and if any expression it contained could at all tend to give offence, I hope that the determination I have just received is, in your eyes, a sufficient punishment for a crime of much greater magnitude.
>
> As Lord Longford's determination is founded upon prudential motives and may be changed should my situation be altered before I return to Ireland, I hope you will believe that should anything occur which may induce you and him to change your minds, *my mind will remain the same*. In the meantime with best wishes for your happiness, believe me your most obedient servant A. Wesley.

So, Arthur on his way to his first campaign in Holland had committed himself, in his opinion, for ever. The 33rd Foot sailed in June and spent nineteen days at sea before reaching Ostend, where Arthur soon found himself commanding a brigade of three battalions. The Duke of York's little army and the Dutch troops now endeavoured to keep the French invaders at bay. It was an ignominious campaign. The French seized the ports and after a series of minor actions at Boxtel, Nijmegen and Arnhem the British troops retreated through Germany and eventually re-embarked at Bremen in April 1795. Arthur had mildly distinguished himself in the Boxtel skirmish and learned a certain amount of the hardships of war in the long Dutch winter. Illness, disease, the winter ice and snow killed many more British troops than fell to French shot and bayonet. Back at HQ Prince Adolphus reported that 'the life was not the most amusing: we are however now pretty well off for girls and this renders it less tiresome!'

In rather cavalier fashion Arthur abandoned his regiment in Bremen, and when they were next stationed in Essex left them behind again. In the meantime his elder brother Richard had eventually made an honest women of his French mistress and married her in London. They had already produced five children and this scandalous relationship had shocked the rather prudish Pakenham family and further reduced Arthur's chances.

During 1795 Arthur spent his time mainly in Dublin, still as MP for Trim and ADC at the castle. He continued to make occasional speeches in parliament and from time to time visited London to see his brother Richard and ladies of the town. He soldiered half-heartedly with the remnants of his 33rd Foot, who had suffered heavily on the retreat from Holland to Germany the previous winter.

He met Kitty on many occasions at the usual festivities, dinners, theatres, concerts and balls, but the embargo remained on writing to her and visiting her at Pakenham Hall. In his frustration he decided to leave the army, and applied to the lord lieutenant and to Richard for a post in the Irish Revenue and Treasury Boards. After all he had made a good job of the regiment's account books – but he had no luck. He was not at all well that autumn and winter: unhappiness and frustration can be debilitating, and his strong physique was always prone to colds and fevers. Orders to sail to the West Indies with his regiment were thwarted by intense gales in November, December and January.

Shortly after the New Year of 1796 he was made full colonel of the 33rd and, although an invalid convalescing in Dublin in April, sailed for India in June. His regiment had already sailed and he expected to rejoin them at the Cape, having settled most of his debts and said farewell to his constituents at Trim. As the ill, unhappy and frustrated twenty-seven-year-old soldier sailed south, his Gallic rival across the Channel had already won spectacular victories at Lodi, Mentenotte and Mondovi.

And pretty little Kitty, the 'Longford Lily', was left behind in gay Dublin.

Chapter Three

'THAT IS ALL INDIA'

The young pink-faced bachelor left Portsmouth in the summer of 1796 on the S.S. *Rockingham* with a large library and high hopes. Nine years later he returned with a smaller, more frivolous library, a small fortune, loaded with honours and still a bachelor – a middle-aged bachelor. The innocent young colonel of the 33rd Foot returned as a 'Sepoy' general, a less innocent sun-tanned major-general, with the Order of the Bath and a different name. He went as Arthur Wesley and returned as the Hon. Sir Arthur Wellesley KB, the victor of Assaye and of half-a-dozen lesser battles. He also left behind several attractive young matrons who were most reluctant to see him depart. His first port of call *en route* for India was Cape Town. He was accompanied by a shrewd young officer called Captain George Elers of the 12th Regiment of Foot, who also kept an interesting diary.

Arthur Wesley was described as 'all life and spirits', a man about 5 foot 7 inches tall (he was in fact a few inches taller), with a long pale face, a remarkably large aquiline nose, a clear blue eye and the blackest beard necessitating two shaves a day. He was noted as extremely clean in his person and bearing a resemblance to the well-known actors John Philip Kemble and Charles Young.

Among his companions on board ship were two sisters, daughters of the second-in-command of the Madras Council. One of them, nineteen-year-old Miss Jemima Smith, was described as 'a most incorrigible flirt, very clever, gay, very satirical with a pretty little figure, lovely neck and bosom, who had made a conquest of the young Colonel Wesley'; her sister Miss Henrietta Smith, aged seventeen also had her charms.

George Elers, a very particular observer, noted in his diary that Arthur Wesley spoke very quickly with a very slight lisp. He had a very narrow jaw-bone, with a peculiarity in the shape of his ear similar to Lord Byron, the lobe of his ear uniting to the cheek, and a habit of pursing up his mouth when he was pleased and when he had been thinking abstractedly. Arthur had obviously told his junior shipmate that he had left debts behind in Dublin. A small tradesman in Dublin had been of great assistance to him with a loan of £500 – equivalent to a year's pay – which on his arrival in India he duly repaid. Elers recounts how on his return to Dublin, Arthur walked into the tradesman's shop, a boot and shoemaker, and asked if the trader remembered him. 'No,' was the answer. 'Well can I be of service to you?' 'I want nothing for myself but I have a son . . .' 'Give me his name, you did me a kindness once and I do not forget it.' Arthur obtained the shoemaker's son a 'place' at £400 per annum. Elers was delighted with this anecdote which proved that the returning hero 'had a very tender and feeling heart.' Elers was a cousin of Maria Edgeworth but may not have been aware of Arthur's attachment to Kitty Pakenham.

The final half of the voyage, from September to mid-February 1797, was on the S.S. *Princess Charlotte* – a 'most tedious' voyage to Madras with no recorded ship-board romances. From Madras they sailed to Calcutta where another diarist was in residence. William Hickey was on the payroll of the East India Company – a *bon viveur*, interested in acquiring a fortune as soon as was convenient and to return to England as a rich Nabob.

The society in Calcutta was in many ways reminiscent of the Dublin Castle environment; the race meetings, supper parties, mess dinners, governor-general's levée, morning rides and social calls. But there was one main difference: the British in India were dominated by the male sex, of whom many were bachelors (like William Hickey), either on the make or in the midst of their career with John Company or the army. As a consequence there were few unattached ladies, and married ladies were very much in demand. The gallant young colonel of the 33rd Foot met many such married women, among them a Mrs Mitchell and wrote a letter to commend Captain Mitchell to Richard, Lord Mornington, who was soon to appear on the scene. He met Mrs Floyd ('to whom a thousand thanks') who arrived on Choultry Plain, Mrs Lewis, Mrs Walker and many others, and he was a wedding witness in 1798 to 'Belle' Johnstone's marriage.

The others included a certain Mrs Sturt, and we are indebted to Captain George Elers for this story. She was a beautiful woman on the establishment of a notorious madam living in Berkeley Street, London. The lady had married a Major William Ashley Sturt of the 80th Regiment. Attractive London courtesans frequently did make good matches. Mrs Sturt arrived at Madras in 1801 without a sixpence to her name. She knew Arthur Wesley who was then serving at a palace of Tipoo sahib's outside the fort of Seringapatam. She enquired his whereabouts on arrival and wrote to him – her old friend Wesley – who by return of post sent her a draft for £400. A few years earlier this had represented a year's income. But then she was a very beautiful woman. George Elers noted in his diary that Arthur Wesley had a very susceptible heart, particularly

> I am sorry to say, married ladies and his pointed attention to Captain Macintire's young pretty wife gave offence not to her husband but to his ADC Captain West, who considered it highly immoral and indecorous.

The pale elegant ladies of Calcutta, according to Hickey, smoked cheroots with grace, went to theatres or, together with the colonel of the 33rd Foot, organised their own theatricals. The regimental messes produced lavish meals with the best of claret, Champagne, Madeira and brandy, followed by songs, catches and glees, billiards, horseplay and severe hangovers. The morning races helped to clear the officers' heads – after all there was no war on. They also played backgammon, known as trick-track, most mornings.

Arthur had few letters from Ireland and once went for a year without news. When Richard arrived in 1798 as governor-general and promptly changed the family name, to Wellesley, the pace of social 'ton' grew more frenetic. Richard not only lived 'like a lord', he lived like a 'King-Emperor'. Nothing was spared, no expense omitted to ensure that his court was as near regal as money could make it. His cavalry bodyguard was increased four-fold to 300 men and two guns, and a year later to 400 men, two guns and a band with sentries everywhere.

There were three more ladies with whom Arthur Wellesley was involved at this time. The pretty young wife of Colonel Stevenson was to be seen daily in 1801 in the fashionable Dowlaut Baug in Calcutta. Arthur was in nearby Bombay and the lady's husband was commanding in Mysore during the governor's absence. She was presented with rose trees and vegetable plants such as cabbage and celery from Arthur who was now a keen gardener having realised the dietary value of green vegetables. He also stood godfather to Mrs Stevenson's son.

Amateur theatricals were taken very seriously. Arthur purchased for his account '1 Book plays', '8 plays', Schiller's *Robbers* and Davies' plays written for a private theatre. His reading reflected his interests at that time, French novels and the *Novelists Magazine*. Mrs Gordon of Bombay was another of Arthur's favourites. She was the wife of his paymaster and for a time the Gordons lived in Arthur's house while their own was being built. His correspondence from Chinchore during 1804 included requests for her to send pickled oysters at their best and safest, when the rains commenced.

Don't send them by Coleman as he will eat more than his share before he reaches camp, nor by any of your great eaters or I shall get none of them. Tell Colonel Gordon (the lady's husband) that I see that all the offices of a subordinate Collector (of Taxes) in Malabar are filled up and that his brother in law has no chance. But as a recommendation from a Great Man is always a good thing, I wrote this day to Lord William Bentinck to recommend Captain Watson to him.

Mrs Gordon had had a tiff with the colonel because he had been too busy to pay her proper attention. Soon she wrote 'Since your absence, Seringapatam has not been half so gay, no dinner parties at least I have been at none'. Luckily the oysters were received and everybody liked them. Arthur continued:

As for your susceptible youths, I consider three days full enough for them at Bombay particularly when I want them elsewhere. But whenever you have a mind to detain one of 'my champions' as you call them, you have my permission to do so, and I shall not be the 'Deaf Adder' of the reasons which you will give for detaining them, provided that you don't allow them to marry. After that they would not answer my purpose. We get on well, but we want you to enliven us. Allow me to prevail upon you. If you'll come I'll go and meet you with my servant at the top of the Ghaut, so that you will only have 24 miles to travel in a palanqueen. There is excellent galloping ground in the neighbourhood of camp and the floor of my tent is in a fine state for dancing and the fiddlers of the Dragoons and 78th, and the Bagpipes of the 74th play delightfully.

Later on he wrote from Bombay to Mrs Gordon of his 'great dinners daily, sufficiency of dances together with the general's (i.e. himself) gallant wishes for her return to Bombay in high health and beauty, to be again its ornament.' He was godfather to her child born in 1802.

Towards the end of his stay in India, he sat to a painter, Mr R. Home, for a head and shoulders portrait at the modest price of 500 rupees and other portraits were painted for his lady friends. He purchased for one of them '1 Brilliant hoop Ring and 2 pearl guards, to ditto for 150 Rupees', and also a pearl necklace with some bracelets and a silk-worked shawl.

Which of his beautiful ladies received the paintings and the rings and necklaces? Was it Mrs Stevenson, Mrs Macintire or Mrs Gordon? Most certainly one other lady would have received tributes from the new major-general with 'strange and penetrating clear blue eyes.' The pretty Mrs Macintire's husband was a brave and active officer but unfortunately had indulged in entrepreneurial activities by stealing saltpetre.

Two colonels, Saxon and Mandeville, and the latter's wife, were caught and convicted at a court martial and disgraced. The young Captain Macintire 'must inevitably be ruined' as his colonel, Wellesley put it. His successor was Captain John William Freese, of the Madras Artillery.

The new Commissary of Stores at Seringapatam, in July 1802, had a pretty young wife whose portrait still hangs proudly at Apsley House, the Duke of Wellington's town mansion. She was the daughter of General Stuart, and gave birth to a son that same month. Arthur Wellesley stood godfather and the infant was given his name, in all by the time he left India in 1805 he had acquired three godchildren. The brown-haired Mrs Freese and Arthur fell in love and several people were deeply shocked, including again his ADC, Captain West. The romance continued until the major-general returned to England. Many of his Indian friends, Colonel John Malcolm and Captain Barclay wrote to Arthur in England and always gave him news.

> I never saw Mrs Freese better and your accounts of Arthur which she read today have made her mad with joy. Why do you shave the poor boys eyebrows and endeavour to alter Gods works? In Scotland red hair is a Beauty at least it was five centuries ago.

Arthur Freese had been sent back to a healthier climate in England but on his arrival the boy found his aunt dead, so his godfather (and his new wife) took him in to live with them. Mrs Freese's three other sons were sent to an uncle in England. The biographers note a trifle anxiously that Captain Freese and the young son Arthur Freese both had *sandy* hair.

Captain George Elers describes the colonel's dining habits,

> He kept a plain but good table. He had a very good appetite, favourite dish was roast saddle of mutton and salad. Very abstemious with wine: drank four or five glasses with people at dinner and about a pint of claret after [hardly little or no wine]. He was even in his temper, laughing and joking with those he liked, speaking in his quick way – talking about the campaign plans was the usual topic of conversation after dinner. He was severe upon any neglect by the commissariat department.

Elers played billiards frequently with his colonel and usually beat him. The colonel's dress was a long coat, uniform of the 33rd Regiment, a cocked hat, white pantaloons, Hessian boots and spurs, a large sabre with a handle of solid silver with gilt mounting on the scabbard. His hair was cropped close, but not powdered as being prejudicial to health. The Beau also purchased eight pieces of the finest lush linen to make dazzling new shirts and to impress the desirable young matrons. He also told

Elers that his highest ambition was to be major-general in Her Majesty's service. That was in May 1801 and within the year his 'highest ambition' was achieved. One feels some sympathy for poor Captain Elers who had neither the capital to purchase a majority nor the patronage to further his career. Four years of campaigning in the Mahratta wars turned Arthur Wesley into a professional army commander. Victories at Seringapatam, the defeat of Tipoo sahib, the bloody battle of Assaye, the siege of Gawilghur and many other sucessful battles all ensured Arthur's promotion in April 1802 to major-general.

He was now richer with a small fortune of £42,000, but his health had deteriorated with his campaigning and he suffered from rheumatism, lumbago, ague and constant fever. He was cheered however by the award of the Order of the Bath on 1 September 1804 and by a presentation in Mysore; 'We, the native inhabitants of Seringapatam have reposed for five auspicious years under the shadow of your protection . . .'

For a variety of reasons – the end of campaigning, his health, the advancement of his career and for one important romantic reason – a return home to England and Ireland was deemed essential. To Richard he said 'Send me all your commands to England. I shall have nothing to do excepting to attend them and I will exert myself to forward your views.'

Farewells were made to the officers and men of his successful army – particularly to Sir John Malcolm, Colin Campbell, 'Beau' Cradock and, of course, Colonel Stevenson. Suitable farewells and gifts were made to the array of beautiful young matrons as, on 10 March, Sir Arthur Wellesley sailed on HMS *Trident* with Captain Page. Part of his luggage included an amazing array of romantic fiction, *The Rival Mothers*, *Love at First Sight*, *Illicit Love*, and a dozen others including *Fashionable Involvement*. He also took with him ten pairs of ladies' shoes! To Mrs Wilks who was on board ship on the voyage, he confided that he now had scarcely any rheumatism or lumbago. 'If I had not quitted India I shall have had a serious fit of illness. I was wasting away daily and latterly when at Madras, I found my strength failed.' The ship reached the island of St Helena on 9 July 1805, from where he wrote to Colonel Malcolm back in India. He also wrote to Mrs Stevenson and to Mrs Freese 'a full account of all our adventures.'

Chapter Four

MARRIAGE

The *Trident* sailed from India towards home waters in company with a fleet of forty ships described as 'Indiamen and Chinamen' in the summer of 1805. The major-general had been partaking for the last four years in a stately quadrille, or perhaps even a pavane, an equally slow, delicate and infinitely sad musical lament. It had started with – on the face of it – an innocent letter from Colonel M. Beresford to Arthur Wellesley written in January 1801. After tributes about the recent military successes in India, he gets to the point:

> I don't know what your objects at home may be, but I am certain that you will not take amiss what I say. I know not if Miss Pakenham is an object to you or not – she looks as well as ever – no person whatsoever has paid her any particular attention – so much I say, having heard her name and yours mentioned together. I hear her most highly spoken of by Mrs (Olivia) Sparrow. She lives so retired that nobody ever sees her. One night, Tom Pakenham took me to sup to Lady Longford's – I could not avoid looking with all my eyes at the lady and thinking of you and former times. I happened on this just as your letter from the banks of the Nevbruda reached me – but I had not nerves to say anything about you . . .'

The crafty colonel enclosed for the recipient a letter from Mrs Sparrow, a young matron, wife of General Sparrow, a born matchmaker and Kitty's most intimate friend. That was the first step in the slow, inevitable sequence of events that led to Major-General Sir Arthur Wellesley's marriage.

At the time that this letter was conceived and wended its way very slowly across the oceans to India, little round-faced Kitty was embroiled in a second courtship with Galbraith Lowry Cole, son of the Earl of Enniskillan, who commanded a regiment at the age of twenty-two. He was an old friend of the Pakenham family and now commanded in the Coldstream Guards after distinguished service in the West Indies. Although a second son, and the same age as Kitty, he was on the staff of the commander-in-chief, Lord Carhampton, and in many ways was an ideal suitor for Kitty, encouraged by both families. From her point of view there was no commitment to Arthur, she was not allowed by the conventions of the time to write to him. She had not the slightest idea what his prospects were in India, nor, more importantly, what his future intentions might be. Lowry Cole was a handsome professional career soldier, on the spot, and Arthur was ten thousand miles away and for all she knew, might *never* return to court her again. Lowry Cole was a local hero during the Irish Rebellion and had been elected MP for County Fermanagh. Kitty was twenty-seven, an age at which most of her friends were already married and mothers. Lowry Cole was seriously involved with Kitty, but by April 1801 he had been posted to service in the Mediterranean. Shortly afterwards his brother wrote,

> Since that love affair with Kitty Pakenham, he seems like a burnt child to fear the fire and not to have any wish to hazard his happiness any further.

Arthur of course knew none of this but assuredly Colonel Beresford and his ally Olivia Sparrow did! In midsummer 1803 the Cole brothers were writing,

> Kitty is at Cheltenham. I am beginning to think she wishes to bring on the subject again with Lowry, but he fights shy. She will deserve it as she treated him cruelly . . .

The second stage in the long distance romance was that Arthur, who could never resist answering a letter, any letter, wrote to Olivia Sparrow in August 1801:

> You may recollect a disappointment I met with about eight years ago in an object in which I was most interested. Notwithstanding my good fortune and the perpetual activity of the life which I have led, that disappointment, the object of it and all the circumstances are fresh in my mind, as if they happened only yesterday. How much more would they bear upon me if I was to return to the inactivity of a home life? I have answered your questions candidly and have stated facts which tend rather to my own humiliation. But I do so because I am convinced that you have always been acquainted with the circumstances to which I have alluded: because I wish to shew you the merit of your friend is still felt and because I know you will not mention them (to more than six full assemblies)!
>
> You are so kind as to enquire after my health. It is excellent. Excepting what I have above mentioned to you, I have reason to be satisfied with everything. Fortune has favoured me upon every occasion and if I could forget that which has borne so heavily upon me for the last eight years, I should have as little care as you appear to have.

> When you see your friend, do me the favour to remember me to her in the kindest manner. You see that I have written you a long letter. I expect a longer answer . . .

This letter took nine months to reach its destination.

Arthur Wellesley had the *esprit* of most young men. He liked handsome young women but the prospects of marriage during his military tour in India, which extended to nine years, were nil. He could and did flirt with attractive married ladies – the Stevensons, Gordons, Freeses and others – and perhaps occasionally the flirtations were serious. But the fading romance with the 'Longford Lily', the girl he had left behind, outweighed anything else.

Meanwhile Olivia Sparrow, the matchmaker, duly showed or communicated the contents of Arthur's letter to Kitty, who in May 1802 wrote to her closest friend,

> God Almighty forbid he should remain an exile from his country or be unhappy in it. Olivia, you know my heart, at least I believe you do, as well as I know it myself. You know how sincerely I am interested in his happiness and can imagine what gratitude I feel (indeed much more than can be expressed) for his kind remembrance. My dearest Olivia, you know I can send no message: a kind word from me he might think binding to him and make him think himself obliged to renew a pursuit which perhaps he might not then wish or my family (at least some of them) take kindly . . . Longford expressed pleasure which I am sure was sincere at his success.

Olivia's letter with a summary of Kitty's honourable but perplexed views took ten months to reach Arthur.

The slow pavane continued with letters between Olivia Sparrow and Arthur Wellesley, each one taking a minimum of nine months to reach the recipient. Olivia's brother was serving in Calcutta in 1804 and Lowry Cole's younger brother was serving with the East India Company. In addition to Arthur's notable successes on the battlefield, his other amatory successes were also reported back in the Irish countryside. He wrote from Fort William in August 1804 to Olivia:

> Opinion and sentiments respecting the person in question are the same as they have ever been. They were the result of a long and intimate acquaintance in the course of which I declare I do not recollect one action that I did not approve and that was not consistent with her character and the whole tenor of her life . . . Will public service be allowed as a set-off against the faults imputed to a man's private life by scandal and calumny? Will she whose penetration nothing can escape, believe in the affection of

one against whom the scandalous world has said so much? ... As I suspect from a conversation which I had with Lady William (Bentinck), or rather a lecture she gave me, that the scandalous world had attacked me again and that the reports which they have circulated to my disadvantage may have reached England. It is not necessary that I should enter into a discussion regarding the truth or falsehood of the reports, although I by no means allow that they are true ...

On his passage home from India he met a gentleman who had been in Dublin society when the love affair terminated. He said that Catherine Pakenham had long given up Society and was 'wearing the willow for him in an Irish village.' Lady Frances Shelley recounted this story in her diary many years later.

In most romantic novels the hero home from distant parts gallops at high speed to greet his long lost love and vaunt his new title and worldly goods. What actually happened in this strange courtship proves beyond doubt that Arthur Wellesley was an honourable, prudent, and wary man.

Initially he had several conferences with Prime Minister Pitt in Downing Street on the state of affairs in India, there was no need to sing his brother's praises since Pitt already knew Richard well before he was sent to India. In London he also met Lord Nelson by chance in a waiting room in the corridors of power. Arthur had reached England in September but his meeting and eventual marriage to Kitty took place nearly eight months later.

In the outside world Napoleon had been crowned emperor and was triumphant at the battles of Ulm and Austerlitz. Nelson was chasing Admiral Villeneuve to the Indies and back to bring about a major battle and prevent a French invasion fleet sailing for our shores. The battle of Trafalgar and Nelson's death in action took place six weeks after Arthur's return.

In this eight-month period letters were exchanged at a slightly brisker rate between the marriage-broker Lady Olivia Sparrow and the separated lovelorn couple. Olivia accused him of neglecting Kitty, to which he replied,

All I can say is that if I could count myself capable of neglecting such a woman, I would endeavour to think of her no more ... What is to become of your friend in the winter? Does she remain in Ireland? Shall I go over to see her? I am very apprehensive that after having come from India for one purpose only, I shall not accomplish it. I think it is not improbable that if troops under orders for embarkation should be sent to the Continent, I shall be ordered to go with them and possibly never see you or her again.

Arthur was in London and set out to enjoy himself. There he met Harriette Wilson and Mrs Sturt's courtesan friends and enjoyed their favours. He went to the theatre, where his mother was agreeably surprised to see him again. He purchased clothes, chinaware, books and from Robert Birchall's music shop in New Bond Street, a variety of music; Beethoven and Mozart sonatas and a score or more of romantic songs, duets and trios and he visited his mother in Cavendish Square.

Despite his obvious good health he spent a few days taking the spa waters at Cheltenham. His mother, Lady Mornington, wrote to a handsome young French lady, the Duchesse de Gontaut 'A.W. knows nobody: he is coming to Cheltenham to rest on his laurels, it will be a charity if you will pay him some attention.' According to the duchesse's memoirs – she was then the young Vicomtesse de Gontaut-Biron – through her friend Mrs Wellesley-Pole (Arthur's new sister-in-law, William's wife), she agreed to meet Arthur in Cheltenham. She was delighted with the commission to meet a handsome titled major-general and perhaps have a discreet flirtation with him. Not so her two friends Lady Templeton and Miss Upton, who had perhaps heard of the 'Sepoy General's' penchant for married ladies. She visited the Pump Room with the reluctant Miss Upton in tow, scanned the list of new arrivals and found the name Wellesley on the board and read it aloud. It was a difficult name for the French to pronounce. A gentleman beside her was similarly engaged: he put his finger on a name, smiled and turning to the lady, observed 'Madame de Gontaut?' '*Rien de plus piquant*' she wrote afterwards 'we had never seen each other before and here we were already acquainted.'

Sir A.W. gave his arm to the vicomtesse and they left the salon. Suddenly the lady was covered in confusion, for an inefficient garter left its post and fell at the feet of her cavalier. 'To lose one's garter in broad daylight! In full view of everyone! In England! I confess it made me blush!' Sir A.W. picked it up and with a gracious smile and in excellent taste observed 'Now surely is the moment to say "*Honi soit qui mal y pense*"' showing off his Etonian education. Miss Upton said rather dryly 'It's lucky it was a new garter!' Lady Templeton invited A.W. to dine everyday where Miss Upton sang and he was delighted with her talent. 'As for me I was enchanted with this simple candour: he talked to us of India, never of his victories which we heard of through every letter that came to us.' He confided in his beautiful new-found friend

In a few days I shall leave Cheltenham on account of a very grave matter which will decide my whole future life. When I was very young I became attached to a Miss Pakenham, a very nice person, pretty and sweet and we became engaged. We were both very young. I had an ardent desire to enter the Army and I was obliged to leave her though we both cherished the hope of being one day re-united. Years passed. In the meantime Miss P. had the smallpox. She wrote to me that remembering our promise she must warn me that she had lost her beauty. It appeared that the smallpox while destroying her beauty had not deprived her of her memory.

The vicomtesse noted that his manner of saying that phrase was so peculiar and so like him that she could not help laughing.

But she has my promise and my honour demands that I should keep it: it was rather fine of her to write to me with so much simplicity and truth. So I shall start for Ireland at once. I have very little time to lose. Perhaps I shall come back this way alone or with her.

He went and eventually Kitty and he returned together on their honeymoon, she in the carriage alone and he on the box. 'My protégé of Cheltenham became in due course the Duke of Wellington.'

Arthur spent the first three weeks of October in Cheltenham staying at the Plough Inn where Mr Joseph Bickham served him dressed salmon or roast fowl or mutton chops, his favourite, accompanied by a half bottle of Madeira wine. That is when he was not dining with the vicomtesse, Lady Templeton and Miss Upton. But he did meet General and Mrs Sparrow who told him that Kitty's sentiments were still the same.

During this period Kitty was exchanging long dramatic letters with Olivia Sparrow. Her conscience and her love for the stranger from India are immediately apparent.

You assure me he still regards me, he has authorised you to renew the proposition he made some years ago . . . It is quite impossible for me to express the apprehension that preys upon my heart at this moment. I think he wishes to be ordered abroad and perhaps he is right for I am very much changed and you know it, within these last three years – so much that I doubt whether it would be in my power to contribute to the comfort or happiness of anybody who has not been in the habit of loving me for years – like my brother or you or my mother. Read his letter again, my dear Olivia. Is there one expression implying 'Yes' would gratify, or that 'No' would disappoint or occasion regret?

Seventeen years later Arthur confided in his mistress, confidante and friend Harriet Arbuthnot and she, in turn, recorded the conversation in her diary:

> ... my astonishment at his having married such a person, for that however pretty she might have been, she never could have had more mind (than she had now) and that it was quite inconceivable! I could not help laughing at his answer. He said 'Is it not the most extraordinary thing you ever heard of!! Would you have believed that anybody could have been such a *damned fool*? I was not the least in love with her. I married her because they asked me to do it and I did not know myself. I thought I should never care for anybody again and that I should be with the army and in short I was a fool. I will tell you that whole story if you like.' He then said that he was quite young when he first liked her: he would not allow that he was very much in love, but he asked her to marry him and she refused him. He then went to India, remained for some years, and thought no more about her. On his return to England, Lady Olivia Sparrow sent for him and told him that Miss Pakenham had continued to like him, that she had refused other offers on his account and advised him to renew his offers which, *in an evil hour*, he did. He said she was quite indifferent to him but that he had liked her, he did not care a pin about anyone else or what became of himself. He told me however, that some months elapsed between his writing to her to offer himself and his marriage and his mind misgave him many times: they corresponded and her letters gave him offence. However he ended by going over to Ireland and being married and he has repented it ever since.
>
> I told him that in all my life I had never heard of anybody doing so absurd a thing, that there could be but one justification, his having been desperately in love with someone who had ill used him and being in a state of desperation at the time and even for that he was too old. He agreed cordially in my abuse of him and said I could not think him a greater fool than he did himself.

'He was too old' was only too true. Arthur was a veteran of thirty-six. Not only was he unmarried but there was no one else in mind except the timid little country mouse, good, worthy, sweet and quite useless to him – as events proved. Kitty's niece, Mrs Foster, wrote many years later that after his return from India all the gay and fair flocked admiringly round the gallant and attractive young officer. But by 4 November he had committed himself.

In January 1806 the Prime Minister, William Pitt, died, probably as a result of hearing the dreadful news of the Allied defeat at Austerlitz. Arthur was daily awaiting orders to embark for north Germany with an infantry brigade – a token force to help the beleaguered Russian and Austrian troops. The abortive campaign that took place was a classic disaster, even worse than his first service in Flanders eleven years earlier. Embarking in storm and tempest nine troop ships sank and three thousand officers and men perished in the icy North Sea. Not a shot was fired by the English survivors in the make-believe war that followed. Arthur was back in England again by the end of February after six pointless and dangerous weeks near Bremen. During that winter he visited Richard's children. Their father had been dismissed from his post in India and had left that country in time to greet and say farewell to his friend Pitt just before he died. Ironically the elderly Lord Cornwallis, who had succeeded Richard, died in harness three months later. On his return home Richard was impeached on charges of squandering money, which, no doubt, he had done.

Arthur was in effect downgraded after the abortive campaign in north Germany and returned to being colonel of the 33rd Foot in Hastings. His Indian rank of major-general was not substantive in the English army. The new Prime Minister, Lord Castlereagh, offered him the seat of Rye, in Sussex nearby to Hastings, partly so that he could defend Richard in the House of Commons from the back benches. He was granted leave and decided in April to visit Ireland and marry his little Irish bride.

'She has grown ugly, by Jove,' he muttered to his brother Gerald, the clergyman in the family, who was to marry them. The ceremony took place in the Rutland Square residence of the Longfords on 16 April 1806 in the parish of St George's, Dublin. Arthur's brothers turned up in force as witnesses, as were most of the Longfords and Pakenhams, but the recently widowed matchmaker Olivia Sparrow was absent. 'The Honble. Sir Arthur Wellesley K.B. to the Honble. Catherine Dorothea Sarah Pakenham of this parish by the Rev. G. Wellesley' were the words recorded on the marriage register.

It must have been a most unsatisfying sexual relationship. Kitty was assuredly a virgin, a nervous, shy, timid, unassuming virgin and Arthur would not have been much help in the construction of a happy and sensual partnership. His experience would have been confined to a few paid performers in Dublin and London – such was the fashion of the day. Although Harriette Wilson must have given him enormous pleasure and sexual satisfaction in the period after his return from India – and indeed many times after that! It is possible that one, or more than one, pretty young matron in India may have helped him and given him some unexpected and perhaps sophisticated pleasures of the bed.

Arthur was now aged thirty-seven and Kitty thirty-four. She wrote to her stepmother on 1 May, 'Sir Arthur is handsome, very brown, quite bald and a hooked nose.' She was always very short-sighted and believed her husband to be 'quite bald' whereas he kept an excellent thatch of hair until the day he died nearly half a century hence. Mrs Calvert in her Journal *Irish Beauty of the Regency* met the newly weds a little later.

> I went to see my mother and found Lady Wellesley with her. She is just married to Sir Arthur W. She is now about two or three and thirty and he is about seven and thirty. He must have found her sadly altered for she was a very pretty little girl with a round face and a fine complexsion. She is now very thin and withered (I believe pining in his absence helped to make her more so). I think she looks in a consumption, which idea, a short cough increases and I know Sir Walter Farquhar [her doctor] has desired her to take great care of herself. She is gentle and amiable. I hear that when someone told Sir Arthur he would find her much altered, he answered that he did not care: it was her mind he was in love with, and that could not alter.

Meanwhile Maria Edgeworth's stepmother was writing,

> one of those tales of real life in which the romance is far superior to the generality of fictions. I hope the imaginations of this hero and heroine have not been too much exalted, and that they may not find the enjoyment of a happiness so long wished for, inferior to what they expected.

Arthur had drawn up a beneficial marriage settlement whereby in the event of his death a fund would be created to take care of Kitty. The Longfords guaranteed £4,000 for Kitty plus an extra £2,000 from her mother, whilst the 'Sepoy General' put half his Indian fortune of £40,000 into the marriage trust. An honourable action in view of his many expressed doubts before the wedding.

The young honeymooners lived initially at No. 14 Clifford Street and then later in Harley Street. Many diaries and journals record their varied society engagements. Kitty appeared at Queen Charlotte's drawing room where the queen told her,

> how happy to see you at my Court, so bright an example of constancy. If anybody in this world deserves to be happy, you do! . . . but did you really never write one letter to Sir Arthur Wellesley during his absence?

To which little Kitty replied, 'No, never, Madam'. The queen continued, 'And did you never think of him?' 'Yes, Madam very often.'

During the summer of 1806 Arthur was sometimes in Hastings with his regiment, sometimes in London with Kitty and also in Ireland to inspect the coastal defences. Meanwhile 'My dearest Kitty' was getting into a muddle with her household expenditures and to her husband's annoyance she was also pregnant with their first child. Sir Arthur was longing for resumed action. The débâcle in the North Sea and in Bremen was not of his making, but commanding a small brigade on the Sussex coast was a distinct comedown for the victor of Assaye.

A small British army now soldiered in Calabria and produced a modest victory at Maida. The war with Spain promised another forlorn hope of going to Argentina to capture Buenos Aires. The British High Command have had a long record of sending ill-equipped expeditionary forces off to the remotest parts of the world with the utmost lack of military logic. The command was offered to Sir Arthur, who shrewdly wrote a long memorandum for the prime minister pointing out whether it be Argentina or Mexico the whole scheme was quite impracticable. He offered them an attack on Jamaica as a sop to the armchair warriors. Arthur was now quite desperate for a command, even as second-in-command.

Beresford was on the River Plate on the disastrous expedition to the Argentine. Kitty's erstwhile lover Lowry Cole and John Moore commanded in Sicily, and Arthur was still required to write memoranda for the Cabinet on a Mexican invasion, which he was prepared to undertake with 11,000 men and the appropriate military supplies. He was based in Deal in Kent with his brigade in early December.

In the winter of 1807 young Arthur Richard Wellesley was born, on 3 February at No. 11 Harley Street whilst Sir Arthur hunted with the Salisbury's at Hatfield. Richard's defence in parliament against the threat of impeachment was still rumbling. The Catholic question provoked a change of government and King George III sent for the veteran Duke of Portland with Canning as Foreign Secretary and Lord Castlereagh back at the War Office. Nobody wanted the role of Lord Lieutenant in Ireland and the Duke of Richmond, who reluctantly accepted the post, asked for his young friend Arthur as his chief secretary at a salary of £6,566 a year. With no overseas command in sight and his London expenses unexpectedly high, Sir Arthur had little hesitation in accepting. Richard was offered the Foreign Office but declined, brother William was made Secretary to the Admiralty and Henry made a Secretary of the Treasury.

Kitty was proving to be singularly inept at managing the domestic finances but her problems were compounded by the arrival of little Arthur Freese, Sir Arthur's godson from India, by childish diseases, by domestic dramas (her maid drowned herself of love), and by the fact that in the spring, at the age of thirty-seven, she was pregnant again.

Already the writing was on the wall. Kitty filled the house in Harley Street with her family and friends from Ireland with their homely, gossipy small-talk. They had nothing in common with Sir Arthur's military and political colleagues. And indeed, what had always been clear to the onlooker, Kitty and her husband had no common ground at all except for the two young children (Charles was born in June 1808). Kitty had her painting, a little music, her charities for her 'pensioners', books (despite her short-sight) and little else to offer her husband.

The beautiful young Lady Salisbury, who was to become a very close friend of Arthur's, enticed him to amusing and interesting weekends at Hatfield in Hertfordshire where he could ride and hunt, shoot rather dangerously and take part in the admirable discussions with men and their wives (and mistresses) who controlled the country's destiny. 1806/7 was the time which was to alter Sir Arthur's lifestyle. For the next half-century, apart from his famous Iberian campaign, he would be found wining and dining in the society of the country's ruling élite. He would there be found in flirtatious mood with the beautiful young matrons whose views influenced their husbands and lovers.

In April 1807 he was summoned to Dublin Castle and Kitty joined him in May. He was besieged by requests for preferment from both families, and managed to refuse most of them relatively politely. He was back in London in June, the month when Bonaparte annihilated the Russians at the battle of Friedland, and signed the strange Treaty of Tilsit on the River Nieman. Another military expedition was planned by the Whitehall warriors and, to clear the decks, Sir Arthur sent in his resignation on 1 June to Lord Castlereagh.

On the last day of July Sir Arthur embarked at Sheerness and sailed on the SS *Prometheus*, a fire-vessel, on a secretive mission. The Foreign Secretary, George Canning, had decided that Scandinavia should be kept out of Bonaparte's clutches by neutralising or capturing the Danish fleet, much as Admiral Nelson had so brilliantly achieved six years earlier. Sir Arthur now made his second will, leaving the bulk of his estate not committed to Kitty's trust, a matter of £20,000, for his young son Arthur Richard.

Arthur was given a brigade to command. His old rival in India Sir David Baird, commanded a division and Lord Cathcart commanded the whole expedition. The campaign went according to plan and Copenhagen surrendered on 5 September, after brisk action on 29 August at Kiöge where the major-general showed his old Indian skills again. He met several of the leading Danes – a gentleman named Rosencrantz, a general, and the indignant Princesse de Holstein who invited him to shoot her coverts '*comme le chevalier est amateur de chasse.*' This was a pleasant interlude and he spent the autumn in Copenhagen concluding the surrender negotiations, before he returned to England on 29 September. When parliament met in February 1807 he was thanked publicly for his zeal, intrepidity, genius and valour – which was perhaps rather overstating a minor brigade action.

After a week or so in London and conferences with Lord Castlereagh he returned in mid-October to his well-paid appointment at Dublin Castle and his lodge in Phoenix Park. Meanwhile the French armies rampaged through Spain and reached the Portuguese seaboard where Marechals Junot and Murat had an easy campaign. For the next nine months Sir Arthur undertook most conscientiously two quite different responsibilities. As chief secretary in Dublin he performed a difficult but unexciting role which included a detailed plan for the defence of Ireland against a French invasion. In Westminster he was much in demand acting as unpaid army chief-of-staff. There were vague plans for another operation in America which meant conferring with the Spanish General Miranda and there were plans for a Swedish expedition under John Moore plus a defensive plan for India should France and Russia invade from the north-west. On 25 April 1808 he was made a lieutenant-general in recognition of the Copenhagen expedition and his planning services to Whitehall. One of the many plans that had been hatched was for an expedition to set sail from Cork for a raid on Venezuela! In May Sir Arthur wrote a military appreciation of the consequences of a revolt in Spain against the occupying French armies, he recommended that the Venezuelan force be diverted to Gibraltar to encourage the Spanish revolt. This plan was well received and in June his more detailed plan was accepted. Predictably he was appointed to command this invasion force, initially in Spain, and if that was not successful, on to Venezuela. King George III signed Sir Arthur's commission on 14 June and he dined that night in Harley Street with Kitty and a certain Mr John Wilson Croker whose 'Correspondence and Diaries' contains a wealth of anecdotes. He soliloquised aloud about his future in Europe fighting the French, who under Bonaparte had out-manoeuvred and overwhelmed all the armies of Europe. Sir Arthur's experience of commanding troops in Europe against first-class opposition was nil. The prospect was enough to daunt any general of the time. 'I am not afraid of them, as everybody else seems to be,' he told his wife and Mr Croker.

Fortunately his rather vague mission was now more closely defined. He might look in at Vigo or Corunna, the two north-western Spanish ports with excellent natural harbours, but his task was to drive Marechal Junot out of Portugal. So leaving a furious General Miranda behind him (no Venezuelan campaign now), and a tearful Kitty with three small children to look after (including Arthur Freese), Sir Arthur set sail on the SS *Crocodile*. In his fortieth year he must have realised what high stakes he was playing for. The young gambler of twenty years ago was taking on the might of Napoleon's highly trained armies with 9,000 men from his base in Cork plus a further 5,000 more troops at sea off Spain.

Chapter Five

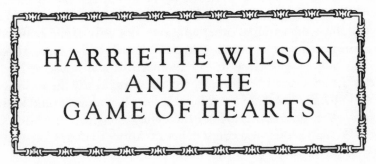

HARRIETTE WILSON AND THE GAME OF HEARTS

John James Dubochet was a clockmaker, a handsome citizen of the canton of Berne in Switzerland, who came to live in London at No. 2 Carrington Street in Mayfair about 1780. His wife, Amelia Cook, bore him a number of charming daughters called Harriette, Fanny, Amy, Sophia and Juliet.

John James was a mathematician with expressive eyebrows, and was regrettably over fond of his charming daughters. Amelia, his wife, occupied herself in London with a stocking repair business. Her daughters grew up in London bilingual, charming and, living near Shepherds Market, accomplished courtesans. Amy, the eldest daughter, was a dark-eyed rather mean virago. Fanny was a sweet, golden-haired child, and Sophia was pretty but glum. But Harriette, who soon changed her name for professional reasons to Wilson, was the pick of the bunch. Certainly most of the members of Whites Club in St James thought so! The members of Boodles and Crockfords were equally enthusiastic about Harriette and her specific charms. The interest that these delightful young ladies had in common – apart from their profession – is that they all married rather well.

Harriette was born in Mayfair on 2 February 1786. She was described rather later by Sir Walter Scott,

> she was far from beautiful but a smart saucy girl with good eyes, dark hair and the manner of a wild schoolboy.

Falling on hard times, relatively speaking, she was persuaded without much resistance, by a slightly unscrupulous London publisher called John Joseph Stockdale in the Haymarket, to publish her memoirs. That was in 1825, and the book was so much in demand that thirty editions were published and some were pirated by printers such as T. Douglas, E. Thomas, Thomas Little and others.

Her published story started in 1801. She was fifteen and living in the Marine Parade, Brighton when she succumbed to the charms of Lord Craven. She soon acquired other admirers, not only of the gentry, but also of the nobility. Her parents meanwhile had moved to No. 23 Queen Street in Soho, quite close to Lord Craven's town house at No. 16 Charles Street. Certainly around 1805 she was already the mistress of the 6th Duke of Argyle. In the following year her admirer (and keeper) was John, Viscount Ponsonby, a handsome young man of whom King George IV was jealous on account of his attentions to Lady Conyngham. Harriette starts her *Memoirs* by saying,

> I will not say in what particular year of his life the Duke of Argyle succeeded with me. Ladies scorn dates. Dukes make ladies nervous and stories dry. Amy my eldest sister had been the first to set us a bad example.

Harriette had immense vitality, considerable wit, no beauty, but took a lively interest in her admirers and, of course, spoke fluent French. She held court in her opera box and offered besides a comfortable bed, a sofa, alcove, hearth, dinner table and a salon in which to entertain her friends. Her main rivals were Julia Johnstone and later on Catherine Walters, known as Skittles. The annual Cyprians Ball, given by the 'Fashionable Impures' (the informal group of demi-reps and courtesans), was held at the Argyle Rooms where the ladies of leisure played hostess to their admirers and protectors. These ladies of the night boasted names such as Laura, Venus and Mendicant, the Mocking Bird, the Brazen Bellona and the White Doe. In addition to the charms mentioned, Harriette's portrait shows a voluptuous bosom, a small waist and altogether a lovely figure. She had a strong determined face and a pleasing smile.

She was kept for a time by the Duke of Argyle, then Lord Worcester, but Lord Ponsonby was the real love of her life. Nevertheless she was on very good terms with Tom Sheridan, the playwright's son, Lord Alvanley, the famous wit, Henry Luttrell, the brilliant conversationalist, Henry Brougham, the great advocate, Beau Brummel the Dandy, Fred Lamb, Lord Byron . . . and the gentleman who in May 1814 became the Duke of Wellington.

The first advance was made to Mrs Porter, a well-known procuress and owner of a notorious establishment in Berkeley Street. This was probably on Arthur's return from India in 1805. The *Memoirs* were written twenty years later and Harriette referred to Arthur Wellesley always in retrospect as the Duke of Wellington.

Who feeling himself amorously given – it was in the summer one sultry evening ordered his coachman to set him down at the White Horse Cellars in Piccadilly whence he sallied forth on foot to No. 2 or 3 in Berkeley Street and rapped hastily on the door which was immediately opened by the tawdry well-rouged housekeeper of Mrs Porter who with a significant nod of recognition led him into her mistress's boudoir and then hurried away simpering to acquaint the good Mrs Porter with the arrival of one of her *oldest* customers. Mrs P. on entering her boudoir bowed low but she would have bowed lower still to His Grace who had paid but shabbily for the last bonne fortune she had contrived to procure him [Mrs Sturt perhaps]. After desultory comments about the weather, His Grace came to the point. 'There is a beautiful girl just come out, a very fine creature – they call her Harriette and . . .' but Mrs P. interrupted him 'My Lord, I have had three applications this very month for the girl they call Harriette and I have already introduced myself to her'. [This happened when Harriette was in Somers Town]. 'It was at the very earnest request of General Walpole. She is the wildest creature I ever saw. She did not affect modesty, nor appear in the least offended at my intrusion. Her first question was "Is your man handsome?" I answered frankly that the General was more than 60 years of age at which account Harriette laughed heartily and then seeming to recollect herself, she said she really was over head and ears in debt and therefore must muster up courage to receive one visit from her antiquated admirer at my house'. 'Well,' interrupted Wellington half jealous, and half disgusted. 'Well, my Lord the appointment was made for eight o'clock on the following evening at which hour the old General was punctual and fidgeted about the room for more than three quarters of an hour. At last he rang the bell violently . . . eventually a lady whose face was covered with a thick black veil arrived in a hackney coach and was shown into the best room. 'She came then?' inquired W. impatiently and blowing his nose . . . The old General in a state of perfect ecstasy begged my pardon for his testy humour and explained that for a year he had been following Harriette . . . Judge our astonishment, my Lord when the incognito, throwing back her veil with much affectation discovered a wrinkled face which had weathered at least 60 summers, aye and winters too . . .' 'My Good Woman' said W. without making any remarks on Mrs P.'s story 'my time is precious. One hundred guineas are yours and as much Harriette's if you can induce her to give me the meeting'. 'My dear Lord,' said Mrs P. quite subdued 'what would I not do to serve you. I will pay Harriette a visit early tomorrow morning although my Lord to tell you the truth I was never half so afraid of any woman in my life. She is so wild and appears to be perfectly independent and so careless of her own interests and welfare that I really do not know what is likely to move her.' 'Nonsense' said W. 'it is very well known that the Marquis of Lorne is her lover.' 'Lord Lorne may have gained Harriette's heart' said Mrs P. just as if she understood the game of hearts! 'However I will not give up the business till I have had an interview with her.' 'And make haste about it' said W. taking up his hat 'I shall call for your answer in two days. In the meantime if you have anything like good news to communicate, address a line to Thomas's Hotel in Berkeley-Square.' These two respectable friends now took leave of each other.

That was the opening salvo in the Game of Hearts. Mrs P. duly interviewed Harriette, who was acutely disappointed that her new client was not the mysterious stranger with the great Newfoundland dog whom she particularly fancied.

'His Grace only entreats to be allowed to make your acquaintance. His situation, you know [i.e. marriage to Kitty] prevents the possibility of his getting regularly introduced to you. Be assured he is a remarkable fine-looking man and if you are afraid of my house, promise to receive him in your own at any hour when he may be certain to find you alone.' 'Well,' said Harriette with a sigh 'I suppose he must come. I do not understand economy and am frightened to death at debts. Argyle [i.e. Lord Lorne] is going to Scotland and I shall want a steady sort of friend of some kind in case a bailif should get hold of me.'

Finally Harriette agreed to an appointment at three for the next day 'but mind, only as a common acquaintance.'

Away winged Wellington's Mercury as an old woman wings it at 60 . . . W. was punctual. He bowed first then said, 'How do you do?' Then thanking Harriette for giving him permission to call he then wanted to take her hand. 'Really for such a renowned hero, you have very little to say for yourself.' 'Beautiful creature!' uttered W. 'Where is Lorne?' 'Good Gracious' said Harriette out of all patience at his stupidity. 'What came you here for, Duke?' 'Beautiful eyes, yours,' explained W. 'Aye man! they are greater conquerors than ever Wellington shall be but to be serious, I understand you came here to try to make yourself agreeable?' 'What, child! do you think that I have nothing better to do than to make speeches to please ladies?' said W. '*Apres avoir depeupler la terre vous devez fair tout pour la repeupler,*' Harriette replied. 'You should see me where I shine,' W. observed laughing. 'Where's that in God's name?' 'In a field of battle,' answered the hero. '*Battez vous, donc et qu'un autre me fasse la cour,*' said Harriette. But love scenes or even love quarrels seldom tend to amuse the reader, so to be brief what was a mere man, even though it were the handsome Duke of Argyle, to a Wellington? . . . W. called on me the next morning before I had finished my breakfast. I tried him on every subject I could muster, on all he was most impenetrably taciturn. At last he started on an original idea of his own 'I wonder you do not get married, Harriette?' (Bye-the-bye ignorant people are always wondering that). 'Why so?' W. however gives no reason for anything unconnected with fighting at least since the Convention of Cintra, and he therefore again became silent. Another burst of attic sentiment blazed forth 'I was thinking of you last night after I got into bed,' resumed W. 'How very polite to the Duchess,' I observed. 'A propos to marriage, Duke, how do you like it?' W. who seemed to make a point of never answering one continued, 'I was thinking . . . I was thinking that you will get into some scrape when I go to Spain'. 'Nothing so serious as marriage, neither I hope,' said Harriette. 'I must come again tomorrow to give you a little advice,' continued W. 'Oh, let us have it all out now and have done with it.' 'I cannot,' said W. putting on his gloves and taking a hasty leave of me. 'I am glad he is off, thought I, for this is indeed very uphill work. This is worse than Lord Craven.'

Up in his highland woods Argyle got to hear of Wellington's latest success and was jealous of his frequent visits to Harriette whose story now continues.

W. was now my constant visitor [after the controversial Treaty of Cintra] – a most unentertaining one – Heaven knows – and in the evenings when he wore his broad red ribbon he looked very like a rat-catcher. 'Do you know the world talk about hanging you?' Harriette asked him, 'Eh,' said W. 'They say you will be hanged in spite of all your brother Wellesley can say in your defence.' 'Ha,' said W. very seriously 'what paper do you read?' 'It is the common talk of the day' Harriette replied. 'They must not work me in such another campaign, or my weight will never hang me!' 'Why, you look a little like the apothecary in Romeo and Juliet already' Harriette said.

Harriette recounts how Wellington came to take hasty leave of her in the summer of 1808 shortly before he sailed. 'I am off for Spain directly.' She became melancholy and remembered that W. had relieved her from many duns which had caused her much unease. She thought she might never see him again, her lover Ponsonby meant nothing to her and was out of town. She said, 'God bless you, Wellington,' and burst into tears. Her journal says,

> the tears appeared to afford rather an unusual unction to his soul and his astonishment seemed to me not quite unmixed with gratitude. 'If you change your home,' said W. kissing her cheek, 'let me find your address at Thomas's Hotel as soon as I come to England and if you want anything in the meantime write to Spain, and do not cry; and take care of yourself and do not cut me when I come back. Do you hear?' he said, first wiping away some of her tears with her handkerchief and then kissing Harriette's eyes, he said 'God bless you!' and hurried away.

She recorded in her journal,

> Argyle continued to correspond with me but if one might judge from the altered style of his letters, Wellington had made a breach in his Grace's late romantic sentiments in my favour.
>
> Breach-making was Wellington's trade, you know, and little as men of Argyle's nation might be expected to care about breaches, yet the idea of Wellington often made him sigh . . . I have often seen his Grace [she meant W.] in his cotten nightcap. Well then the terrific Duke of Wellington! The wonder of the world! Having six feet from the tail to the head! So leaving out his dimensions etc, etc, it was even the D. of W. whose laurels like those of the giant in the Vicar of Wakefield had been hardly earned by the sweat of his little dwarf brows and the loss of their little legs, arms and eyes . . .

The next adventure recalled by our courtesan must have been in 1809 when she was twenty-three and Wellesley was forty. He arrived back in town from Spain and,

> cannons were fired and much tallow consumed in illumination. His Grace of Argyle came to me earlier than usual on that memorable evening but being unwell and love-sick he found Harriette in her bed-chamber who said '*Quelle bizarre ideé vous passé par la tête?* Surely you have forgotten the amiable Duchess, his bride and all the fatigue his Grace [i.e. W.] encountered enough to damp the ardour of any mighty hero or plenipotentiary for one evening at any rate – therefore trust me. W. will not disturb us tonight!' At that very moment a thundering rap at the door was heard '*Vive l'amour! Vive la guerre*' said Argyle '*Le voila!*' He threw Harriette's dressing gown over his shoulders and putting on one of her

old night caps . . . put his head out of her bedroom which was on the second floor and soon recognised the noble chieftain, Wellington. Endeavouring to imitate the voice of an old Duenna A. begged to know who was at the door. 'Come down I say,' roared this modern Blue Beard [i.e. W.] 'and don't keep me here in the rain, you old blockhead!' 'Sir,' answered A. in a shrill voice, 'you must please to call your name, as I don't dare to come down robberies are so frequent in London, just at this season and all the sojers, you see, coming home from Spain that its quite alarming to poor lone women.' W. took off his hat and held up towards the lamp a visage, which late fatigue and present vexation had rendered no bad representation of that of the Knight of the Woeful Figure. While the rain was trickling down his nose, his voice trembling with rage and impatience W. cried out, 'You old idiot, do you know me now?' 'Lord, Sir,' answered A. anxious to prolong this ridiculous scene, 'I can't give no guess and do you know Sir, the thieves have stolen a new waterbutt out of our airy not a week since and my missis is more timbersome than ever.' 'The Devil!' vociferated W. who could endure no more and muttering bitter imprecations between his closed teeth against all the duennas and old women that had ever existed returned home to his neglected wife and family duties.

Harriette's journal was written some years after the events actually took place and she gave the impression that the Duke had returned from Spain on more than one occasion – which of course he had not. The following anecdote logically follows after the hilarious scene caused by Argyle.

I was surprised by a visit from the D. of W. who had unexpectedly arrived from the Continent the night before.

'How do you do? What have you been about?' asked his Grace, then fixing his eyes on my pale, thin, careworn face, he absolutely started as though he had seen the ghost of some man he had killed, honestly of course!

'What the devil is the matter' inquired W. 'Something has affected me deeply' answered I, my eyes again filling with tears, 'and I have been ill for more than two months.'

'Poor girl,' said W. as though he really would have pitied me, had he but known how and then added, 'I was always dreading your getting into some scrape. Do you recollect I told you so? How much money do you want?' said this man of sentiment, drawing near the table and taking up my pen to write a draft. 'I have no money, not a single shilling, but this is not the cause of my sufferings.' 'Nonsense, nonsense,' rejoined W. writing me a cheque. 'Where the devil is Argyle? Why do you not make him pay your debts? I will give you what I can afford now and you must write to me *as usual* at Thomas's Hotel, if this not sufficient. Good God! How thin you have grown were you sorry I left you? I remember you shed tears when I told you I was off for Spain. I am a cold sort of fellow, I dare say you think so and yet I have not forgotten that either, because there is no humbug about you! and when you cry you are sorry I believe: particularly one night I remember I dreamed you came out on my staff.'

W. consoled me as well as he could and sat with me nearly three hours. His visit made no impression on me except that I was grateful for his kindness in leaving me the money I wanted.

On another occasion,

I was interrupted by a visit from W. Here is a thing in the shape of an intellectual companion thought I. After W. had left me I entirely forgot him: nay, before, for now I recollect this he said something about my bad taste in talking on subjects irrelevant to what was going on, such as a remark I might have made about my rose-tree or my dinner, when I ought to have been all soul. No matter. The soul's fire is partly kept alive by dinner or whether it is, or not still dinner, or even a rose-tree is infinitely more interesting than the Wellington!

She wrote to one of her lovers Richard William Meyler,

My old beau Wellington is going on famously thanks to the fineness of his nerves and his want of feeling and his excellent luck. I do not mean to say he has not a good notion of commanding an army for though I do not understand things I am willing to take it for granted that this is the case . . . Nevertheless *tel qu'il est*, he has made I understand a desperate conquest of Lady Caroline Lamb: but then her ladyship was never very particular.

Harriette's sister Sophia was then the mistress of Lord Deerhurst at the age of thirteen but later married Thomas Hill, Lord Berwick. Amy lived with a Count Palmella who paid her £200 a month, and Fanny lived as Mrs Parker with a certain Colonel Parker. Another anecdote concerns Harriette's clientele.

Leinster was my next visitor, and then Lord Robert Manners dressed in a red waistcoat, corduroy breeches, worsted stockings and thick shoes which had nails in them: yet in spite of all this he looked very handsome. The D. of W. came next 'Why the devil did not your servant tell me that all these people were here?' whispered the merely mortal hero, as he bolted downstairs and ran foul of Lord William Russell in the passage.

Harriette describes her costume,

My crimson velvet pelisse trimmed with white fur and my white beaver hat with the charming plume of feathers were spread out in my dressing room ready for Hyde Park and conquests.

Her real genuine love was for the Marquess of Worcester and she lived with him in Charmouth for a time. In 1812 Worcester's father, without his son's knowledge, asked Wellington to appoint him his ADC in Spain. Harriette commented that Worcester had sworn not to leave London unless he was allowed to spend a whole fortnight entirely with her. She knew she would never be permitted to follow the army in Spain. At that sad news she burst into (another) violent flood of tears. But when peace was declared Lord Worcester returned, a 'cold blooded shameless profligate like the great glorious wonder of the age – Wellington.' But Harriette who was living in Paris in 1814/15 met the Duke again. She was taking a solitary drive up the Champs Elysées on the way to the Bois de Boulogne, as the Duke galloped past her carriage. He at once recognised her and returned to greet her,

'I thought it was you,' he said. 'I am glad to see you are looking so beautiful, I'll come and see you. How long have you been in Paris? When may I come? Where do you live? How far are you going?' 'Which of these questions do you desire to have answered first, Wellington?' she enquired. 'I want to know where you live?' 'At No. 35 Rue de la Paix'. 'And may I pay you a visit?' 'Whenever you like.' 'I'll come tonight at eight o'clock – will that suit you?'

Harriette agreed and shook hands with the Duke. She went on in her diary:

His Lordship was punctual and came to me in a very gay equipage. He was all over orders and ribbons of different colours, bows and stars and he looked pretty well. 'The ladies here tell me you make a bad hand at ambassadorship.' 'How so?' he replied. 'Why the other day you wrote to ask a lady of rank if you might visit her, à *cheval*? What does that mean pray?' 'In boots, you foolish creature! What else could it mean?' 'Why the lady thought it just possible that the great VILLAINTON being an extra-ordinary man might propose entering her drawing room on the outside of his charger as being the most warrior-like mode of attacking her heart.' 'You are a little fool' said Wellington kissing me by main force, 'And then your Routs are so ill-conducted, the society so mixed.' 'What is that to me? I don't invite the people. I suppose they ask everybody to avoid offence. Who the devil was that old women last Friday?' 'What do you mean? I was not there. What sort of old woman do you allude to?' Harriette inquired laughing. 'An old woman with a piece of crape hanging down here,' said he pointing to his breast, 'and ragged red shoes.' 'How am I to know all your ragamuffins?' I hope my readers, [went on

43

Harriette,] have now had enough of the immortal W. In short they must e'en be satisfied whether they have or not, for they will get nothing better out of him. W. was no inducement for me to prolong my stay in Paris and as Buonaparte was now on his way from Elba, I began to prepare for my departure. The English were all hurrying away in a state of great alarm. My mother and Amy were settled in a small house just out of Paris and determined to stay where they were.

We will never now who took the initiative to write, produce and print Harriette Wilson's memoirs. Was it the rather shady John Joseph Stockdale or was it Harriette herself, always broke despite a settlement of £1,200 from Lord Worcester's father, the Duke of Beaufort. Stockdale approached all of Harriette's clientele and demanded a payment of £200 for the omission of the appropriate name from her *Memoirs*. Some paid up but others, including the Duke, said, 'Publish and be damned' or the equivalent.

In a long postscript in her book Harriette makes much of the Duke's refusal to pay.

His Grace in the meek humility of his heart has written to menace a prosecution if such trash be published. What trash, my dear Wellington? Now I will admit for an instant, and it is really very good of me, that you are an excellent judge of literature and could decide on the merits or demerits of a work with better taste and judgement than the first of the Edinburgh reviewers. Still in order to pronounce it trash we should fancy that even W. himself must throw a hasty glance on one of its pages at least. Quite the contrary, W. knows himself to be the subject and therefore wisely prejudges the book trash one fortnight before it sees the light! So far so good! But when my own W. who has sighed over me and groaned over me by the hour, talked of my wonderful beauty, ran after me, bribed Mrs Porter over and over again after I refused to listen to *her* overtures, only for a single smile from his beautiful Harriette! Did he not kneel? And was I not the object of his first, his most ardent wishes on his arrival from Spain? Only it was a pity that the Duke of Argyle got to my house first. Therefore what could my tender swain W. do better than stand in the gutter at two in the morning pouring forth his amorous wishes in the pouring rain in strains replete with the most heart-rending grief, to the favoured lover who had supplanted him ... When I say, this faithful lover whose love survived six winters, six frosts, six chilling, nay, killing frosts when W. sends the ungentle hint to my publisher of hanging me, beautiful, adored and adorable me, on whom he had so often hung! *Alors je pend la tête.* Is it thus he would immortalise me? I do not need to say that W. threatened to hang me in so many words. Nevertheless since he has threatened to bring forward my soft epistles in which I remember I wrote that old frights like himself, who could not be contented with amiable wives, but must run about to old procuresses, bribing them to decoy young girls, who are living in perfect retirement in Dukes Row, Somers Town and not dreaming of harm, ought to pay us for the sacrifice they tempt us to make, as well as for our secrecy. However all I entreat of my late tenderly enamoured wooer is that he forthwith fulfil his threat to produce those said letters in court, and lest a small trifle of hanging should be the result, but whether of him or me is yet to be seen, I'll e'en make my Will and so goodbye to ye, old BOMBASTES FURIOSO.

Actions for libel were taken out, not by the nobility, but in 1826 by Mr Blore, a stonemason of Piccadilly, and by Mr Hugh Evans Fisher.

Stockdale wrote his threatening letters in December 1824 to all the members of Whites, Boodles and Crockfords who had at one stage been Harriette's lovers. When Harriette Wilson's diary was published in 1825, several of the Duke's friends made their own comments on it. Sir Walter Scott wrote, 'Here is some good retailing of conversations in which the style of the speaker, so far as known to me, is *exactly* imitated.'

The American Mrs Betsy Patterson wrote to Lady Morgan,

What do you think of Miss Harriett Wilson's life written by herself? Every one reads it. She is living in Paris which seems to be the favourite residence of all naughty English women. Miss H. is married to a very handsome man willing to make an honest woman of her.

This was Colonel Rochefort and the couple lived at No. 111 Rue de Faubourg St Honoré, a very smart address. Harriette was certainly in Paris in 1814 and from 1820 onwards. She charmed the ambassador, Sir Charles Stuart to allow her correspondence to go in the Foreign Office bag.

Harriet Arbuthnot wrote to her husband on 3 February 1825 from Brighton,

By the bye I have seen here Miss Harriet Wilson's book. It is great nonsense but very little indecency, indeed none. What she says of the Duke is so ridiculous and so unlike him that I should doubt her knowing him except for his generosity in giving her money *whenever she wanted it* and I should not think he wd care about it except for the bore of having his intrigues shewn up.

And in her journal in March 1825 she wrote,

the merits of an infamous book lately written by a common street walker giving a history of all her adventures! This woman I understand had turned into ridicule the Duke of Wellington who she claimed as one of her lovers. I asked him if he knew her and he told me he had known her a great number of years ago, so long tho' that he did not think he shld remember her again, that he had never seen her since he married tho' he had frequently given her money when she wrote to beg for it and that she had offered to leave him out of her book if he wd pay. This of course he refused and has never given her a farthing since she threatened him.

There is little doubt that her *Memoirs* were substantially correct. The Duke would naturally, as was his wont, have destroyed all Harriette's letters to him, but what about his letters to her?

Chapter Six

THE PENINSULAR WAR AND THE PORTUGUESE AND SPANISH LADIES

Sir Arthur sailed for the northern shores of Spain and Portugal on 12 July 1808. Apart from the period 4 October to 22 April 1809, he spent the next six years campaigning against the best of Napoleon's generals until on 23 June 1814 he arrived at Dover after a few days spent in Paris.

Sir Arthur's little family of ADCs at his HQ consisted of young Lord Burghersh, eldest son of the 10th Earl of Westmorland, who in 1811 married his favourite niece Priscilla Wellesley-Pole, William's daughter; young Lord Fitzroy Somerset, who was destined to become Lord Raglan of Crimea fame – a handsome, brave, dashing young man who married Emily Wellesley-Pole in August 1815, another favourite niece and Sir Colin Campbell, a young hero of Assaye. They all served with distinction in the Peninsular. Adam Neale and John Hume were Wellesley's key doctors, the latter's daughter Elizabeth being a close friend of Kitty's.

The expedition called briefly at Corunna where the Spanish Junta was contacted. They wanted arms and money but not British reinforcements. The general then called at Oporto, 150 miles further south, where he drank some vintage Port and met the influential Bishop of Oporto, head of the supreme Junta of Portugal. Soon the first successful blending of the Portuguese with the British armies took place. General Bernadin Freire and his army of 6,000 Portuguese troops were to meet Wellesley's army of 9,000 men and advance and capture Lisbon. The British landed at Figuera da Foz, a pretty fishing village, on 30 July.

The first successful battle was at Rolica fifty miles north of Lisbon where the veteran French General Laborde was forced to retreat. Reinforcements from England arrived plus a senior lieutenant-general, Sir Harry Burrard. He wanted to wait for Sir John Moore's force to arrive before tackling Junot's 30,000 French veterans. The British in Portugal could not afford to lose a single battle. There was nowhere to retreat except into the Atlantic Ocean. However the French resolved to attack the lines of Torres Vedras from the east into Vimeiro village (south-west of Rolica on the coast) and northwards from Lisbon. A sharp action followed and the French were defeated and forced to withdraw. Old Sir Harry refused to take advantage of Sir Arthur's success – 'Sir Harry, now is your time to advance. The enemy are completely beaten and we shall be in Lisbon in three days.' Yet another even more elderly and more senior lieutenant-general appeared on the scene – Sir Hew Dalrymple.

To everyone's surprise the French now sued for temporary peace and the Convention of Cintra was signed by which the French were to evacuate Portugal. Frustrated by the convoluted negotiations by the senior generals Sir Arthur went on leave and arrived back in Plymouth on 4 October after barely three months away with two classic battles to his credit. Back in London he was forced to defend at a tribunal his agreement to the Convention of Cintra in which the French army had been allowed to leave Portugal unchallenged, although the two senior generals were entirely responsible for drafting it. He now spent six months in England before returning to campaign in the Peninsula.

The angry Whig opposition members, particularly William Cobbett, took the opportunity to attack the Wellesley family in its entirety. William was at the Admiralty, Henry at the Treasury and Richard was busy negotiating in the corridors of power and with his various mistresses. Sir Arthur first reported to Lord Castlereagh and gave his account of the Portuguese campaign. He saw Harriette Wilson in London and Kitty in Dublin. He went to a royal levée, and in mid-November spent much time attending the tribunal sittings at the Chelsea Hospital. Seven general officers were members of the panel effectively proffering judgement. The consensus of opinion was that after two successful engagements, the terms made with the French were too lenient, even casual. By mid-December the tribunal agreed by six votes to one that the terms of the armistice were acceptable and that of the convention by four votes to three. William Wordsworth and Lord Byron were both quite apoplectic when the results were made known but Sir Walter Scott praised Sir Arthur's conduct. Sir Arthur was now back at his old job as chief secretary in Dublin Castle. The House of Parliament in London voted Arthur their thanks for Vimeiro and Kitty gave a ball in his honour in Dublin.

The gallant Duke of York of Flanders fame was under serious attack as commander-in-chief of the army because of his mistress' speculations. Mrs Mary Anne Clarke, a 'demi-rep' of the same standing as Harriette Wilson had been conducting a skilful entrepreneural business selling commissions, promotions and exchanges in the army presumably with the Duke of York's approval, tacit or otherwise. The little harpy even brought Sir Arthur's name into the scandal that followed when her peccadilloes became known.

Disaster struck the British army at Corunna on 16 January 1809 and Marshal Soult was back in Oporto by March. On 17 March the Duke of York resigned and at the same moment a major scandal shook the Wellesley family. Lady Charlotte Wellesley, Henry's wife and mother of four children eloped with Henry Lord Paget, himself a married man. Henry was ill, desperate and unhappy. But March was not out yet: Kitty's brother Henry Pakenham had substantial gambling debts and that too provoked a major outcry. Despite these scandals Sir Arthur had persuaded Lord Castlereagh to mount another expedition in Portugal with specific conditions that it should be made up of a minimum of 20,000 British troops including 4,000 cavalry and an integrated Portuguese army. Sir Arthur resigned his post as Chief Secretary of Ireland to be succeeded by his friend John William Croker, the diarist. He said goodbye to Kitty and his two young children at Goodwood. He also said farewell several times to Harriette Wilson and sailed for Lisbon, arriving there on 22 April.

There were great rejoicings in the Portuguese capital. Ballads were composed in his honour. At the theatre and opera at San Carlos he was wildly fêted and he was made major-general of all the forces in Portugal, superseding his old friend from Indian days 'Beau' Cradock. The battle for Oporto that took place on 12 May was probably Sir Arthur's most audacious action. His skills in Spain and later in France were usually based on a strong defensive position which the impetuous French generals always attacked – '*toujours l'audace*'. This time he reversed his normal strategy and undertook a brave, almost foolhardy boat-crossing of the wide River Douro which gave the Buffs of the 3rd Foot a toehold, then a foothold and soon a torrent of redcoats stampeded Soult into retreat in heavy rain. French savagery with the local peasantry was met by equal brutality as the wounded and any stragglers were slaughtered.

Soult and Ney were at loggerheads. Junot, Mortier, Kellerman, St Cyr, Lapisse and Sebastiani were scattered over the vast plains of Spain, harassed by Spanish guerillas and with only tenuous communications with King Joseph Bonaparte in Madrid. Napoleon was busy in central Europe and had little time to spare for the problems of the Peninsular.

Sir Arthur's main concerns in the summer of 1809 were the lack of funds to pay his troops and officers and to obtain commissary supplies. His army squandered their energies on plundering, despite the new military police and frequent hanging of offenders. Sir Arthur could only control his own generals by sheer willpower. Daddy Hill, impetuous Picton, Beau Cradock and others all had their moments of irresponsibility if they were out from under their master's eye. Marshal Beresford of the Portuguese army had delusions of grandeur. Lastly his relationship with the errant Spanish generals, Cuesta, La Romana, Venegas, Castanos, Odonoju and others was unsatisfactory.

When discussing the cowardly sprint by deserting Spaniards, Sir Arthur told Croker long afterwards that he never minded troops running away. 'They all do at some time or other, as long as they *came back*.' He could not have believed that his Guards, nor the Buffs, nor his beloved 33rd Foot would actually run! At the battle of Talavera Marshal Victor had 40,000 men and the British/Portuguese/Spanish force only 20,000. On 28 July the French attacked and were shot down. They regrouped, attacked and were shot to pieces despite a totally unjustified charge by a brigade of Guards and the king's German legion, who lost heavily in the process. The British cavalry charged as usual gallantly, as usual out of control, and lost heavily as well. They never learned – it was the fox-hunting tradition, of course, trot, gallop, charge, and the devil take the hindmost.

Sir Arthur thought that Talavera was the hardest fought battle of modern times, even worse than Assaye. The Allies lost 5,000 men, a quarter of their force, and the French over 7,000, but were forced to withdraw. It was Sir Arthur's first major European victory. His brother William, back at home, chose the title for him that King George III would confer on the victor of Talavera. The Viscount Wellington of Talavera now takes over from Sir Arthur Wellesley.

A major risk of starvation soon meant that it was impossible to stay in Spain. Wellington retreated and his brother Richard, Lord Wellesley, arrived as British minister in Seville, accompanied by a demi-rep, a courtesan called Sally Douglas, with a 'grand establishment.' The Wellesleys never did anything by halves. If it had to be a scandal, it was a scandal on the grand scale.

In addition, brother Henry's troubled marriage continued to contribute to the family notoriety. He had divorced his Cadogan wife in June but was again living with her. Lady Charlotte produced a daughter in 1810, of whom Lord Paget was the father. It was just as well that, 'Lord Wellington laughs at all the calumnies the papers publish.' But it was not only the papers that reckoned the Wellesley family was in trouble.

Lady Sarah Napier, mother of the gallant sons who so distinguished themselves in Portugal and Spain, wrote to her friend Lady Susan O'Brien,

> Now for my military news from officers who have returned. The position of Lord Wellington is bad for the sick and they don't recover. They were all nearly starved for one fortnight by the failure of Spanish faith and neglect of the English commissaries. Whose fault is that? Why the Commander in Chief's to be sure ... and then you well know that a Commander in Chief *who publickly keeps a mistress at headquarters* does not give all the attention to the care of his army and disgusts his army who lose all confidence in him.

In December Lady Sarah wrote, 'he is an ambitious Englishman who wanted all the glory for himself ... I wonder how long we shall hold Portugal?'

Who was this mistress at Wellington's headquarters? One rumour current was that it was Lady Albert Conyingham. Sir Charles Oman wrote that Lord Wellington's relations with 'the other sex were unedifying'.

Wellington was in Lisbon on 10 September to prepare his secret defences of Torres Vedras, north of Lisbon, with his chief engineer, Colonel Richard Fletcher. He found the army at Lisbon in disarray, and reduced all leave to a minimum. No one needed to stay in bed with the same woman longer than forty-eight hours, was the edict that he issued to his army in Portugal. In a court martial of a certain Lieutenant Pearse he decreed that the word honour should not be linked with the act of going to a brothel.

That winter he made Viseu his army HQ – a pretty village in the mountains east of Lisbon near the Spanish frontier. Napoleon by now had increased his veteran army in Spain to over 30,000 troops and his ambition was to drive the 'Leopard' into the sea; Wellington was still army commander of the 'Leopards', that large dangerous breed of wild cats. 'When I shall show myself beyond the Pyrenées the frightened leopard will fly to the ocean, to avoid shame, defeat and death.'

The victory at Talavera brought Wellington an additional pension of £2,000 per annum. Even Creevey, the diarist who disliked him, wrote,

> All our indignation against him ended in smoak. Better still his army under his eagle eye – and nose – was at last improved.

Wellington was, as usual, everywhere. In Badajoz hunting red deer, in Seville, and he saw Richard in Cadiz before his return home. Even his old rival for Kitty's hand, Lowry Cole, now a divisional commander under him, wrote,

> I never served under any chief I like so much, as Lord W. He has treated me with much more confidence than I had a right or could be expected from anyone.

His staff gossiped and preferred 'writing news and keeping coffee houses' and positively 'croaked' to their friends and relations back at home. Sir Charles Stewart, adjutant-general and Castlereagh's half-brother was the leading 'croaker'. The Lisbon opera was a great attraction with Catalini, Collini and Naldi singing to the cosmopolitan audience, and Sir William Peacocke, the governor of Lisbon was host to many of Wellington's officers.

The winter of 1809/10 had its compensations despite Lord Byron's caustic verse:

> How many Wellesleys did embark for Spain
> As if therein they meant to colonise?

Riding to hounds was a favourite sport. Lord Wellington had his own pack, as did several other officers including young Harry Smith, who later on married a beautiful Spanish bride. Lord W. found the Spanish and Portuguese señoras and señoritas very attractive.

On 14 October 1809, in Badajoz, a great ball was given by Donna Payna and Donna Anna Fortunata of Elvas to honour King Ferdinand VII's birthday. Lord W. was impressed by the boleros and fandangos danced by the hostess and a second lady, a handsome widow named Donna Manuela, who sang a Spanish ballad accompanied by the guitar. Country dances and cotillons were formed and Lord W. joined in the singing. Another Badajoz hostess was the Marchionesse of Monte Salud; no beauty, but very intelligent, who entertained her guests to musical evenings with piano, flute and guitars. Most of the officers agreed the Marchionesse D'Almeida was the youngest and loveliest Spanish beauty present. The ladies, including Donna Josepha Basquez, sang and danced boleros accompanied by Señor Fuentes, the guitarist. This type of soirée was called a Tertulia, and was popular with the musical general.

The memoirs of Charles Greville quoted in 'Epitaph of the Beau' written in 1852 noted:

> In his younger days he was extremely addicted to gallantry and had great success with women of whom one in Spain gained great influence over him and his passion for whom very nearly involved him in serious difficulties. His other ladies did little more than amuse his idle hours and subserve his social habits and with most of them his liaisons were certainly very innocent.

Captain Thomas Bunbury's journal tells of,

> a Canon from the Cathedral of Lamego, whose niece or daughter was *always* at the parties given for or by the English officers in Oporto and elsewhere. The young lady was good looking with light coloured hair. She went by the name of 'The Lorda', a soubriquet she had acquired from having been a great favourite of Lord Wellington who was so much pleased with her performance on the pianoforte at the Convent of Viseu where his Lordship and staff were wont to repair almost every day during their stay there, that he made her a present of a piano which he had sent out to her from England.

Bunbury mentioned that she certainly played well and was about to take the veil and be engaged as organist at a convent in Oporto where none but ladies of rich and noble families professed. They even had theatrical performances and other amusements in the convent of the order she was about to enter. 'I know this world is all vanity and folly' wrote the captain of the 50th Regiment of Foot!

Captain William Stothert of the 3rd Foot Guards who were stationed at Viseu guarding the army HQ noted that there were two monasteries. The British officers, including their commander-in-chief, preferred to visit the St Josephine monastery to watch and hear the fair novice Donna Antonia Maria, who entranced them with her playing on the organ and pianoforte. The probability is that pretty little 'Lorda' did not hie her to the convent after all, because *four years later* on the anniversary of the siege and storming of Ciudad Rodrigo on 8–19 January 1812, a grand fête was held at which Lowry Cole was awarded the Order of the Bath.

A grand dinner and a ball was followed by supper for sixty-five people including Spanish and Portuguese dignitaries. The supper rooms were hung with crimson, satin and gold. At the ball there were 150 officers and forty ladies including the Marquis D'Espesa *and two nieces of a 'chanoin'* who danced the bolero and fandango and played music. Many toasts were drunk in claret and the Portuguese wine of Lamego. Sir Colin Campbell and General O'Lalor managed the fête and Lord W. was as usual in high spirits.

Ensign Cowell Stepney was at Elvas on the Portuguese frontier in March 1812 and dined at Wellington's HQ. Lord W. was in high spirits and most attentive to two pretty Portuguese girls who inevitably formed the centre of attraction. They spoke French well and displayed good manners and gratified Lord W.'s taste for music by singing many pretty airs. A gallant troubador Colonel Hon. Thomas Fermor of the 3rd Guards was so inspired as to indulge the ladies *en revanche* with several French romances. Lowry Cole's friend George Bell who kept a journal reported:

> We had some very handsome Spanish senoras who looked on and laughed through their bright eyes but understood nothing [this was at the General's HQ at Curia]. There was one fair and beautiful Englishwoman always present, joyous and happy, a charming representative of those bright stars of Albion, whose presence was always cheering amongst so many redcoats, the only lady at HQ, wife of Colonel C---, General Hill's ADC who fell afterwards at Waterloo.

She may have been Lady Albert Conyngham.

On the other hand Francis Larpent, Wellington's judge advocate-general, was rather dubious about the social climate.

> At W's H.Q.'s there are no books, no women but ladies of *a certain description* and as to living, you would be surprised what good living is here except at Lord W.'s table and about two more and even at those, no port wine, only thin claret, and the country wines of Lamego and Portuguese brandy. Major and Mrs Scobell – she is the only *English lady* here, and one Portuguese lady, niece to Captain Mor, but ugly, smells of oily saltfish. The H.Q. in three wretched villages four miles from Freinada and eight from Castell Bom.

Freineda is in Portugal a few miles west of Fuentes D'Onoro on the frontier: it was Lord W.'s HQ for two successive winters.

Captain Cooke of the 43rd Light Infantry wrote in his journal that the Señora Maria Josepha of Fuentes D'Onoro was one of the girls who sang very pretty airs in praise of the renowned chieftain. She was the happy

Moza or Muchacha with striking castanets whose charms were extolled at this period at HQ's and elsewhere. Lady Sarah Napier wrote to Lady O'Brien on 25 October 1809,

> I heard today what Lord Wellington's ideas were of what was to be done in Spain and to my humble conception they are a bubblemaking, a plausible sounding appearance and must break and vanish into air.

Her three young sons Charles, George and William, had fought with Sir John Moore and were now soldiering with some success under Lord W. Their mother wrote,

> what is their object in life – fame – and where can they learn to deserve it better than in such a moment? A good cause, a good commander and good climate at an early age when zeal is warm in their hearts and gilds every horror of war. Happy age!

She was less hostile to the C-in-C when he promoted George and William from captains to brevet-majors.

Lord Wellington spent little time in Lisbon even during the long winter quarters of the next two years. The next three years of campaigning were all of a similar pattern. The Anglo-Portuguese armies would make determined forays into Spain punctuated by successful set-piece battles with Wellington usually in a defensive position, nearly always heavily outnumbered. The highly skilled British infantry would outshoot the French grenadiers and the British cavalry would fail to follow up successfully. The French marshals would in due course bring up very heavy reinforcements and the Anglo-Portuguese armies would retreat losing no battles but with many casualties through sickness and wounds. The Spanish guerillas would hamper the French, and Wellington's superb defences at Torres Vedras were never really tested. For the French to lose a battle was important mainly in terms of prestige, but for the Allies to lose a single battle would have been a major disaster and might have resulted eventually in the loss of Portugal. Savage battles took place at Ciudad Rodrigo, Busaco, Fuentes d'Onoro and Badajoz with similar results – heavy casualties on both sides but the Anglo-Portuguese army undefeated.

Most of the 17,000 Allied sick and wounded slowly recovered in the winter of 1811 while Wellington attended dinners, balls, an occasional theatre and opera, amateur theatrical, and hunted. On 27 June 1811 Wellington wrote to a love-sick major requesting leave to save his fiancée's heart from breaking,

We read occasionally of desperate cases of this description, but I cannot say that I have ever yet known a young lady dying of love. They contrive in some manner to live and live tolerably well notwithstanding their despair and the continual absence of their lover and some even have been known to recover so far as to be inclined to *take another lover, if the absence of the first has lasted for long.*

After his third successive winter quarters in Portugal, Arthur must have hoped that it would be his last. Rather surprisingly he commenced campaigning in the winter of 1812. The troops marched through the snow, and after a twelve-day siege took the fortress of Ciudad Rodrigo from under the nose of Marmont, who was at Salamanca. All the diarists present there – Kincaid, William Bragge, Private Wheeler, Harry Smith and others describe the siege and the subsequent bloody sack of the town. The Allied army lost 1,100 men and the French 2,500 including prisoners. A grateful government and Prince Regent in need of good news created Arthur, Earl of Wellington, with an increased pension of £4,000. Money was now flowing in from all directions. The Spanish Cortes created Arthur Duke of Ciudad Rodrigo and a Grandee of Spain. His devoted Spanish ADC, General Don Miguel de Alava carried his victory despatch to Madrid. Alava, who was two years younger than Wellington, always looked ten to twenty years older. He had fought at Trafalgar in the Spanish part of the Franco-Spanish fleet. He had estates and a mansion near Vittoria, and was a great patriot and raconteur. An ugly little man, he adored Wellington and did his best to stay close to him for the rest of his life. Alava had a fund of anecdotes and it is a pity that his memories were not translated. One famous remark of his was, 'J'en ai pris en horreur, les deux mots "daylight et cold meat".' The ritual conversation between the two men was 'When do we start?' and 'What would there be for dinner?'

Colonel Cadogan wrote:

Lord W. is particularly gay and playful in conversation, enjoys fun, always the first to promote amusement. Always able to sleep at any moment rolled in his cloak on the bare ground, his slumbers are as peaceful and profound as those of a child. When he awakes he is immediately in possession of his faculties.

Major-General Long (not his favourite cavalry officer) wrote:

The Spaniards appear thunderstruck with this miraculous change in their affairs and they begin to think Lord W. is *really* a General and they are piously given to call him an Angel.

The next target was Badajoz – for the third time. The siege began in March and the attack was launched on 6 April, Easter Sunday. If the storming of Ciudad Rodrigo was cruel, that of Badajoz was like battering at the gates of Hell. The storming was disastrous and 5,000 officers and men were killed and wounded – four times that of the earlier siege. It is difficult to understand why Wellington was prepared to take Badajoz – *come what may*. He knew only too well the difficulties of a set-piece siege against resolute and well-armed defenders. Wellington blamed the slaughter on the lack of engineers, miners and sappers. But for an army commander who (like Monty a century and a half later) husbanded his major resource, the British infantryman, his decision to throw them away, to waste them, was incredible. The great man cried after the slaughter.

Even worse was the slaughter of the defenders and the rapine that went on for three days. The diarists who were present – Bragge, Kincaid, Donaldson, Leith-Hay, Tomkinson, Grattan – all agreed that plundering and looting were appropriate actions. Leith-Hay wrote 'the immemorial privilege of tearing the town to pieces.' He should have added 'and the occupants.'

That summer Wellington had, as usual, a variety of choices. He could march north, or south, or east. In the event in June he marched with his Allied army of nearly 50,000 men towards Salamanca. The Beau decided to invade that city and eventually with little loss entered it on 27 June. His reception was chronicled.

> Lord W. was in great danger of being smothered by the crowds of women who aspired to the honour, of not only seeing, but I believe kissing his Excellency. The twenty seven nunneries were all thrown open and the repeated shouts of '*Viva los Ingleses*' have made my head ache. [Tomkinson wrote] The inhabitants were out of their senses at having got rid of the French and nearly pulled Lord Wellington off his horse. The women were the most violent, many coming up and embracing him. He was writing orders on his sabretach and was interrupted three or four times by them. . . . Salamanca . . . excited women crowded around him with tears and kisses, almost pulled from his saddle.

Goya painted him unshaven, wild, hollow-eyed with damp hair, a most unfamiliar Wellington. A *Te Deum* was sung in the cathedral and the magistrates of the city gave him a ball. The joy of the inhabitants who cried and embraced him was immense. One *old* woman hugged and kissed him, to his great annoyance.

After Ciudad Rodrigo and Salamanca there were 'gaieties, fêtes, balls without end and masquerades' to celebrate the French defeats.

Several fascinating descriptions of the Spanish ladies were written down by the Peninsular journal-keepers.

> At Mass they dressed in black: the wealthy in silk, the others in camel hair trimmed with velvet and lace. They wore white silk stockings and shoes, white gloves to the elbow and short skirts with fringes six inches in length. Their calves were pretty, they had small kissable feet and wore black veils which they held with two fingers in such a way as to conceal half their faces and to leave room for their dark eyes to flash between. Their hips were well developed and their arms and breasts very full. But their waists made one long to clasp them and their whole figures were charming, well rounded but slender. Their gait was regal. The church bells were pealing the whole day but they were well tuned and not unpleasant!

Several Spanish families 'of rank' discussed with their saviour the merits of sending their children for education to Catholic schools in England. Lord W. wrote off to England on their behalf for details of suitable schools. He purchased three female dresses for his nieces in England so that they could use them for masquerades. They were covered with hand work, embroidery, lace and gold and he paid 2,000 'dollars' for them. He was called Vellington or Belinton or even Velliston, the letter 'W' being unfamiliar to the Latin races. He wrote to his brother William,

> The people of Salamanca swear that my Mother is a Saint and the daughter of a Saint to which circumstance I owe all my good fortune!! Pray tell her this.

Although Marshal Marmont had been badly wounded, Wellington's own generals were in worse shape – Beresford, Lowry Cole and Cotton wounded and Graham and Picton still sick. Of his various options a march on Madrid seemed the best and three weeks after Salamanca the Allied army entered the Spanish capital in triumph. On 12 August Captain Bowles wrote 'They appear to consider Lord W. as a species of divinity.' Shawls and mantles were spread for his horse to tread upon and when he dismounted he was so violently embraced by feminine admirers, being handed from one to the other that he became fairly exhausted by their uncontrollable attentions. He wrote to Sir John Malcolm,

> I am among a people mad with joy for their delivrance from their oppressors. God send that my good fortune may continue and that I may be the instrument of securing their independence and happiness.

Back in London Lady Bessborough was cheered by an enthusiastic little

Spanish lady who clasped her hands together in ecstasy at the mention of Wellington's name and said in pretty broken English 'a most great Capitan or sooner a Gode gone to save my poor country.' In Madrid, Frederick Ponsonby wrote,

> if Lord Wellington would have let them they would have knelt and prayed to him! A ballet of delectable young ladies were present with offerings of grapes, sticky sweet, laurel leaves and divine worship. Old Duero was high-nosed, aloof and silent with wild brunettes covering his hands, sword, boots and horse with kisses. And the bells rang all day.

He was made Marquess of Wellington on 18 August and the next month Generalissimo of the Spanish armies, a role he was reluctant to accept. Control of their own armies by the Spanish generals such as Cuesta was so limited, that how could he, from afar, control the Spanish commanders?

William Grattan of the Connaught Rangers found himself at St Ildefonso, a suburb in Madrid, and commented favourably on the magnificent waterworks, elegant gardens and pleasure grounds.

> In the evening at 6.30 p.m., and this was mid-summer, the fountains were playing and inspiring airs wafted over the gardens from the musical bands. At 8 p.m. Lord W. was surrounded by a number of generals, a splendid staff and many grandees of Spain to the tune of 'See the Conquering Hero comes'. The females disregarding all form of etiquette broke through the crowd to get a nearer view of his Lordship and many embraced him as he passed down the different alleys of the gardens. Songs were followed by bolero-dancing and later waltzing – one of the most intoxicating and delightful nights of pleasure that we had ever witnessed. The great street in Madrid was Puerto del Sol filled with merchants, dealers, higglers, charcoal vendors, fellows with lemonade on their backs, girls with pannellas of water crying out *Quien quiere agua?* Nothing could stop the populace which mixed with us. The officers were nearly all forced from their horses in the embrace of the females and some there were who actually lost their seats, if not their hearts.

It was in this heady excitement that Wellington met the beautiful Spanish Duchess of San Carlos and Benavente/Ossuna. She considered herself indebted to him for everything, having been made an exile by the French government of Spain from her immense possessions. Fortescue recounts how W. spent sixteen days in Cadiz in early 1812 riding through winter floods on a 'romantic visit'!

The estates of Ossuna and Benavente were near the Spanish border with Portugal. The palace of the Duke of Ossuna with its lofty towers

The Young Commander –
'food for powder and
nothing more' . . . 'a
charming young man.
Handsome, fashioned, tall
and elegant . . .'

The Game of Hearts –
'Harriette Wilson, far from
beautiful but a smart, saucy
girl with good eyes, dark
hair and the manner of a
wild schoolboy . . .'

Kitty Pakenham, the 'Longford Lily', the belle of Dublin, Duchess of Wellington. 'Very amiable, very religious, entertaining for her husband unbounded admiration, she could not bring herself to take the slightest interest in the subjects which mainly engrossed his attention . . .'

was in Beja, not far from Salamanca. That of Benavente near Villa Franca, Astorga and Labaneza. The Beau was in both regions in the spring of 1813 and he would have met the duchess again at either of these estates.

Wellington's private papers include a revealing letter to him from Madrid dated 11 *de enero*. It was a missive of thanks from *La Duquesa de San Carlos* for sending her 30,000 reales. She promised to repay them '*pronto posible*' and signed herself his '*apasionada Amiga*' which says it all.

The Duke's Spanish estate when he was given the titles of Duque de Vittoria, and separately of Ciudad Rodrigo, were at Soto de Roma near Granada. He never visited them but later in his life under an English manager, they produced wine and olive crops. He never drew any income from his Spanish estates. Later on in life the Duke's favourite order to wear was the Spanish Order of the Golden Fleece given him by the Princess of the Peace (Maria Theresa de Bourbon, niece of King Charles IV of Spain). It was a superb creation of diamonds suspended by a red ribbon, plus medals for Vimeira 1808, Talavera 1808/9, Torres Vedras 1809, Ciudad Rodrigo 1812, Badajoz 1812, Salamanca 1812, Vittoria 1813, Toulouse 1814. Wellington regarded his success in Spain as due to being a '*conquerant sans ambition*'. He had for a time sovereign power but no one had suspected him of any design to become king of Spain or Portugal. 'I *was* almost King of Spain.'

Wellington was installed at the Palacio Real, the royal palace, and immediately put out a proclamation to maintain law and order. The constitution of Spain was established by the Cortes in the name of King Ferdinand VII. The proclamation was signed by the Duque de Ciudad Rodrigo. A minor engagement then followed to capture 2,000 French soldiers with 200 artillery pieces holding out in the Retiro Citadel. The bizarre uniforms of the Spanish guerillas with mantles and plumes were now much in evidence. Wellington had always praised their role behind the lines of communication. He now had verses composed to him:

> 'Velinton' en Arapiles
> A Marmon y a' sus parciales
> Para almorzar les dispuse
> Un gran pisto de tomaates
> Y tanto les dio
> Que les fastidio.

He was painted again by Goya, this time from life, he attended balls, concerts and serenades, festinas, theatre, opera, corridas (which the English found abhorrent, particularly the blood lust displayed by the

Spanish ladies) and in turn he and many other officers gave balls.

> Proud Wellington prances, we march at his bid
> And bad plays shall be acted again in Madrid

Private Wheeler was enchanted by the pretty pale-faced black-eyed maids who modestly offered him nosegays or sprigs of parma or of olive while,

> others of the sex more bold would dash into our ranks, take off our caps and place a sprig of laurel, then seize our arm and sing some martial air to the memory of some immortal patriot. Thus we slowly moved on amidst the sweet voice of thousands of the most bewitching and interesting little devils I had ever seen. The people were mad with joy. They called us their deliverers, their saviors '*Vivi Vellinton, Vivi les Angoless, Vivi les Ilandoes.*' Every bell that had got a clapper was set ringing the windows were ornamented with rich drapery embroidered with gold and silver. The whole of the windows and tops of the houses were crowded with Spanish beauty waving white handkerchiefs. The people endeavoured to drag us inside their houses.

Despite Bonaparte's increasing commitment and losses on the Russian steppes there were still three substantial French armies in Spain. King Joseph's was near Valencia, Soult was in Andalusia in the south and Clausel was still in the north-west in Burgos. The autumn of 1812 was a difficult time for Wellington. At the back of his mind was the site of his winter quarters. All the military historians write of this crucial period. One view was that the occupation of Madrid was a political sop to help the government at home. But if the Anglo-Portuguese armies were fated to leave Madrid and scuttle back to Portugal for the winter surely Madrid's occupation was of no help to anyone, least of all to the excited Madridilenos who had no idea how short the occupation was going to be. The British occupation of Madrid was for less than a month. Burgos was unsuccessfully besieged and Wellington began yet another long, painful and very costly retreat back into Portugal, losing thousands of men *en route*.

It was probably the darkest period in his life and many eye-witnesses commented on his bad humour, almost despondency. He was forty-three, with titles and military fame but the French were just as powerful in Spain as ever before. Possibly there was some consolation in that Bonaparte's retreat from Moscow was on a scale ten times more deadly than his own. Wellington had lost 5,000 men, on his retreat, but had sent 20,000 French prisoners back to England. But 'All the French gentlemen were NOT safe on the other side of the Ebro' as he had hoped. In December he was in Cadiz for sixteen days to see his brother – and also to see his charming Spanish duchesses.

Chapter Seven

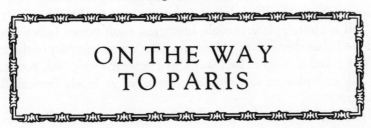

ON THE WAY TO PARIS

The emperor was back in Paris with his defeated '*Grande Armée*' but he still had 200,000 troops in Spain, double those of the Allies.

Wellington now in his winter quarters appeared to concentrate on hunting Portuguese foxes with over 20 couple of hounds. There were however many agreeable dinners at HQ to celebrate former victories: Christmas dinner was served at Freinada, and visits to the theatre and the opera in Lisbon were made. As usual amateur theatricals were popular with the Light Division at Gallegos. But the main occasion was the grand ball to celebrate the anniversary of Ciudad Rodrigo. Wellington's favourite song was '*Ahé Marmont, onde vai Marmont*' accompanied by a guitarist with dark flashing eyes.

More honours flowed towards him – the colonelcy of the Blues and the Order of the Garter and even more pensions.

He was still in winter quarters by the spring of 1813, but by the end of May had again occupied Salamanca. He had divided his army into two parts and they eventually linked up at Toro, a town on the Spanish section of the River Duero west of Vallodolid. He had marched 400 miles in 40 days! By 21 June he had deployed his full army of 78,000 men against King Joseph's 57,000 troops a few miles west of Vittoria. The unusual, as always, happened. A Spanish brigade fought well and took the hill of Puebla. The Earl of Dalhousie, commanding the 7th Division, and Picton's 3rd got lost. Dalhousie had distinguished himself the year before by getting lost on the retreat from Burgos. The Hussars committed mass suicide in Arinez. Young Harry Smith performed well. Picton shouting, cursing and screaming, encouraged his 3rd Division to achieve miracles. By 5 p.m. King Joseph Bonaparte accepted defeat, leaving much of the 'whole wealth of Spain and the Indies' available for looting and pillage by the Allied troops. The predictable result was that the French as usual succeeded in getting away despite losses of 8,000 compared to the Allies' losses of 5,000 troops. They lost 150 field guns and immense quantities of ammunition.

For at least a day the Allied army gave up fighting and abandoned itself to looting the five million dollars – the whole of the French army's pay – as well as church plate, medals, uniforms, snuff boxes, ladies' dresses (and the ladies themselves). General Gazan's wife was part of the spoil. She was asked if another lady was also a general's wife. '*Ah, pour cela – non, elle est seulement sa femme de campagne.*' A lovely cynical Gallic comment.

King Joseph managed to get 55,000 men safely over the Pyrenées and back into France, due to, as Wellington put it 'our vagabond soldiers . . . totally knocked up' by their day and night of looting and plunder. On 2 July he wrote his famous letter,

> It is quite impossible for me or any other man to command a British army under the existing system. We have in the service the scum of the earth as common soldiers . . .

The British army were volunteers, the French were conscripts and the standards of discipline were correspondingly low – and high.

The Prince Regent made Wellington a field marshal. Napoleon's huge losses in Russia meant that at long last his armies in Spain had been reduced and whittled down to the point where Wellington had, for the first time, military superiority in numbers and could thus develop a consistently stronger offensive. A Spanish proverb ran, 'In Spain a small army is defeated and a large army starves.' Wellington knew this full well and managed to keep his armies just of sufficient size not to be defeated, nor to starve! The king of Spain said of him '*Yo quiero mucho a Wellington: es un gran General*'. But perhaps the greatest accolade of all came from the defeated Bonaparte, who said of Wellington that the Duke equalled him in everything and excelled him in one thing – caution.

San Sebastian and Pamplona were still garrisoned by the French and Clausel had a strong force at Logrono, as did Foy near Bilbao. Suchet was resisting strongly on the east coast near Tarragona. By the end of June Marshal Soult, who had replaced King Joseph, had reorganised his forces on the French side of the Pyrenées, now joined by Clausel's, Foy's and some other units. San Sebastian looked like falling quite soon but Pamplona was well fortified and did not warrant a costly siege. The

Anglo-Portuguese army of 50,000 men was now confronted by a French army of about 84,000 who were still in a state of shock after their ignominious retreat from Spain. Wellington's Spanish army of 25,000 was now discouraged from straying outside their home country, so they blockaded Pamplona, and also guarded Irun on the main coast road.

On 7 October 1813 Wellington invaded France after five years of more or less non-stop campaigning. Beating the Frenchies on their own home ground was a novel concept to the Europeans who had suffered at Boney's hands for exactly twenty years. Bordeaux and Toulouse were the two prime targets with the prospect of bitter and determined resistance by Soult's army. Rain, more rain and the flooded River Disassoa, were the initial deterrents. The Spanish contingent looted the village of Ascain and Wellington sent them packing back into Spain and was prepared, although outnumbered, to take on Soult. The Portuguese, who had always fought well when integrated with the English brigades, were wanted back in their home country in case the *Spaniards* decided to invade Portugal. Marshal Beresford was sent back to Lisbon to delay any rash decisions for a recall.

Wellington's headquarters were at St Jean de Luz, a large, attractive fishing village south-west of Bayonne. Soon winter fox-hunting, reviews, dinners and theatricals were the non-martial order of the day, and on 18 January 1814 Wellington gave a grand ball to celebrate the queen's birthday. It was attended by quite a few English ladies, mostly married. One officer present noted 'We have still only four of the legitimate kind of lady'.

Wellington gave another ball on the 11 February. There were now many anniversaries to celebrate. He frequently wore the sky-blue Salisbury coat presented to him by his admirer, Emily Mary, at Hatfield House. His brother-in-law Culling Smith found him more hounds and horses for the winter chase. Little Captain Gronow noted,

> Lord W. with his hounds, dressed in a light blue frock coat (colour of Hatfield hunt), a present from Lady Salisbury, then one of the leaders of the fashionable world and an enthusiastic admirer of His Lordship.

By the middle of February Wellington took the initiative and decided to bypass Bayonne. Perhaps the siege of San Sebastian was fresh in his memory. The River Adour was now a significant water barrier swollen by the winter flooding. Both Wellington and his faithful Spanish ADC General Alava received minor wounds on 27 February. A bullet struck W.'s sword-hilt, badly bruising his thigh, and he could not ride for a week afterwards. Rumours were now circulating that the Prussian and

Allied armies were converging on Paris and indeed the Treaty of Chaumont was signed on 31 March as the Allies really did enter Paris. The news sadly only reached Wellington a week later, by which time the assault on Toulouse had started. 'A very severe affair' it was too, in Wellington's words. Soult was driven out of the town on 10 April at a heavy cost to the Allies of 4,500 casualties, to the French loss of 3,200. News was brought from Bordeaux by Colonel Ponsonby (Harriette Wilson's lover) that Napoleon had abdicated, and King Louis XVIII had been restored. At the grand dinner in Toulouse after the battle was over much champagne flowed; General Alava proposed 'El Liberador de Espana!' and the celebrations lasted all night. The war was over at last, even though game old Marshal Soult, then in the beautiful walled city of Carcassone, refused to surrender. Worse still the Governor of Bayonne decided to go down fighting to the bitter end, and both sides lost a thousand casualties in pointless savage combat, in which General Hay was killed and General Hope wounded. There was a short time before the little army disbanded – some troops were sent to the American war – the Portuguese went back home, and the rest sailed from Bordeaux. The cavalry rode overland to the Channel ports.

Lord Byron, as radical as ever, wrote 'Buonaparte has fallen – I regret it – the restoration of the despicable Bourbons – the triumph of tameness over talent.' He was undoubtedly the only man in England to lament the downfall of the Corsican.

On 3 May Arthur Wellesley was made Duke of Wellington and he wrote this to his brother Henry in Madrid, 'I believe I forgot to tell you that I was made a Duke.' He went by coach to Paris and arrived for the great parade of Allied troops before Louis XVIII, which took place on 4 May. Under his round top hat, and white neckcloth there was his familiar blue frock-coat, a sombre contrast to the fineries of Russia and Prussia. He stayed in Paris for a week, and then went by coach to Madrid to see the king, his brother Henry and the Spanish duchesses. On 17 May with General Alava and Lord Fitzroy Somerset, the king of Spain received them very well at a ball in their honour.

After the difficult victory outside Toulouse the Duke, as he then was, spent several weeks in Madrid and its environs. He knew it well and particularly the palace of La Granja with its courtyards and fountains. In May and June he was back in Toulouse to see the French actress Madame Georges play Voltaire's *Semiramus*. He stayed in the Hotel de France and was seen to be in the company of Madame C---, a Spanish beauty married into a French family of rank. She lived in one angle or *apartement* in the same hotel and ADC's were discouraged from making visits.

Henry Wellesley, minister at Madrid after Richard's tenure, wrote to Arthur on 15 May 1815, 'After all you have gone through, you will find diplomacy a very pretty amusement.' Was Henry only referring to the future appointment for Arthur as ambassador in Paris, or to the pretty amusements in Madrid the Duke had noticeably enjoyed? De Monvel wrote that 'W. was accompanied everywhere by a tall dark creature who had followed him from Spain as his mistress.'

Chapter Eight

KITTY AT HOME

When her husband sailed for Spain in July 1808 on the *Surveillante*, the relationship between Kitty and Arthur, after a little over two years of marriage, had been clearly established. Despite his impeccable manners Sir Arthur was obviously disappointed in his little Irish bride. Before he left for India he was convinced that she held high moral principles, had a sense of duty and was a strong minded young woman of great charm, interested in the arts and literature. He knew that she wrote verse, painted, was musical and that she read a lot. She would have been a gregarious young lady surrounded by a large family (and for her brothers he had a great respect and liking) and by many friends. The Pakenham's were fecund and Arthur wanted a family, particularly and traditionally, of sons. And in this respect on the balance sheet of two years Kitty had performed admirably, but in every other way he weighed her in the balance and found her wanting. According to G.R. Glieg, his earliest biographer, Kitty had broken another engagement to marry Arthur, who reckoned he had been grossly deceived.

Looking back objectively on all Arthur Wellesley's relationships with a score or more of women, it is probable that he wanted, like most men, the best of all worlds. The carnal joys of Harriette Wilson, the intellectual stimulation of Madame de Staël, the political cut and thrust of Harriet Arbuthnot, the diplomatic intrigues of the Princess Lieven, the warm undemanding, platonic love of Lady Shelley, the spiritual challenge produced by Miss Anna Maria Jenkins and the passion that he enjoyed with Madame Grassini, Mrs Patterson and several others.

Very soon he discovered that he and Kitty had nothing in common except the two young children. She was indiscreet, tactless, quick tempered, and gossiped too much, so that he kept her in ignorance of his plans and his problems. She had not the interest in either his political or his army career to warrant any discussion nor the merest mention of them in his letters to her from Portugal and Spain. She was no longer either good looking nor well-dressed – two attributes which Sir Arthur required from his ladies. She could not manage her household budget and accounts, she was incompetent. Her little charities siphoned off money due to pay tradesmen (who then dunned her husband). She was weak and unreliable, and lack of reliability was for Wellington a cardinal sin in man or woman. Her lack of logic annoyed him and her arguments and 'lame excuses' just made him ignore, even avoid her. She had no sense of humour, and drama and tragedy were essential to her daily life. As the children grew older, she became over-protective, inspiring them to fear their father and eventually to avoid him for months, occasionally years at a time. There came a stage when he was mildly ashamed to bring his friends to Stratfield Saye. Harriet Arbuthnot, Lady Shelley and several others were unanimous in their dislike, tinged with pity, for his unsuitable wife. The sad thing is that Kitty adored her husband and made the greatest efforts to keep his love – but totally failed.

Some of her poetry was circulated within the Pakenham family and their friends.

On the death of Sarah, a nurse

> Let one short word her various worths include
> Can eloquence say more than 'She was good'.

On her own grave illness in 1796

> Returning from the gates of death
> Within whose awful porch I lay
> Again to draw the vital breath
> And view the cheerful day.

On the shores of Lough Eske seeking spiritual guidance

> May my firm soul the impious wit detest
> With scorn discourage the unhallowed jest
> Teach me to live as born one day to die
> And view the eternal world with constant eye.

One might have expected that their love of music would have kept Kitty and Arthur in some harmony. She played the harp and pianoforte but gave them up fairly soon. Later she rather vaguely took up the harp again, and many years afterwards decided to buy a new pianoforte. She was so short-sighted that her music making was not particularly skilful.

She painted flower studies in watercolour and took months to actually complete any work. Being a dilettante, she decided to take drawing lessons from the painter Josiah Slater, but never finished them. Kitty took up shoe-making, a fashionable pastime for bored young ladies, but made very few. 'I have completed a galoche this evening.' She made smocks for the children and hemmed handkerchiefs for Arthur. Her reading included most of Sir Walter Scott's works including *Lady of the Lake* and *Waverley*, and she frequented the local libraries, mainly to read the daily papers seeking news of her absent husband. *Roman Comique de Salon*, Espriella's *Letters from a Spaniard*, *Memoirs de Sully*, *Gil Blas*, and *Revolutions in Portugal* were some of the books she read.

Kitty took up riding but was never a competent equestrienne. One of the reasons why Wellington in Paris after Waterloo was so intensely taken with the lovely Lady Shelley was that she was a superb rider and he could take her with complete confidence to his military reviews in front of the crowned heads of Europe. Alternately very active taking long walks with the boys, Kitty was then totally jaded with deep Irish depression when nothing went right. Her confidence in herself was reduced by Arthur's cool indifference, and she disliked appearing in public for a variety of reasons. One was that she was so short-sighted that she could not recognise people. Another that she did not dress as well as any of Arthur's lady friends, partly from lack of taste and partly from lack of funds in the early days of their marriage. Nevertheless she was received at Court, went to musical evenings, occasional theatres, and later on in Paris, made a brave show as the ambassador's wife (for a week or so before being sent back home).

Kitty, like many of her friends, decided in 1809 to compile a daily journal and these are some extracts from it.

> If I delay any longer what I have proposed to do every day from the 8th of April will probably never be ever begun. Three months have passed of which I can give no account . . .

> Rose very late from fatigue.

> Longford and I dined early and went tête à tête to the play 'The Foundling in the Forest' and 'Killing no Murder'.

> I propose beginning a regular plan of occupation tomorrow.

I feel indolence is again creeping about me. I am fatigued by a regular course of insignificant occupations and dissatisfied with myself when idle.

Fatigue and cold oppress me.

Ill and idle. I have nothing to say of this languid day.

Alone and sad.

Made as yesterday, languid and dawdling.

But amongst her daily ennui there were signs of her romantic love for Arthur,

Surely Heaven will protect the good, brave man!

She wrote frequently to Sir John Malcolm, Arthur's great friend from their days in India. Her high romantic hyperbole continued in the same vein,

I have always seen him [her husband] in my mind protected by a transparent, impenetrable adamantine shield and settled that he could not *be touched even*: so precious a life so invaluable – surely the almighty hand of God will protect him.

This was on hearing of Arthur's minor thigh wound at St Jean de Luz.

After she gave birth to two sturdy sons in her late thirties Kitty's strength and health were never great. In her diary she describes the many colds and fevers that she caught.

My health nearly as it was – delicate, not positively unhealthy . . .

Each day she gave the three young children (including Arthur Freese) their lessons, and in the summer at Broadstairs or Ramsgate, took them to bathe in the sea and walk on the pier. She bought a barrel organ to amuse them. With her companion Martha the children were well looked after. She read Psalms to them on most days and taught them French, Geography and the Catechism. She adopted young, motherless Gerald Wellesley, Henry's son. The boys' uncle Gerald Valerian was then a chaplain to the Royal Household at Hampton Court.

Kitty, although she accused her husband with some justice of being 'neglectful', put a brave face on their relationship. She wrote to Richard, Lord Wellesley, after Arthur had sailed for Portugal,

I am a soldier's wife and the husband of whom it is the pride of my life to think, shall find he has no reason to be ashamed of me. All promises well, the Cause is a glorious one and please God we shall see our friends return safe and successful . . .

And her best friend Maria Edgeworth wrote of her,

charming amiable Lady Wellington as she truly said of herself she is always Kitty Pakenham to her friends . . . her dignified graceful simplicity 'not to be compared to the beaux esprits, fine ladies and fashionable scramblers for notoriety.'

Perhaps the marriage would have been more successful if she had been a 'beau esprit', but a *reliable* one of course.

From time to time Arthur *did* remember his wife. On leave in 1809 in Dublin he purchased for her three plain hairbrushes set in gold. He sent a Spanish shawl to Lady Liverpool who kindly gave it to Kitty, who suspected it was not *really* meant for her!

But his letters to her from the Peninsula were short, terse even, with no love and few and far between. She was reduced to seeking news from his relations and friends and from the library newspapers. Each week she posted him a copy of Cobbett's *Weekly Register*. She also sent him little home comforts; shirts, stockings, boots, a knitted blanket, two books (Dr Neal's *Letters from Spain and Portugal* and *Life of Cobbett*). Curiously enough she kept none of his letters and he, predictably, none of hers. Throughout the campaign he kept no portrait of her with him, but in the lid of his campaign dressing case he kept a watercolour of his two young sons that Kitty had sent him.

After her misappropriation of the housekeeping money, both in Dublin and in London, Arthur had rather unkindly forbidden Kitty to return to Ireland with the children to stay with her family. He was afraid that she would end up heavily in debt and that even more tradesmen would be dunning him for bills she chose not to pay, or simply forgot to pay. Luckily most of her Irish friends, including Mrs Calvert and Maria Edgeworth, visited her in London, as did her brother Lord Longford, who by now was worried about Kitty's relationship with her absent husband. Her old suitor Galbraith Lowry Cole called from time to time when he was on leave. She wrote to Colonel Torrens, the War Office secretary at the Horse Guards, for news from the battlefronts. Although brother Longford was most helpful to Kitty and his nephews, she also saw her brothers Hercules and Edward when they were on leave. In London she occasionally visited Lady Mornington, her mother-in-law, and received visits from William and Henry Wellesley 'much dejected' since his wife had eloped and he was ill with fever and liver attacks. Once or twice the great Richard condescended to visit her and wrote her a 'penitential' letter.

She went on visits to Tunbridge Wells and Brighton and rented houses there in Arthur's continued absence, although once he sent his ADC Captain Burgh to see her in London with the news of the victory at Bussaco. Even the Prime Minister Lord Liverpool called on her once and offered her the use of his house at Coombe Wood and invited her to dine at Fife House. As her husband became more famous, so did visits from the famous become more frequent. Richard Wellesley now came often to Broadstairs to see her and in town, Lady Liverpool became her confidante. Frequently however she refused invitations and left the particular town she was staying in to avoid the embarrassment of meeting strangers. Meantime the honours poured in – she became a countess, then a marchioness and finally duchess. By now Arthur had begun to acquire a penchant for other duchesses.

Little Kitty, to her everlasting credit, took all this fame, or rather the marriage to fame, in her stride. She stayed sweet and modest, argumentative and weak, incompetent, plain and dowdy.

Chapter Nine

PARIS AND BRUSSELS – 1814

Richard Wellesley had hoped to take over Castlereagh's responsibility for negotiating the complicated peace terms with France. Instead Castlereagh offered Wellington the key role of the Paris embassy. Apart from the American campaign, there was little likelihood of any more campaigning for a long time to come – or so Europe considered.

On his return from Madrid, Wellington spent a few days in June in Paris where he first visited Madame de Staël's famous salon.

July and the first week of August were spent in great triumph in London before he decided to take up his new appointment in Paris. He attended levées, a Thanksgiving ceremony, was painted by Lawrence, and attended a party for Marshal Blücher.

But first he spent two weeks with the Prince of Orange inspecting the frontier fortresses in the Low Countries, which seemed, with the benefit of hindsight in the following year, to have been a far-sighted decision. He found many 'advantageous positions' for defence between Brussels and the border with France, which stood him in great stead. He had time to attend a ball in Brussels, a theatre or two and several concerts. He also met a whole host of beautiful young women, English, Irish, French and Italian. Some of them became his mistresses, some became his romantic lovers, but all of them remembered him with the greatest affection. Amongst them were the attractive Annesley sisters, Catherine, the younger girl, was about to marry Lord John Somerset, who was a brother of Fitzroy Somerset, Wellington's devoted ADC. The elder sister, Lady Frances Annesley, had recently married an obnoxious Hussar officer, James Wedderburn-Webster. Their father was Arthur, 1st Earl of Mountnorris who had married Sarah Cavendish. This Irish family was related to the Wesleys.

For reasons of economy the Duke and Duchess of Richmond lived in Brussels. Charles Lennox had been Lord Lieutenant of Ireland and was a close friend of Wellington's. The young Lennox sons were also now ADC's to Wellington and the young Lennox daughters, who used to go riding in Dublin parks with their father's ADC, were now high-spirited young ladies. Particularly Lady Georgiana who soon became known to Wellington as 'Dearest Georgy'.

The Greville family were rather more complicated. Colonel Charles Greville and his wife Lady Charlotte had been friendly with Kitty at Tunbridge Wells. They had three young children including two sons: Charles, who became a very celebrated diarist; and Algernon, who became in later years Wellington's confidential secretary. 'La Coquette Gentille' or 'the Chrysolite' were nicknames for the delectable Lady Charlotte, the eldest daughter of the 3rd Duke of Portland. She was also, for a number of years, Wellington's mistress.

The glamorous Caton sisters from Baltimore were soon to figure on the scene, along with their sister-in-law Mrs Betsy Patterson, better known as Madame Patterson-Bonaparte. Mrs Mary Anne Patterson, née Caton, together with Lady Charlotte Greville and later Harriet Arbuthnot, were the three true loves of the Beau's long life.

The young matron who could ride like a dream was to soon appear on the Duke's horizon. Lady Frances Shelley captivated the Duke and accompanied him on all his military reviews as his dashing unofficial ADC. A further significant meeting that year was with Harriet Fane, the younger second wife of Charles Arbuthnot, a great friend of Wellington's brother Henry Wellesley. She was twenty-six years younger than her husband.

Wellington soon acquired a varied French contingent of beauties and admirers. As usual there were a clutch of duchesses plus a princess, the most remarkable female intellectual in Europe, and two of Europe's most talented singers and actresses. Coincidentally Arthur seems to have taken up where his defeated rival, Bonaparte, left off.

The painter B.R. Haydon wrote of Paris in 1814 that it had 'an air of mortified vanity and suppressed exasperation which was natural.' The city was a curious mixture. Thousands of wounded French veterans mingled with the returning émigrés, who after twenty years absence living on their wits and charm in London, were delighted to be back. High-waisted coats and tall feather-trimmed hats were the rage that summer. The centre of Paris was full of the occupying armies. The Cossacks were camped out in the Champs de Mars, the English in the Champs Elysées and the rough boisterous Prussians who annoyed and terrified the Parisians, were stationed in Luxembourg, Tuileries and the Concorde. The 30,000 English troops were the best disciplined and the most popular with the French population and their disciplined field marshal was the most popular of the leaders of the Allied powers, more popular than old Marshal Blücher, the king of Prussia or the tsar of Russia.'

Wellington returned to Paris on 22 August 1814 and placed his embassy in the Hotel de Charost in the Rue du Faubourg St Honoré. No spoils of war, even though the mansion belonged to the absentee 'petit caporal'. It was usually occupied by his sister, the amorous Princess Pauline Borghese who was then in Naples and preparing to join her brother on the island of Elba. The British government paid 870,000 francs for the new embassy, which bordered on the Champs Elysées. The first French duchesse to be encountered was the Duchesse de Angoulême, who was flattered and proud to meet him, as the first English ambassador 'Le justement célèbre Lord Duc de Wellington.' He went to her soirées at the Pavillon de Flore and chased stags with her husband. The wretched and greedy King Louis XVIII had returned from exile in Hartwell – a sad gargantuan figure. Lord Byron certainly had a point about the Bourbon restoration. Wellington hunted with the royal family, held reviews and discussed the 'horrible' slave trade, which Britain was now trying to abolish.

The next duchesse he met was Claire de Duras, a pretty little woman, both clever and witty, nicknamed 'Mouche' and wooed by Châteaubriand and Benjamin Constant. She was soon remonstrating with the Duke on the subject of France's looted art treasures; his correct policy was to return the treasures to the country from which they had been stolen by Napoleon's light-fingered marshals. She thought that Wellington was looting the Louvre to send valuable paintings and statues as his presents to the Allied leaders. The Apollo Belvedere was given to the Duke by the Pope, and the duchesse asked him what he was proposing to do with the valuable statue. 'Why pack it up and send it to London,' he answered. 'Then England will have one statue the more, but one man the less,' she said. She told him forthrightly that he may have gained honour on the battlefields of Europe but it would all be sacrificed if the Apollo went off to Apsley House. It stayed in Paris! He wrote to Madame de Staël '*La Duchess de Duras ne me sourit plus. Enfin je suis delaisse.*'

He met his delightful old friend from Angers days, the Duchesse of Sabran, and reminisced about his idle year at the school of equitation.

Aglaé Ney was the beautiful wife of the 'bravest of the brave' Michel Ney, Prince of Borodino and Moskowa. She was falling in love with a young Englishman called Michael Bruce who in turn was being pursued by the wild young Caroline Lamb! Within two years the Duke was due to have acute problems with the Ney family. In the meantime he met his old adversary hunting in the Bois, and his wife in the salons of Paris.

Princess Pauline Borghese had returned to the capital and was certainly one of the two most beautiful women there. Wellington described her to his niece Lady Emily Bagot, then wife of the British minister in Washington, 'I have seen a good deal of your friend Pauline, who talked of you sometimes. She is a heartless devil . . .'

He met the young Duchesse de Berri, whose husband thought and said that Wellington was a '*parvenu*' or upstart. The Beau in turn said that she was a,

curious character of which folly is the prominent feature: one of those foolish people who imagine that to will a thing is sufficient. No such nonsense.

'*On peut tout faire, il n'y a qu'a le vouloir*' the beautiful young duchesse cried out. '*Oui Madame mais il faut avoir aussi les moyens*' replied the experienced middle-aged field marshal.

Adele D'Osmonde, the Duchesse de Gontaut-Biron, was the Duke's very friendly acquaintance of Cheltenham spa days – the lady of the delinquent garter – who was delighted to make his acquaintance again and claim him as one of her lovers. In Paris in September 1821 she was said by the Duchesse d'Escars (Louis XVIII's Chamberlain) to have been

> un peu la Maitresse de Monsieur, un peu beaucoup la Maitresse du Duc de Berri et aussi un peu celle du Duc de Wellington.

But the Duke disclaimed that distinction for himself!

The reigning beauty in Paris was Madame Juliette Récamier née Bernard, beloved friend of Madame Germaine de Staël and an acquaintance of Kitty's cousin Maria Edgeworth and of Wellington's friend the first Lady Salisbury.

On Wellington's arrival in Paris Sir Charles Stewart, the brother-in-law of Lord Castlereagh and English commissioner to the Allied army, gave a magnificent ball at which most of the sovereigns of Europe were present. The emperor of Russia and the king of Prussia danced several polonaises. The Duke appeared for the first time in public in Paris with his two nieces, Priscilla, Lady Burghersh and Emily, Lady Fitzroy Somerset hanging on each arm. There were no eyes for anyone else. The Duchesse de Boigne recalled:

> this ball where grandeur abounded, everything gave way to military glory. That of the Duke of Wellington was brilliant and unalloyed and a lustre was added to it by the interest that had long been felt in the cause of the Spanish nation.

But out of all these magnificent ladies it was the Italian Madame Guiseppina Grassini who in 1814 captured Wellington's heart. A most unlikely choice but she had sung her way into the hearts of every audience in Europe. A Bonapartist lady circulated stories about a Prima Donna even though Kitty was in Paris and said 'if Grassini smiled who could resist?'

The four theatres where Wellington and the Castlereaghs had permanent boxes were the Grand Opera, le Français, le Fédeau and de Variéties.

Although the actress Madame Mars was reported to have snubbed the Duke, her colleague Marguerite Josephine Weimer, whose stage name was Mademoiselle Georges, used to boast of her success with both Napoleon and Wellington. '*Mais Monsieur le duc etait de beaucoup le plus fort.*' John Cam Hobhouse described the lady, then aged twenty-seven (whom Wellington had met in Bordeaux and Toulouse earlier in the year) as, very large with a fine face and strong lines with expressive action, so as now and then almost to remind me of Mrs Siddons.

She played at the Comédie Francaise and lived until 1867. At the time when Wellington knew her she was described as,

> still beautiful, somewhat large and when she played Hermion in *Orestes* she combined the majesty of Mrs Siddons with the grace and sweetness of Miss O'Neil.

She was painted in her role of Cinna by Lagrenée.

Victor, Duc de Broglie wrote of the Duke in his *Souvenirs*,

> He was a true Englishman, a piece of the old rock, simple in mind, straight, solid, prudent but hard, tough and a little narrow. The clumsy and pressing gallantries he permitted himself towards pretty young women, he pushed as far as they would let him!

The Congress of Vienna had opened on 15 September 1814, with the five victorious powers – Russia, Prussia, Austria and Britain and, rather surprisingly, France (represented by Talleyrand) congregating to produce a plan for more or less permanent peace in Europe.

Kitty had arrived in Paris in October to join her husband and gossipy Lady Kinnaird reported on 'the follies of the Duke of Wellington's public addresses to Grassini, who lived in the same house with the Duchess', which was not completely accurate. Kitty did however meet Madame de Staël who was by now well acquainted with the Duke, and acquitted herself nobly in the encounter that followed. Kitty, who was not interested in her clothes, now tried hard and wore a silver cloak, blonde mantilla and regulation lappets!

The English government were worried about Wellington's safety in Paris. There were rumours of assassination plots and Lord Liverpool looked for a solution to bring the Duke out of Paris with dignity. The Treaty of Ghent was signed on 24 December bringing peace to the American war, so there was no question of the Duke being sent across the Atlantic, not that he would have gone. Finally the Prince Regent wrote to the king, Louis XVIII, on 18 January 1815 to request permission for Wellington to be the British representative at the Congress of Vienna (to take over from Lord Castlereagh). He arrived there at the beginning of February, leaving behind Kitty and their two sons, who had arrived in Paris two days after Christmas.

A superb painting by Isabey depicts the Congress of Vienna of the winter of 1814/15. There were twenty-one leading diplomats and foreign ministers. The British contingent of eighty was the largest, represented by Lord Castlereagh, Wellington, Stewart, Clancarty and Cathcart. In Vienna the Duke was seen by Lord Strangford playing ecarte with Maria Louise, Duchess of Parma, the ex-Empress Maria Louisa, who after Josephine had been divorced, became Napoleon's consort on 1 April 1810. The two settled their accounts in gold 'napoleon' coins. At one stage the empress and Wellington had been served by the same cook, and the lack of the latter's roast mutton available in Vienna was regretted by the former. They talked uninhibitedly about the absent Napoleon, and Wellington found her son 'a fine lad, educated just like the Arch-dukes!' Maria Louise was very civil to the Duke and they dined together at Schonbrun early in the year.

As there were no coffee houses of 'repute' in Vienna, the diplomats met daily either at Lady Castlereagh's supper parties 'where we have curious medleys almost every night', or at Lord Stewart's house where balls were frequent. The emperor of Russia danced polonaises with Lady Castlereagh and country dances with Lady Matilda. The archduchess polonaised with Monsieur Planta.

The Prince de Talleyrand's niece Dorothea acted as hostess for her uncle during the course of the five month conference. She was quite outspoken in her adoration of Wellington because he had saved the Palais Royal in Paris from destruction by the Prussian troops. She herself was half Prussian but her sympathies were entirely French. Sainte-Beuve noted that her blue black eyes always burned with an 'infernal fire' which turned night into day! Talleyrand, who now knew the Duke well, told that keen little observer Captain Gronow,

> watchfulness, prudence and experience of human nature were the only means he employed . . . by the use of these simple agencies he acquired great influence . . .

Through this influence the Duke persuaded King Louis XVIII that Talleyrand should work jointly with the English to block a Russian plan to absorb Poland. Talleyrand was probably the most devious, cynical and successful politician in Europe. To have survived thirty years of politics in France under Napoleon and the Bourbons was a triumph. His praise of Wellington, the conqueror of France, was thus all the more surprising. But the alliance of Russia and Prussia was infinitely more dangerous than La Belle Alliance. '*Le Congres ne march pas, mais il danse*'.

On 7 March 1815 after Wellington had been in Vienna five weeks, and just as he was about to go out hunting, the news of Napoleon's bolt from Elba on the brig *Inconstant* with 1,200 troops was relayed to him. Castlereagh wrote immediately to the Duke and offered him the choice of staying at Vienna or command of an army in Flanders.

Of course there was only one decision that could be made. All was in the melting pot again. The Tsar said to the Duke, 'It is for you to save the world again.'

Before he left Vienna all the beautiful women kissed him soundly and promised even more kisses when he had reconquered Paris. They all knew in their heart of hearts that the little Corsican – as usual – meant business.

Chapter Ten

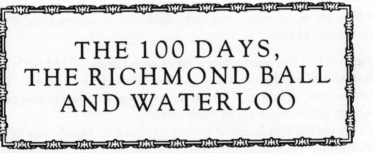

THE 100 DAYS, THE RICHMOND BALL AND WATERLOO

Napoleon raised his standard at Fréjus on the Golfe de Juan on 1 March and entered Paris without a shot being fired in anger twenty days later. The bloated Bourbon king, 'poor old Bungy', fled to Ghent and Wellington's old adversaries stayed in Brussels – Marmont at the Hotel d'Angleterre, Victor at the Hotel Wellington and Berthier with friends. But the 'bravest of the brave' had been despatched by Louis to bring Bonaparte back to Paris in an iron cage. Ney then decided on the night of 13 March to change sides back to his old master Napoleon. Undeniable loyalty since he owed the Bourbons nothing, but treachery also. By now Marshals Soult and Grouchy were on active service with Napoleon.

At the end of March Wellington was appointed commander-in-chief of the Allied armies in Flanders and he reached Brussels on 4 April and took a house in the Rue de la Montagne du Parc.

His veteran 'Spanish' troops, his old Anglo-Portuguese army, had long since been disbanded. Out of the twenty-five battalions of English troops available to him, only six had served with him in the Peninsula. The Portuguese refused to supply him; the Dutch were of poor standard; the Belgians quite unreliable; and the mercenary Hanoverians were the best of the Allied troops. He had asked for 40,000 British infantry, 15,000 cavalry, 150 guns and staff and generals of his choosing. He received just over half his requirements including 7,000 veterans. By the summer he had an Allied army of 80,000 more or less under control. Marshal Blücher had a larger Prussian army of 130,000 stationed to the east.

Fortunately many of the Peninsular Generals rallied to the flag, including a reluctant Thomas Picton, Hill, Pack, Kempt and others. Wellington agreed a policy plan of action with Marshal Blücher on 3 May, and by the middle of June he had made the best he could of his large rather motley crew.

> I have got an infamous army, very weak and ill equipped and a very inexperienced staff.

Bonaparte had recruited a more experienced army of 122,000 quickly and efficiently and his obvious move was to attack and defeat each of the Allied armies separately. During the ten weeks of hectic preparation, Wellington was as always in 'high spirits'.

Kitty was back in England having left Paris in March, but Wellington's mother was still in Brussels. The 'ton' and high society revolved round the gregarious Duke and Duchess of Richmond and around Wellington. In the last week of April he was present at a concert given by Madame Angelica Catalani '*la première cantatrice de l'Europe*' who had been a great success in London. *L'Oracle* noted '*Le Duque assiste aux concerts de Mme C. était grand amateur de musique.*'

On Saturday 22 April 1815 the Beau met the diarist Thomas Creevey who wrote in his journal afterwards,

> I thought several times he must be drunk but drunk or sober he had not the least appearance of being a clever man. I have seen a good deal of him formerly and always thought the same of his talents in conversation.

Creevey was rather inconsequential, poor, with no influence, non-military and obviously not worthy of social effort by the Duke. A few days later, on the twenty-seventh, he gave a ball at the grand concert hall near the Porte de Louvain, Rue Ducale where the Italian nightingale sang the 'air de Porto-Gallo' and the orchestra rendered a Haydn symphony.

He was charmed with Cataline, ardently applauding whatever she sang, except the 'Rule Britannia', then with sagacious reserve he listened in utter silence . . . he felt it was injudicious to sing it outside England.

Meanwhile Lord Byron wrote predictably,

> Oh France! retaken by a single march
> Whose path was through one long triumphal arch!

There is little doubt that Arthur Wellesley had a penchant for beautiful young ladies less than half his age; in particular the Richmond daughter, Georgiana Lennox, and the Annesley sisters. Georgiana was now nearly twenty, small in stature, well proportioned, regular features, beautiful hands and feet and a delicate and transparent complexion. She had first met him in 1806 on his return from India and for forty-six years she was known to the Duke as 'My dearest Georgie'.

On 2 May Georgie rode with him on reviews to see Colonel Vilvorde of the Brunswick troops. It rained heavily and she returned in a soldier's greatcoat escorted by General Alava. The Rev. Spencer Madan was the tutor to the young Lennox ladies and he commented:

> No one would suppose hostilities will soon commence judging by the Duke of Wellington. He gives a ball every week, attends every party, partakes of every amusement that offers. Yesterday he took Lady Jane Lennox to Enghien for the cricket match and brought her back at night apparently having gone for no other object but to amuse her. At the time Bonaparte was said to be at Maubeuge, 30 or 40 miles off.

On the twenty-ninth the Duke gave a grand fête at the Hotel de Belle-Vue. Also during this time M. Ruxthiel of Liège sculpted a bust of him. Wellington was enjoying every moment of this exciting nerve-racking build-up towards the inevitable decisive encounter which would be on double the scale of any Peninsular battle. He was now aged forty-six in the high summer of his life.

Lady Caroline Capel wrote in her diary of 2 June

> The D. of W. has not improved the Morality of our Society as he has given several things and makes a point of asking all the ladies of Loose Character – Every one was surprised at seeing Lady John Campbell at his House and one of his staff told me that it had been represented to him her not being received for that her Character was more than suspicious. 'Is it by God,' said he, 'then I will go and ask her Myself,' on which he immediately took his hat and went out for that purpose. But Nobody can guess the Lord Wellington's intentions and I dare say Nobody will know he is going till he is actually gone. In the meantime he amuses himself with Humbuging the Ladies particularly the Duchess of Richmond.

Her son, Wellington's ADC, described him, 'He was gay even to sportiveness all the evening.'

On 6 June Wellington warned Lady Charlotte Greville that her mother, the duchess, who was planning a picnic to Tournai or Lille for the eighth, should not go. 'You'd better not go, Say nothing about it, but let the project drop.'

The relationship between Wellington and Georgie was surprisingly close. He had commissioned a portrait of himself by a Belgian artist, an 'original miniature', which he gave her on the fateful evening of the fifteenth. Her brother George was his ADC, her brother March was ADC to the Prince of Orange, and her father was most anxious to take part in the fighting still to come.

One of the other two close attachments the Beau had was with the pale, delicate young Lady Frances Wedderburn-Webster. Basil Jackson, a staff officer, in his *Reminiscences* quoted a 'glowing episode' that took place in Brussels in June.

> He was sitting in the park when a Very Great Man walked past and immediately a carriage drove up and a lady got out of it and joined him. They went down into a hollow where the trees completely screened them. Another carriage then arrived and from it alighted Lady Mountnorris who went peering about searching in vain for her daughter, Lady Frances Webster.

Lady Charlotte Greville was a more serious contender for the Duke's heart. If he did not see her each day, he wrote to her. This loving friendship was one of the most serious in the long life of the Beau. Thomas Creevey noted that Lady Charlotte was visited frequently by the Duke when she was living at the Hotel d'Angleterre.

Benjamin Robert Haydon had described a Wellington Fête of July 1813 to celebrate the Duke's victory at Vittoria.

> While the Hussars with their golden tassals and rich boots their warlike heads and dark mustachios with a sort of martial condescension were bending down to whisper to lovely women whose graceful floating feathers would intermingle as they held up their head with their rough sweeping horse hair. As day dawned the groups in front were lit up by its silvery light, while those within were still engoldened, by the deep yellow effulgence of the lamps. The crimson, golden beaming dress of the Soldiers, the satinny, creamy feathery lightness of the delicious women whose bright eyes rained influence gave it an air of chivalrous enchantment or fairy land – to my dying day I shall never forget it.

This description could have equally suited the Duchess of Richmond's ball two years later, a few hours before Quatre Bras and Waterloo.

The Duchess of Richmond had enquired of Wellington whether the timing of her ball was indiscreet in relation to the forthcoming battle. To which he replied 'Duchess, you may give your ball with the greatest safety, without fear of interruption.' Their 'wash-room', a large room used by a coach builder, had been decorated in style; decorated with paper trellis adorned with roses. Attending were three duchesses, one marquise, nine comtesses and one baronne, but the ladies were still outnumbered by five to one. Amongst that plethora of beauty, Lady Charlotte Greville hung on the Duke's arm, although he talked to 'Dearest Georgy' Lennox and Lady Hamilton-Dalrymple, whilst messages poured in with news from the front. The Marquise d'Assche was cross at the ease of the Duke's conversation with Lady Frances Wedderburn-Webster to whom he paid ardent court.

It is impossible not to admire the insouciance of the Duke on this exhilarating occasion. He had made his military dispositions as best as he could. He had never fought the great Corsican before and he was not happy with the composition of his own army. Although he had met Marshal Blücher on several occasions he could not place any great confidence in his large Prussian army. So when he blurted out to his close friend the Duke of Richmond at midnight 'Napoleon has humbugged me, by God! he has gained twenty-four hours march on me' he was telling the truth. He also asked his host for a local map!

During the Highland reels, the valses and the romantic episodes of the ball his greatest adversary had stolen a march on him. The dancing had continued to 2.30 a.m. and the Duke was up at 5.30 a.m. giving his final orders, specifically to the Duke of Brunswick and the Prince of Orange.

Before dawn on 16 June the balance of his forces had left Brussels for the first engagement at Quatre Bras. By noon he had ridden six miles to greet Blücher again to agree their final plan of campaign.

Many years later he was to recall the drama of that day with some of his admirers; Lady Salisbury and Lady Shelley, and at Harriet Arbuthnot's dinner parties. It was undeniably a close-run thing.

Lady Caroline Lamb wrote to Viscountess Melbourne from Brussels on 16 June. She was a wild, attractive, slightly unbalanced young woman half in love with the Duke.

Dearest Lady Melbourne, The great amusement at Bruxelles indeed the only one except visiting the sick is to make large parties and go to the field of Battle – and pick up a skull or a grape shot or an old shoe or a letter and bring it home . . . There is a great affectation here of making lint and bandages, at least it is an innocent amusement. It is rather a love making moment, the tall wounded Officers reclining with pretty ladies visiting them – it is dangerous. Lady Conyngham is here – Lady C. Greville – Lady D. Hamilton, Lady F. Somerset, Lady F. Webster most affected and Lady Mountnorris who stuck her parasol yesterday into a skull at Waterloo. Perhaps a certain rivalship makes me see her less favourably, but indeed Lady F. Webster is too ridiculous. Mr Bradshaw an amiable Dandy close by me, says it makes him ill for 2 hours after he has seen her. I conclude that you have heard that the Duke of Wellington fell desperately in love with her and 2 others, which was the cause of his not being at the Battle in time. The Duchess of Richmond's fatal Ball has been much censured; there never was such a Ball – so fine and so sad – all the young men who appeared there shot dead a few hours after.

And Caroline Capel wrote too 'our Great Hero must have been deceived for he certainly has been taken by surprise.'

Many people think of Waterloo as being a single decisive battle (which it was) but it was in fact the final of four consecutive battles.

Napoleon's tactics were simple. Despite gathering most of his old veterans to join him by early June, he had only a relatively small but experienced army of 125,000 men. His glittering array of marshals had diminished in his absence on Elba. Berthier had died in strange circumstances, Murat had been rejected, Massena had been dismissed. The Armée du Nord now had Ney on the left flank and Grouchy on the right. Under them served Kellerman, D'Erlon, Reille and Milhaud. Marshal Soult was his chief-of-staff and Marshal Davout was left behind as governor of Paris with a small army. His spies had told him that gallant old Blücher had gathered together 125,000 men and that Wellington's motley crew numbered about 68,000. Bonaparte had to act quickly to drive a wedge between the converging Allied armies, possibly by threatening the Channel ports to the west. If he could deploy the majority of his troops against either Blücher or Wellington with more or less equal numbers he was totally confident he could beat both separately, but not together. He was caustic about the failure of his many generals to inflict a single defeat on Wellington in the Peninsular campaign of nearly five years duration. In early June 1815 he had nothing but contempt for Wellington's tactics and career to date.

By 14 June Napoleon had reached Beaumont, south of the River Sambre and Charleroi, a vital town on the river. At Charleroi the main roads divide. One due north to Brussels and the other north-east towards Liège.

The two Allied armies originally planned to halt the French on a lateral road five miles north of Charleroi between Quatre Bras to the west and Sombrette to the east. Napoleon planned to hold the British, Dutch and Belgians in the west and defeat Blücher in the east. His speed of deployment caught Wellington by surprise and he was lucky that Ney, for a variety of reasons, also reacted very slowly.

On 16 June two battles were fought simultaneously seven miles apart. At Quatre Bras, six miles north of Charleroi, Wellington had to fling troops in piecemeal with very mixed results against Ney's divisions which were superior in numbers and quality. By luck, skill and considerable personal bravery Wellington just produced a draw out of thin air. The Allied losses were nearly 5,000 and the French 4,000. It was a desperate affair which Ney should have won comfortably and pushed Wellington's advance Guards easily out of Quatre Bras – but he failed, although the young Prince of Orange was nearly killed in action.

In the east everything went as Napoleon planned at the second battle at Ligny. The emperor and Marshal Grouchy gave Blücher's troops a mauling on a battlefield which Wellington had inspected and found wanting. By nightfall the Prussians had lost 16,000 men and the French 12,000. The Prussians were in retreat and Marshal Gneisenau wanted to scuttle back to the Rhine. It is very much to Blücher's credit that he had given his word to support Wellington and come what may, he was determined to do so. Napoleon also managed to keep the two Allied armies apart – quite vital for any chance of success.

On the following morning Wellington was in no doubt what action was required. Retreat. He said to Captain Bowles, a Coldstreamer,

> Old Blücher has had a damned good licking and gone 18 miles to the rear [to Wavre]. We must do the same. I suppose they'll say in England we have been licked. Well I can't help that.

The third battle in the sequence was Napoleon's follow-up on the retreating Prussians. He deployed Grouchy with 33,000 men to keep up maximum pressure to ensure that the two Allied armies, both in full retreat, did *not* converge.

Two days of pouring rain hampered all the cavalry movements and slowed down the ebb and flow of the four opposing armies. Napoleon was not at all well and Ney was irascible, by turns dilatory and pugnacious. It is possible these problems affected their individual judgements.

By the morning of the fateful 18 June, Wellington had deployed his army of 68,000 men and about 160 guns along a three-mile ridge at

Mont St Jean athwart the Charleroi-Brussels road. He had in front of him on the slopes three defensive strong points. To the west the château of Hougoumont, the farmhouse and orchard of La Haye Sainte to his front, and another farm of Papelotte to the east. Meanwhile Blücher was regrouping eight miles to the east around Wavre, but with thick woods, called the Bois de Paris, between them.

Napoleon had already made one major error and was about to commit another. He had deployed too many troops to chase the fleeing Russians. Grouchy's army corps of 33,000 men was in the event only partly required to keep the Prussians on the defensive. As a result he faced Wellington, who was in an excellent well-planned defensive position, with a nominal superiority in men and an extra 100 guns (which could have been decisive). All his life he had taken on his opponent generals outnumbered, often dramatically. Parity in numbers and guns to spare against the Sepoy General looked like a remarkably odds-on bet. As a result of his over-confidence he fell into the trap which no single Latin general could resist. *Toujours l'audace, l'attaque.*

It was a classic battle. The best general in the world on defensive ground of his choosing against the best attacking general in the world. So the second mistake was to commit all his troops all day, piecemeal, driving them onto the English guns and troops. An outflanking move to the west would soon threaten Wellington's flanks, who would want to defend Brussels at all cost, and force him out of his defensive lines. The story of the battle is well known.

After a thoroughly wet miserable night, Wellington woke at 5.30 a.m. and half-an-hour later rode out of Waterloo village to inspect the defensive lines. Napoleon started his main attack at 1 p.m. and expected the day to be won before dusk. The terrain was waterlogged and his superior cavalry forces could not deploy and charge effectively.

Marshal Soult asked if Grouchy's 33,000 men could rejoin them, and predictably the little Corsican was scathing, 'this affair is nothing more than eating breakfast' he said. At 11.30 the former artillery officer unleashed his huge barrage of covering fire mainly directed to the west, to give an impression of possible outflanking manoeuvers.

There were savage attacks all day on Hougoumont, which was sorely battered, taken and retaken by the Guards. Marshal Ney's main frontal attack started at 1 p.m. towards La Haye Sainte, defended by the German legion. Sir Thomas Picton was killed in action. Pack's Highland Brigade counter-attacked ferociously. The Household Cavalry and the Scots Greys charged the French guns, gallantly but uselessly, and were decimated. Ney's magnificent cavalry equally gallantly, and equally uselessly, charged in the centre against British redcoats in squares reinforced with horse artillery. By 4.20 p.m. the French cavalry withdrew to lick their wounds. Wellington had been hoping for the Prussians to arrive in mid-afternoon, but they were still several miles away. Ney now launched his second wave of cavalry, this time under Kellerman, which also failed. Next came a mixed force of 6,000 infantry and cavalry, also in vain. The 'bravest of the brave' had four horses killed under him and was fighting like a demon. Wellington on the ridge was everywhere at once giving firm, crisp orders and in danger on a score or more occasions.

By 6.30 p.m. La Haye Sainte farm redoubt was taken as the gallant German legion ran out of ammunition and defended with their bayonets. Two attempts to relieve the farm were made without success. Flushed with this success at long last, Ney asked his master for reinforcements as the British centre was now seriously endangered.

Napoleon made his last serious blunder of the day and sent the precious reinforcements to help Grouchy contain the Prussians on the eastern flank.

At 7 p.m. Napoleon launched his final gamble. His army was too deeply committed to withdraw. He himself led his 'Immortals', the 15,000 strong Imperial Guard. At least he led them on as far as La Haye Sainte only a few hundred yards from the remnants of the British lines to shouts of 'Vive l'Empereur'. Most of the German legion were dead, five fresh battalions of young Brunswickers had run, the Cumberland Hussars from Hanover left the field, one Dutch Belgian regiment refused to charge, other Belgian regiments skulked at the rear and refused to come out of the woods. It was indeed a thin red, bloody red line. Marshall Ney led the Imperial Guard up the final slopes. He was black with gun smoke and had lost his fifth horse.

Miraculously Wellington was still riding Copenhagen and took charge himself of the English Foot Guards. The British artillery, and particularly Mercers Royal Horse Artillery, were literally having a field day. The holocaust continued until nearly 8 p.m., although the Prussians had been seen fighting about two miles away to the east. Eventually French cries were heard 'La Gard recule', 'Nous sommes trahis' and finally 'Sauve qui peut'. Despite a last stand by Napoleon's Old Guard, the day was lost and the emperor was nearly taken by Prussian cavalry. An hour later and the two formidable heroes Blücher and Wellington met and shook hands near La Belle-Alliance. Gneiseneau, who had doubted and mistrusted Wellington's abilities and courage for the last few weeks, was put in charge of the follow-up of Napoleon's broken army, and harried them all the way back to Paris. Marshal Davout, with 117,000 troops, put up a spirited resistance. Bonaparte's marshals advised him to surrender and he abdicated on 22 June. Paris fell on 3 July.

Napoleon's armies lost nearly 30,000 men at Waterloo and another 27,000 in the continuous battles against Blücher. They lost half of the Grande Armée which crossed the Belgian borders to 'humbug' Wellington, and all their artillery as well.

The Allies mustered a total of 209,000 men at the start of the campaign. Wellington's appalling casualties amounted to 15,000 at Waterloo, and the Allies lost 55,000 men altogether since the fighting started on 15 June.

It was appropriate that Wellington's last campaign and battle should be the finest and most glorious of all, although the death roll of his friends was appalling. Nearly 50,000 dead and wounded men were left on the field; French, Prussian, German and British. He said to the ubiquitous Creevey,

> It has been a damned nice thing, the nearest run thing you ever saw in your life. By God! I don't think it would have done if I had not been there.

He was right of course, none of the British generals were in his class.

The Duke wrote to his best beloved young women. He wrote to Lady Frances Wedderburn-Webster at 3 o'clock on Sunday morning 18 June.

> We fought a desperate battle on Friday in which I was successful though I had but very few troops. The Prussians were very roughly handled and retired last night which obliged me to do the same to this place yesterday. The course of the operations may oblige me to uncover Bruxelles for a moment . . . for which reason I recommend that you and your family should be prepared to move to Antwerp at a moment's notice. I will give you the earliest information of any danger that may come to my knowledge: at present I know of none.

That letter was written a few hours before Waterloo. At Quatre Bras 2,400 British troops were killed and six times that number in the few hours after the letter was written. He wrote to Lady Frances again on 19 Monday after the battle, with the phrase 'The finger of Providence was upon me and I escaped unhurt.'

Wellington wrote to 'Dearest Georgy Lennox' once before Waterloo and again afterwards, as he did to Charlotte Greville in the centre of Brussels, who passed on the news from the battlefront as it came in.

To Georgy he wrote, 'It is a dearly bought victory, we have lost so many fine fellows.'

High Summer

Chapter Eleven

'CRIM. CON.'
LADY FRANCES
WEDDERBURN-WEBSTER

The Princesse de Lieven wrote in her private diary the intimate details of her passion for her lover Prince Metternich, of her deep companionship with her husband, the Russian ambassador in London, and also of her curious love-hate relationship with the Duke of Wellington. On 18 April 1821 she wrote:

> Let me introduce the characters of my story. Lady Frances Webster married to a jealous husband who has reason to be jealous. She is a young and rather pretty woman although she is a little too washed-out for my taste. But my taste has nothing to do with it and other people admire her: for instance the Duke of Wellington who had certain passages with her at Brussels five or six years ago and nearly forgot in her company that he had the battle of Waterloo to win. There was talk of a lawsuit but he avoided the scandal by paying down some thousands of guineas ... That is my first character ...

The *St James Chronicle* on 3 and 5 August 1815 published scandals about the Duke copied from a local paper.

FASHIONABLE ALLITERATION

'In the letter W there's a charm half divine War – Wellington – Wedderburn – Webster and Wine'. F. The cessation of warfare has in Paris enabled scandal to resume her usual influence on the public mind. A report is very prevalent in the first Parisian circle that a distinguished commander has surrendered himself captive to the beautiful wife of a military officer, high in rank in a manner to make a very serious investigation of this offence indispensable.

The Chronicle went on to surmise that this 'amour' would end with a 'criminal conversation' which was the legal term of the day for divorce proceedings.

But it is hoped that it will turn out to be nothing more than a tale of malevolence. It was said at Brussels that when the Duke of Wellington returned after the battle of Waterloo (which *en passant*, ought to be called the battle of Mont St Jean) he came to visit the wounded; perhaps the wounded heart was meant! A word to the wise!

The article continued,

The husband has laid his damages at £50,000 which it is said the fortunate lover offered to pay: but this affair was too notorious for composition or, the party injured had too much sensibility to be content with wearing 'gilded' horns.

The *St James Chronicle* continued to feed its readers with conjecture.

Several of the public prints have in some particulars gone too far in their statements respecting a high military character and a blooming bride of 22 and have blazoned their CRIM. CON. and damages in their usual sweeping way. A very beautiful woman of Irish extraction is said to be a party in the amour at Brussels which has made so great a noise on the Continent.

Wellington was naturally deeply disturbed by the newspaper articles and told his Spanish ADC General Alava,

That's too bad – the writers a walking lie – never saw her alone in my life – this must be checked.

The lady had a pale sensual face which contrasted with her Bible reading habits. Lord Byron claimed that she made him a certain proposal which he was foolish enough to ignore, both his diaries and those of Tom Moore mention this beautiful enigmatic lady on many occasions.

James Simpson was an observant young advocate who visited Paris via Waterloo and persuaded his friend Sir John Malcolm, who was also Wellington's closest ex-India colleague, to secure him a ticket for the Duke's first victory ball. Malcolm suggested to the Duke that more guests could be invited if the gardens of the Duke's 'Hotel' (which was Marshal Junot's house on the corner of the Place Louis XV near the Place Vendôme) were illuminated with candles, some music was played outside and juggler-comedians employed to amuse the extra guests. Simpson describes the ball with eloquence. The king of Prussia, the Duke of Mecklenberg, the wounded Prince of Orange, Marshal Blücher, were there. Lady Castlereagh was acting as hostess for the Duke, entertaining Talleyrand, Metternich, Fouché, Nesselrode and Schwartzenberg amongst other European notables.

'Nothing is more *agissant* but Lady Caroline William Lamb in a purple riding habit . . . primed for an attack upon the Duke of Wellington . . .'

Below: Lady Charlotte Greville née Bentinck, mother of Algy and Charles. A beautiful woman known as *La Coquette Gentille*, her house in Brussels was the centre of Society, and undoubtedly 'she conquered the Conqueror of France'.

Above: 'There are three powers in Europe, England, Russia . . . and Madame de Staël.' Author of *De l'Allemagne, Delphine* and *Corinne,* she wrote to the Duke of Wellington, *'Vous qui êtes des nôtres'*.

Guiseppina Grassini, *cantatrice Amie de Napoleon*', opera singer and actress who was the leader of the 'ton' in Paris and also Wellington's mistress.

Madame Juliette Récamier – the languid, elegant beauty to whom Wellington boasted of Napoleon *'Je l'ai bien battu'*.

To his surprise young Simpson finds in a salon off the main ballroom,

> there sat two very beautiful Englishwomen of high fashion, Lady Webster
> Wedderburn and Lady Caroline Lamb keeping a chair vacant between
> them. In a few minutes the Duke of Wellington himself looked into the
> room, when the ladies called to him that they had kept a place for him.

He joined them and Simpson noticed that above the Duke's head on the
wall was a bust of Napoleon!

> The two ladies were then joined by Walter Scott, the poet, and the four
> formed a very merry supper party. Lady Caroline Lamb startled us by an
> occasional scream. What became of the Crowned Heads and their supper
> I never heard.

The following day on the Plain de Clichy the Duke reviewed the whole
British army stationed in Paris, estimated at 10,000 in number. Simpson
was there and saw,

> The Duke, beside him rode a very pretty woman whom I recognised to be
> Lady Frances Webster whom I had seen at the Ball. The Duke was on a
> white horse, a conspicuous object. After receiving the salute of the line he
> cantered forward followed by ADCs, servants and Lady Frances to pass
> along the line. The Russian Emperor Alexander was a spectator at this
> review.

Lady Frances Shelley, who was a constant companion of the Duke in the
heady days after Waterloo wrote in her diary,

> On Friday I would not go to the opera for fear of being in the Duke's way
> as I guessed Lady Frances Annesley would be there.

Lady Shelley thought that on balance it was a platonic relationship,

> His manner is the most paternal of any one I ever saw, he was simple and
> kind to Lady A in public but nothing more.

Harriet Arbuthnot also wrote,

> At the time of the battle of Waterloo Lady Frances Webster was the
> 'regnante'.

She too was at Brussels!

Tom Moore, a close friend of Lord Byron, who was in Paris at the
time, wrote in his diary later in 1819,

> Met Lady Frances Webster, conversation *chiefly* about Byron – pronoun-
> ces her coldblooded and vain to an excess. I believe her great ambition is

to attract people of celebrity – if so she must have been gratified as the first Poet (Lord B) and first Captain (D of W) of the age have been among her lovers – the latter liaison was at all events – not altogether spiritual as must the character of the man makes platonism not very probable. Her manner to me very flattering and the eyes played off most skillfully but this is evidently her habit – the fishing is always going on whether whales or sprats are to be caught.

Tom Moore was said to have been in love with Kitty Pakenham and wrote of her love for the young Wesley.

> Thou would'st still be adored, as this moment thou art
> Let thy loveliness fade as it will:
> And around the dear ruin each wish of my heart
> Should entwine itself verdantly still

Later that autumn Kitty joined her husband in Paris, which quelled some of the rumours, and the Wedderburn-Websters were persuaded to take out an action for libel against the proprietors of the *St James Chronicle*, Messrs Baldwin and Moody. The Duke of Richmond was a witness at the trial. The Earl of Mountnorris was obliged to go to Paris for the education of his unmarried daughter and Captain Wedderburn-Webster joined his 'Noble Relation' there. The lady in question was seven months pregnant at the time of the battle of Waterloo when the affair was said to have occurred.

The case was heard on 16 February 1816 after several meetings between the Websters and the Duke. Lady Mountnorris had spread rumours, as well she might have done after her forays in the parks. Wellington had continued to write to the Lady Frances. A letter was dated 18 July 1815 from Paris, about Bonaparte's fate, and ended 'I hope to see you soon.' He certainly did see Lady Frances and her sister Lady John Somerset through the autumn and winter of 1815/16.

Probably because of the Duke of Richmond's evidence, who said of the lady that she was of 'singularly amiable and decorous manners', and eulogies to the Duke's martial qualities, the defence's case was upset. Damages of £2,000 were awarded to the married couple. However the views of Tom Moore, Mrs Arbuthnot, and Princesse de Lieven carry more weight than those of the naïve Lady Shelley.

Lady Frances' husband told Byron (October 1813) 'I think any woman fair game because I can depend upon Ly. F's principles. She can't go wrong and therefore I may.' Byron was equally cruel to her and said she was measured for a new Bible once a quarter! It is clear that her passion for Wellington was genuine, a Titan so far removed from her tawdry friends Byron, Tom Moore, and her rather abhorrent husband.

Perhaps the Duke was a little 'economical with the truth'? As a result of her friendship with Byron the Duke had very strong views on poets

I hate the whole race. I have the worst opinion of them. There is no believing a word they say – your professional poets, I mean – there never existed a more worthless set than Byron and his friends for example.

Chapter Twelve

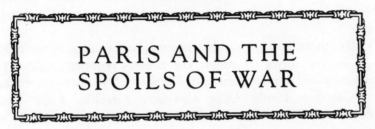

PARIS AND THE SPOILS OF WAR

Wellington spent three days at Brussels and Waterloo after the great victory, comforting the wounded and mourning his dead friends. On 20 June he set off to rejoin the army at Nivelles, and the following day Napoleon reached Paris to try and mend his fortunes. The news of the victory reached London on the night of the twenty-first and the country went wild with delight. English sightseers soon swarmed over the battlefield of Waterloo; the Wordsworths, Walter Scott, John Wilson Croker, even Lord Byron and soon the English beauties too.

The emperor was forced to abdicate by the Chamber of Deputies and the powerful Minister of Police, M. Fouché, although Marshals Davoult, Soult, Ney and Grouchy still commanded the army and could muster considerable forces. Blücher's forces had harried the retreating French army to the outskirts of Paris. Wellington was authorised to inform Louis XVIII that he could return to Paris, provided he accepted Fouché and Talleyrand as his main ministers. Napoleon left for Rochefort avoiding the Prussians, and boarded a British warship *en route* to permanent exile at St Helena. Napoleon II, aged four was in Vienna with his mother, the Empress Marie-Louise.

Several diarists have written of their impressions of Paris that summer of

1815; Captain Gronow, George Keppel, Madame D'Arblay (the novelist Fanny Burney), Madame de Staël and the beautiful Lady Frances Shelley. Very soon the famous Parisian salons were augmented by several English ladies whose evening soirées were attended by the crowned heads of Europe, the defeated French generals, the victorious Allied marshals – and the elegant ladies from France and England. Among these ladies were Madame Crauford, a fat, red-cheeked sixty-seven-year-old woman, the grandmother of Count D'Orsay, who was jolly, not well connected at all but gave parties at her house at 21 rue d'Anjou St Honoré. Lady Oxford took up residence in a hôtel in the rue de Clichy and gave charming soirées. Sir Charles Stuart, the British ambassador, was very popular, and so too was Lady Castlereagh's salon.

To all of them the 'ton' wended their way, often taking in two or more salon's soirées during the night. The English beauties included Lady Conyngham and her daughter Lady Elizabeth, Mrs Harriet Arbuthnot, Lady Caroline Lamb, Lady Charlotte Greville, Lady Frances Wedderburn-Webster and Lady Shelley; all admirers of 'King Villainton'.

On his way to Paris, Wellington was still writing to his young admirers. From Orville on 28 June he wrote to Lady Georgiana Lennox in Brussels,

> Dearest Georgy, I am very much obliged to you for the embroidery [a sash]. If you give your picture, the painter will change it, therefore you should sit with it while he copies it. We are getting on delightfully. Your brothers quite well. Ever yours most sincerely W.

And from Paris on 13 July,

> I don't care how many copies the painter makes of the picture. As you liked it however I recommended it to you not to trust it in his hands. I do invite you to Paris. Your brothers are quite well. I saw William last night [his ADC] such a buck I should not have known him . . .

Dearest Georgy was in Paris in the winter of 1815 and fell ill with typhus. The Duke was,

> most kind sending me dinner every day and convalescent visits, lending me a carriage to drive in. He gave a ball at the Elysée Bourbon and insisted on me going: he sent me a pretty shawl but I spent the evening in an armchair and no dancing.

She was a great favourite of the Duke's and continued to see him in Paris and later in Cambray. In her *Memoirs* she stated that she enjoyed forty-six years of friendship with the Duke. She was a beauty who delayed getting married for many years but eventually, aged twenty-nine in June 1824 she married a cousin, William Fitzgerald de Ros, a captain in the Life Guards. During her long life she met nineteen Prime Ministers including Pitt and of course Wellington, to whom she was always his 'Dearest Georgy'.

One of the most penetrating Parisienne observers was the Comtesse de Boigne, and this account of Wellington's activities and power is fascinating.

> Negotiations for a French loan from Barings and Labouchère ... the Duke of Wellington spared no efforts for this purpose [The English bankers were easily persuaded to lend huge sums to the French Government so that they could repay their enforced debts to their conquerors]. When once he had been induced to adopt an idea and had been persuaded that it was his own, he pursued it energetically.

At the salons and receptions,

> The Duke arrived an hour late according to his custom with his impassive smile on his once handsome countenance, and his 'Oh yes, oh yes' at the service of everybody. This was a sign of good temper. He had the instincts of war to a high degree, though he knew little of the theory [sic]. His judgement upon important questions was sound though he possessed little acquired knowledge. In certain respects his morality was not beyond reproach but he was eminently loyal and straightforward. He never attempted to hide his thoughts of the moment or to evade his promise of the previous evening. But a mere whim was sometimes sufficient to change his intentions entirely. The D. of W. was the most important personage of the time – everybody was convinced of the fact and no one so strongly as himself ... our fate depended upon the goodness of his temper. He alone could take the initiative and tell the sovereigns that the presence in France of the army of occupation of which he was the Generalissimo, had ceased to be necessary to the peace of Europe.

Harriet, Countess Granville and her husband were in Paris from October 1814, left for the 100 Days, and returned after Waterloo. She describes in her diary the main political figures of the day.

> Metternich sat by me at supper at Lady Castlereagh's. I met Talleyrand waddling out; he did not speak to me so I had only the satisfaction of seeing his dirty cunning face and longcoat for a moment. After him came Fouché a little spare, sallow, shrewd looking man who seems to unite all parties in one common feeling – horror of his character! Pozzo di Borgo,

Metternich and Sir Charles Stewart are the only people I like most to talk to here ... Granville laid up with gout so went to see Mlle Mars in *Philsophe Marie*. Talma 'hors' the ranting is magnificent. The Court of Prince Charles (Lord Stewart) and that of Mme de Coigny are two of the major salons. Talma and Mlle Georges act very finely in *Oedipe* and Mme Mars in *Misanthrope*. The theatres are intolerably hot and the carriages rattle more than most.

Nothing is more *agissant* but Lady Caroline William Lamb in a purple riding habit, tormenting everybody but I am convinced ready primed for an attack upon the Duke of Wellington and I have no doubt but that she will to a certain extent succeed as no dose of flattery is too strong for him to swallow or her to administer. Poor William Lamb hides in one small room while she assembles lovers and tradespeople in another. He looks worn to the bone. The D of W talked a great deal about Caroline William. I see she amuses him to the greatest degree especially her accidents which is the charitable term he gives to all her sorties.

The Lambs came to Brussels and Paris three months after Waterloo and still, in theory, married, stayed with Prince Talleyrand. The Duke met them at Lady Kinnaird's and the other fashionable salons in Paris.

Madame d'Arblay, author of *Evelina* described this dangerous young woman,

The famous Lady Caroline Lamb who had been at Mme de la Tour du Pins', dressed or rather not dressed, so as to excite universal attention and authorise every boldness of staring from the General to the lowest soldier among the military groups then constantly pounding la Place – for she had one shoulder and half her back bare and all her throat and neck displayed as if the call of some statuary for modelling a heathen goddess. A slight scarf hung over the other shoulder. As her Ladyship had not then written and could not therefore be considered as an eccentric authoress, this conduct and demeanour excited something *beyond* surprise.

Lady Granville went to the Russian army review and met the three Allied sovereigns. She has even more comments on the Duke.

At St Cloud he called me to sit by him and was quite `a mes pieds` which made Fernan Nunez (bullied by his Spanish Duchess) wink his eyes out and exclaim twenty times in a breath 'Mais voila ce que c'est que les femmes.' The fact is that I really believe the D. finds so few women that do not make up to him. Granville will be pleased to hear of my successes obtained *d'apres ma façon* for an ugly good sort of woman to be attended by a man into whose good graces, beauties force themselves by dint of bassesse – pray forgive my virtuous exultation.

She later noted:

> I quite love the D. of W. He is neither an agreeable man nor in my eyes a 'heros de roman' but he is the most unpretending perfectly natural and amiable person I ever met with.

Harriet Arbuthnot, who was in Paris at the time, wrote in her journal 'The adoration of the ladies for the Duke was given the name '*la nouvelle religion*'.

Lady Shelley described a visit to a soirée at Prince Talleyrand's where Dorothea, Talleyrand's niece, Madame St Edmond Perigord (later Duchesse of Dino), ran up to the Duke and kissed him on both cheeks and called him 'her saviour' with 'most naïve joy'. Lady Shelley admitted,

> She is a very pretty little woman expressing the adoration which we both feel for W. In the carriage home we laughed at her embrace, the D. told me that on the night before he left Vienna all the women at a party embraced him and prophesied that he would conquer Paris, when they would redeem their pledge.

Chapter Thirteen

MADAME DE STAËL 'VOUS QUI ETES DES NOTRES'

By 1765 Ann Louise Germaine Necker's father not only owned his own bank in Paris but had also made a fortune in the shares of the French East India Company. His wife who was a famous writer and scholar ran a fashionable salon in the Rue Michel Le Cômte in the Marais district. From the age of five, young Germaine spent her days in her mother's salon. When she was twenty Germaine married the Swedish ambassador Baron de Staël, and shortly afterwards her son Auguste was born. Three years later King Louis XVI exiled her father who in 1777 had become

French Director-General of Finance even though a Protestant.

At the start of the Revolution Madame de Staël petitioned in vain for the release of Queen Marie-Antoinette. She later became firm friends with Lucien and Joseph Bonaparte, but she and Napoleon disliked each other intensely and the latter exiled her in 1802 because of her royalist sympathies. She regarded the deputies as 'yokels' and founded a society called 'Girondins of the first hour.' The king of Sweden preferred her 'Bulletins de Paris' to his own ambassador's reports. During the terrifying Proscription she saved many of the accused and intrigued to save friends.

Germaine was a large muscular, masculine-looking woman, with rather coarse skin, large bosom and very fine arms. She had dark flashing eyes, beaming with wit and genius. John Wilson Croker, who knew her well, described her as,

> ugly and not of an intellectual ugliness. Her features were coarse and the ordinary expression rather vulgar. She had an ugly mouth, and one or two irregularly prominent teeth which perhaps gave her countenance an habitual gaiety. Her eyes were full, dark and expressive and when she declaimed which was almost whenever she spoke, she looked eloquent and one forgot that she was plain. On the whole she was singularly unfeminine and if in conversation one forgot she was ugly, one forgot also that she was a woman!

She was exiled on several occasions and went to England in 1793–5, to Switzerland, to Germany and to England again in June 1813–May 1814. After her husband's death she acquired various lovers including Benjamin Constant, and eventually married her favourite young lover John Rocca secretly in 1816. He was an intellectual French cavalry officer by whom she had a daughter Albertine, who subsequently became the Duchesse de Broglie.

In England she was accepted into the highest society and was received by the Prince Regent. She made friends with Lord Grey and Lord Harrowby, and 'se brouillait' with the Lansdownes, the writer Thomas Moore, Spencer, James Mackintosh and Wilberforce, the slave trade reformer. She ignored Walter Scott but interested herself in Lord Byron and tried to save his doomed marriage. While in London she met Richard Lord Wellesley and his French wife Hyacinthe, and quarrelled violently with Beau Brummell and the Dandies. Lady Holland wrote to Mrs Creevey at Brighton,

> The great wonder of the time is Mme de Staël. She is surrounded by all the curious and every sentence she utters is caught and repeated with

various commentaries. Her first appearance was at Lady Jersey's. Her personal charms have greatly improved within the last 25 years. She is violent against the Emperor, who she says is not a man *'ce n'est point un homme, mais un système.'* She is much less ugly than I expected: her eyes are fine and her hand and arm are very handsome. She is to live in Manchester St.

In 1813 John Murray published Mme de Staël's book *De l'Allemagne* which had been suppressed in France. *Delphine* had been published in 1802 and *Corinne* in 1807. Her books had strong political messages, against dictatorship, and social ones, against divorce, and were directed at Bonaparte's character and regime. After Waterloo she cried out to her friends in London 'The blow has been cruel, all London is drunk with joy and alone in this great city I feel sorrow.'

Madame de Staël arrived back in Paris on 12 May 1814 with John Rocca and August Wilhelm Schlegel, a philosophical writer of renown, and set up her salon in a dilapidated house in Clichy. 'Why congratulate me? (on my return) Because the Cossacks are in the Rue Racine and I am in despair?' Soon however Paris was saying, 'There are three powers in Europe, England, Russia . . . and Madame de Staël.'

This famous woman was called a 'Brain in the service of a Passion', and to her salon, where the doors only opened at midnight, the 'haut ton' and the intellectuals of Europe crowded. On his way from Bordeaux back to London Wellington called there on 19 June, to take part in one of Madame de Staël's brilliant 'soupers' with Talleyrand, Schlegel, Chateaubriand, Madame Récamier, Lafayette, and a score of others. Her young lover-husband was in the background – passionate, handsome, a violent and sensual man – utterly devoted to his older more brilliant wife. The first night in Paris the Duke dined with Germaine and Benjamin Constant. From August Madame de Staël was writing to him frequently.

For the next three years until her death on 14 July 1817, she met Wellington frequently in her salon or in his house at the Elysée-Bourbon which was close. They corresponded often during 1816, particularly when the Duke was stationed in Cambray. She kept copies of some of her letters to the Duke (he would have automatically destroyed the originals) and she also kept a journal. Some of her letters were written from her château at Coppet in Switzerland near to Lord Byron's villa, and some of the twenty-one letters still surviving of their correspondence are there. Others are in the château de Broglie in Normandy.

Lord W. passed an evening with me the day before yesterday (19 June

1814) of his two days in Paris he gave me one: it is his simplicity that excites admiration.

The Duke's first surviving letter is dated 2 November.

I shall be too tired after todays chasse to sustain with dignity the various attacks which you will make upon me in connection with the events of the last four or five days during which I did not have the pleasure of seeing you! [He also wrote] All I have now is the memory of those happy hours I spent in your house . . . and in your company everywhere.

Although Madame de Staël had helped him draft anti-slavery speeches into precise French (they corresponded and talked to each other in French), her demands on the Duke were continuous. She supported the American side and rejoiced when the War of Independence was over. She was not afraid to be blatantly anti-English to his face.

In a letter to her friend Colonel Guiguer, Madame de Staël wrote,

I have spoken to the Duke about your neighbour at Prangins [near Lausanne]. He has promised me to do everything necessary for M. Joseph Bonaparte [the ex-King of Spain] to be left in peace.

The Duke gave balls on 30 September and 28 October to which Madame de Staël was invited. The Duke met her in the Clichy salon in January 1815 before he went to the Congress of Vienna. During the 100 Days Madame de Staël beat a sensible retreat from her 'bête noire', the emperor, to the safety of her Swiss estate. After Waterloo her return to Paris and her renewed admiration for the Duke reached new heights of ecstasy.

She wrote (translated):

I must see you soon, for in gazing upon you my soul grows stronger [and] When we had the happiness of seeing you in Paris last winter [of 1814] who among us would have believed that your fame had not reached its highest point of splendour! Nevertheless one might say that Bonaparte returned to the soil of France to increase your glory and show the world that he must be vanquished by you (you were able to realise my Lord how great was my admiration for you before these recent events). But you will forgive me for confessing my Lord that the more I admire you, I suffer in admiring you: the more unsullied your glory, the more do I feel the humiliation of my unhappy country. In their misery the French may still look up on the Continental nations with pride, they defeated them once and saw them bend before them but the English led by you are more than human. Before you we blush with shame. England already so noble, free and happy had no need of so much glory. Why did the heavens not make you a Frenchman (to be the liberator) to raise up again our fine nation? . . . Let me plead before you on its behalf as I would plead on my own behalf before that generosity which I adore.

Madame de Staël was trying to persuade the Duke to reduce the size of the occupying armies of some 130,000 men and to reduce the length of the Allied occupation. And to some extent she succeeded, for in February 1816 she wrote to him from Florence the famous phrase '*vous, qui êtes des notres!*'

Wellington, who tried hard to keep out of French politics, sympathised with the party of the right, known as ultras, centred round the ageing king's brother and heir, called 'Monsieur' or the Count d'Artois. Madame de Staël favoured the fanatical left wing in the political spectrum and saw the Allied occupation as an absolute evil, a violation of French self-respect. She quoted to the Duke the rape of Paris by the Prussians who looted and requisitioned all they needed, and the uncontrolled maraudings by the Cossacks and Austrian soldiers. The executions of Marshal Ney and La Bedoyère were seen to be acts of barbarism and a blow to French national liberty, pride and freedom. The Duke's determination to stay in Paris until the French indemnities had been finally paid, was well known. He was also anxious that the last revolutionary vestiges should be eradicated from the system.

The great salons of Paris gave the Duke and Castlereagh a chance to put their views over to the intelligentsia in a way which was impossible outside. Madame de Staël had moved her house and salon to No 6, Rue Royale. The Duke discussed most of his friends (and wife) with Harriet Arbuthnot. Of Madame de Staël she records in her journal,

> When she could be kept from political discussions she was the most agreeable woman he had ever known, so excessively brilliant and '*toute pétillante d'esprit*' but that she delighted in entering into arguments when she lost her head and *déraisonnoit* terribly. He used to say to her '*Je deteste les discussions politiques: je n'en veux pas avec vous*' to which she used to reply '*Eh moi, discuter sur la politique, c'est vivre.*' She let him into all the secrets of the French constitutional party to which she belonged . . . get rid of the Bourbons '*Et alors les émigrés seront pour nous ce que les catholiques étoient pour vous.*'

Madame de Staël wrote at the end of 1816 to the Duke in Cambray that Lord Byron had just published a poem in which he called the battle of Waterloo a 'King making victory'. She was writing a new work in which she said that the Duke's personal character alone had tipped the scales at Waterloo – which of course was correct.

You must become the greatest man, not of our time, but of all times and give us back France. When you come back here my Lord, I will lay my respects on the steps of your altar.

Another letter ended,

let me know when in the coming months I shall hear your name announced in my house. Never has this happened without my heart beating faster . . .'

Madame de Staël fiercely attacked Sir Charles Stuart and Mr Canning about the continued Allied occupation. In January 1817 the Duke recommended a reduction of 20 per cent by each Allied army, a total of 30,000 men. Lady Blennerhasset and the Count de Villele separately wrote in their journals that it was the influence of Madame de Staël on the Duke that caused these sensible troop reductions. That same month she was writing to Wellington,

I have not gone out since I heard you were in Paris, hoping that you might perhaps be thinking of me. Chance has made it so happen that the person who thinks of you most in all the world should also be closest to your residence . . .

Meanwhile she had no luck with Mr Canning about the ending of the Treaty of Paris. She was told,

We have conquered France: she is our conquest and we want to weaken her to the point that she cannot make a move for ten years.

The relationship between the sensual, ugly, intellectual, French patriot and the stern man of probity, the famous English field marshal was extraordinary and touching. During 1816 he saw her practically every day. She was slowly dying of dropsy and died on 14 July 1817. Her last letter in her own hand was written in February, but her daughter, Albertine, continued to write at her dictation to the Duke.

My Lord, My eyes always rest on that bright place above my bed where I saw the Angels of Darkness and of Glory merge into one waiting to decide my destiny. All is as yet uncertain and Providence has not yet become manifest. But the kindness you have shown me will stay in my memory to my last breath: whatever happens it will be the crowning glory of my life and death.

(signed The Secretary – Albertine de Broglie de Staël).

During June 1817 the Duke spent ten days in Paris and visited

Madame de Staël every day. Later the poet A.W. Schlegel wrote to Lady Burghersh saying how grateful and touched all the de Staël family and friends were at the Duke's concern 'such compassion well becomes a hero.'

Germaine de Staël wrote of the Duke during their intimacy, 'Never has God created a great man with less expenditure' which on balance must be presumed to be a compliment! She also said that he had '*pas de coeur pour l'amour*,' to which he answered that she had done everything in her power ' "*pour m'interesser à elle*" what does she suppose me made of?'

The Duke replied to a long, emotional and passionate letter from Madame de Staël with detached logic.

> My presence in this country is founded upon Treaties but you people whose memories are so short and imagination so lively, you forget everything that has brought France to the position she is in now . . . You forget what happened last year [Napoleon's enthusiastic return] . . . I realise someone with your vivid imagination dislikes being referred back to documents for the truth pure and simple: nevertheless it is there you will find it! *Eh bien!* Allow me to give you a little warning, allow me to say as frankly as I would say it if we were sitting alone in front of your fire that you are devilishly indiscreet, that even here [in Cambray] they are telling me you are causing much Mischief and that you put yourself in the wrong with the King . . . Adieu, Madame this is a long letter and I hope it will show you that I am still your most faithfull and sincere Wellington.

In later life he told Lord Stanhope,

> We were great friends and on her deathbed she wanted to see me but I was not in Paris at the time . . . she was a most agreeable woman if you only kept her light and away from politics!

On her deathbed she converted to Roman Catholicism which astounded the Duke 'the truth is that she was terribly afraid of Death . . .'

Of the relatively few letters left to posterity in this three-year affair of two great minds, one from Madame de Staël is most poignant.

> I am French, daughter of a man who loved France above all else and the fate of Poland inspires me with horror for my country. If I had the honour of being English I do not think I would wish to see the destruction of a nation which for five centuries has earned the glory of fighting against England and on the field of Waterloo showed you at least, my Lord, that it knew how to die . . .

Chapter Fourteen

LA GRASSINI –
LA CHANTEUSE
DE L'EMPEREUR

Bonaparte and Wellington had many things in common. Their date of birth in the same year; their genius for making war and high command in the field; their love of beautiful women; and their taste in music.

Despite Bonaparte's undoubted contempt for Wellington, his well-reported jibe about the 'Sepoy General' and his description of Wellington's army as 'an emaciated leopard', there is no doubt of the Duke's respect for the emperor. 'His presence made the difference of forty thousand men.'

The two great men never met but there were several curious links. For instance Wellington inherited Napoleon's mistress 'La Chanteuse de l'Empereur'. Madame Guiseppina Grassini must have been a very satisfactory conquest. Besides her voluptuous charms, her contralto voice and knowledge of fine music endeared her to Wellington in the heady days in Paris during 1814 and 1815. Pauline Borghese, Napoleon's beautiful and seductive youngest sister, may have thrown her elegant cap at the Duke too, since he described her to Lady Bagot as 'a heartless little devil'.

Another connection between the two men was the American Patterson family. If Wellington's dalliance with Marianne had led to marriage, the two military gentlemen would have been related. Betsy Patterson's marriage to Jerome Bonaparte was annulled by the emperor but it was 'a close-run thing'!

Mesdames Catalini and Grassini were acknowledged to be the finest singers in Europe, and they performed before royalty and their courts in every city. Catalini's reputation off stage was impeccable. She was happily married and her husband went with her on her travels. Wellington applauded her arias with enthusiasm in Lisbon, London, Paris and Brussels. 'La Grassini' was *'une contatrice Amie de Napoleon'* i.e. his mistress and she subsequently became Wellington's mistress.

Guiseppina Grassini was born in Varese, Lombardy on 18 April 1773, thus being four years younger than her famous admirers. She lived in Milan at la Casa Arese, Largo San Babola, and made her debut at the Scala, Milan in 1794 as a contralto. The Duke of Sussex was an admirer of hers in 1797. She alternated between Milan and Paris for a number of years and sang at the Fête Nationale in the Champ de Mars in 1800. During 1803 she played for four months in London at the Haymarket Theatre and also sang there later during 1804–6. From 1806–15 she was engaged by Napoleon as the court singer at L'Opéra Buffa and Theatre Italien.

Henrietta, Lady Bessborough, an attractive Francophile, wrote on 13 November 1814 to her lover Granville Leveson Gower,

> The Duke of Wellington is so civil to me and I admire him so much as a hero that it inclines me to be partial to him, but I am afraid he is behaving very ill to that poor little woman [i.e. Kitty]: he found great fault with for it not on account of making her miserable or of the immorality of the fact but the want of precédé and publicity of his attentions to Grassini ... They are calling everyone 'King Pourquoi', pas 'King Villainton.'

La Grassini had fine expressive eyes, large regular features, fine teeth, and tragic dignity. Her language, a mixture of Italian and French with a smattering of English, was distinctly unrefined. She affected a multicoloured gipsy style of dress, and had the Latin temperament, frank to the point of being rude, talkative and impulsive. Although she had no cleverness or wit she had a fund of droll recollections which, spoken in her strong Italian accent, made her the centre of salon society. She possessed a large fortune from the fees she demanded and received, and from sumptuous presents.

> Napoleon gave me this snuffbox. He placed it in my hands one morning when I had been to see him at the Tuileries and he added 'Voila pour toi, tu es une brave fille.' He was indeed a great man but he would not follow my advice 'Il aurait du s'entendre avec ce cher Villainton. By the by c'est ce brave Duc qui m'a donné cette broche. Il me l'a apportée un matin que j'étais encore au lit. Il parlait un singulier baragouin et je ne savais guère l'anglais, mais nous nous entendions tout de même!'*

This was Captain Gronow's account of a meeting with La Grassini.

---

* He ought to have got on with dear Villainton [Wellington]. By the by, it is the good Duc who gave me this brooch. He brought it to me one morning when I was still in bed. He spoke a peculiar gibberish and I know scarcely any English but we got on well all the same!

Andrea Appiani and Madame Lebrun painted her portrait and there is a miniature of her by Ferdinando Quaglia in the Musée de la Scala-Milan.

M. Ferdinand Paet was her directeur general and M. Blangini was her favourite composer. The latter was 'le cavalier servant' of Princesse Pauline Borghese, Napoleon's youngest sister. In his memoirs he recounts a meeting with Wellington and Grassini on 20 July 1815.

Je m'étais remis a composer des opéras (pour Grassini). Je fis representer à Feydeaux La Sourde-Mouette, opéra-comique en trois actes. Le Roi de Prusse, que se trouvait à Paris assista à la première representation. Comme je voyais souvent Madame Grassini elle me conduisit chez Lord Wellington ou nous fimes très souvent de la musique. Là venait assidument Lord Castlereagh, qui chantait avec nous et très passablement pour un ministre anglais. Lorsque Madame Grassini était en petit comité chez Lord Wellington elle declamait et chantait des scènes de la Cleopatra et de Romeo et Giulietta. Seule au milieu du salon elle faisait des gestes comme si elle eut été sur le théatre et à l'aide d'un grand chale, elle se drapait de diverses manières. Je ne me rappelle pas si, dans les séances, elle chanta les arias qui finissent par un squardo d'amor: mais ce que je puis assurer c'est que Lord Wellington était ravi, en extase. Dans ces representations j'étais, a moi seul, tout l'orchestre!*

All the English travellers to Paris came back with various stories about Grassini. John Cam Hobhouse's journal records that Lady Kinnaird told him of the follies of the Duke's public addresses to Grassini, who lived in the same house with the duchess.

On 18 August 1815 the Duke gave a banquet in Paris for the emperor of Russia, the king of Prussia, and all the English nobility in Paris. Walter Scott was there, so was Tom Moore the poet, John Kemble and Talma the actors, and both Madame Catalini and Grassini, who sang for their supper.

---

* I started to compose some more operas (for Grassini). *The Deaf Mute*, a comic opera in three acts, was performed for Feydeau. The King of Prussia who was in Paris attended the first performance. As I often saw Madame Grassini she took me to Lord Wellington's establishment where we often made music. Lord Castlereagh was a constant visitor there and he sang with us, very tolerably for an English minister. When Madame Grassini attended informal gatherings at Lord Wellington's she declaimed and sang scenes from *Cleopatra* and *Romeo and Juliet*. Alone in the centre of the salon she gestured as if she was on the stage and using a big shawl she dressed up in various different ways. I cannot remember if, during these sessions, she sang the arias which end with a 'sguardo d'amor'; but what I am certain of is that Lord Wellington was enchanted, in ecstasy. During these performances I alone was the entire orchestra!

The Comtesse de Boigne recalled an evening at the beginning of 1816;

I remember that upon one occasion the Duke conceived the idea of making Grassini, who was then at the height of her beauty, the Queen of the evening. She was the first professional singer to be admitted to London society. To great talent she added extreme beauty, sound common sense. She was an excellent actress and her principles of singing were admirable. She brought contralto voices into fashion, almost drove soprano voices from the theatre. Her favourite song was 'Paga Fui' from Winter's *Ratto de Proserpina*. The Duke seated her upon a sofa mounted on a platform in the ballroom and never left her side, caused her to be served before anyone else, made people stand away in order that she might see the dancing and took her in to supper himself in front of the whole company. There he sat by her side and showed her attentions usually granted only to Princesses. There were some high born English ladies to share the burden of this insult!

Lady Shelley, with her husband, frequently visited Madame Grassini 'who delighted at my calling, kissed me on both cheeks.' She noted how popular Grassini and Tramezzani the tenor had been for several years in England, and how the Earl of Mount Edgcumbe regarded Grassini's performance in *Gliorazi* and *Curiazi* by Cimarossa as her '*chef d'oeuvre*'.

Madame Grassini told Lady Shelley that French head-dresses half-a-yard high were not worn in good society. She was regarded as the leader of 'ton' in Paris and appeared at the opera in Roman costume, a pair of tight flesh-coloured pantaloons, close-fitting, and over them a thin white shawl drapery that clung in loose folds to her form 'making nudeness more nude'. 'Her acting with Tramezzani was the finest thing I ever saw and I could not repress my tears.'

Charles Greville wrote of the Duke, 'He became the successful lover of Grassini and some women of fashion whose weaknesses had never been known, though perhaps suspected!'

Madame de Staël also wrote that Madame Guiseppina Grassini, the famous Milanese contralto, was widely believed to be *one* of the Duke's mistresses. She was one of several visitors to the Duke's house where there were three noticeable portraits. That of the Pope was flanked by Princesse Pauline Borghese and by Madame Grassini. Madame de Staël said 'Why expose the Pope to such a situation of this sort?' and another French visitor, Monsieur Artois, later Charles X of France, said '*Absolument comme notre Seigneur entre deux larrons* [thieves].'

Grassini rarely sang in public after 1816, apart from two farewell concerts in Milan during 1817, as her voice was fading. Her great affair with the Duke probably started in 1814 and continued for the next three years. He must have thought fondly of the sensual songbird of Napoleon in latter years when he listened at Ancient Concerts (the term then used for classic music) to her Italian niece, Grisi.

Chapter Fifteen

MADAME RECAMIER

The French painters David and Gérard have left to posterity the beautiful features of the Directoire beauty Madame Jeanne Françoise Julie Adelaide Bernard. She was born in Lyons in 1777. Her father was a notary and her mother, a singularly beautiful and attractive woman, was also a successful financial speculator – a rarity in those days. During the Reign of Terror, Juliette (the French call this nickname '*nom de caresse*') married a wealthy Parisian banker Jacques Récamier. He also came from Lyons and he was twenty-seven years older than his child bride of sixteen.

Very soon her beauty attracted the attentions of Lucien Bonaparte and she became his mistress. Lucien wrote her scores of billets-doux – he was 'Romeo' to his Juliette. Not only was she reckoned to be the greatest beauty in France, but also she owned the most beautiful bed. It was made of mahogany, ormulu, and bronze raised upon two steps, and had a coverlet of muslin and gold. Upon this the languid beauty, in fact she had great '*belesprit*', received her guests. Juliette had a clear complexion, a full figure, was tall, and dressed à la mode, often in a white satin gown with a necklace and bracelet of pearls.

During the Peace of 1802, aged twenty-five, she and her mother visited London and became friendly with the Duchess of Devonshire. The Countess Brownlow saw Madame Récamier walking one day in Kensington Gardens in a style she described as,

> *à l'antique* with a muslin gown clinging to her form like the folds of the drapery on a statue, her hair in a plait at the back, and falling in small ringlets round her face and greasy with '*huile antique*', a large veil thrown over the head completed her attire, that not unnaturally caused her to be followed and stared at.

She had by now attracted the attentions of Lucien's powerful brother, the emperor, which she did not reciprocate and of Prince Augustus of Prussia, which were reciprocated, and of the ubiquitous Benjamin Constant. Juliette was fond of the theatre and of Garat's wonderful singing, and was a concertgoer. She became a close friend of Madame de Staël, who initially was enraptured with Napoleon. He was sarcastic with both because he did not like (or was afraid of) intellectual women.

It was in Madame de Staël's salon in 1814 that Wellington first met La Récamier, along with La Fayette, Chateaubriand, Talleyrand, Prince Laval, Canova, Schlegel and old Marshal Blücher.

Juliette kept a journal and some of Wellington's letters to her dated June 13 1814, and other days during that year. She told Madame Lenormant that she did not find the Duke either animated or interesting, and did not follow Madame de Staël's advice 'to obtain influence over him, which without a doubt, she could easily have gained.' She mentioned that he talked of Napoleon to her, knowing that she had been mildly persecuted by the Corsican. '*Je l'ai bien battu*,' the Duke said to her. Apparently Juliette closed her doors against him in disgust!

Paris June 13. I confess Madame that I am not very sorry that business matters will prevent my calling upon you after dinner, since each time I see you, I leave you more deeply impressed with your charms and less inclined to give my attention to politics!!! I shall call upon you to-morrow provided you are at home, upon my return from the Abbé Sicard's and in spite of the dangerous effect such visits have upon me. Your very faithful servant, Wellington.

Another letter was written to her in French.

J'étais tout hier à la chasse, Madame: et je n'ai reçu votre billet et les livres qu'à la nuit, quand c'était trop tard pour vous répondre. J'ésperais que mon jugement serait guidé par le votre dans ma lecture des lettres de Mlle. Julie de l'Espinasse, et je deséspère de pouvoir le former moi-même. Je vous suis bien obligé pour les pampletes de Mme de Staël. Votre très obeissant et fidel serviteur, Wellington. *

Her diary (translated) was written in a staccato jerky style.

---

* I spent the whole of yesterday hunting, Madame; and I only received your note and the books in the evening when it was too late to reply to you. I was hoping that my judgement would be guided by yours in my reading of the letters of Mlle. Julie de l'Espinasse and I despair of being able to accomplish the former myself. I am very obliged for the pamphlets of Mme de Staël. Your very obedient and faithful servant, Wellington.

Madame de Staël's enthusiasm for the Duke of Wellington. I see him at her house for the first time. Conversation during dinner. He pays me a visit the following day Mme de Staël meets him here. Lord Ws visits become frequent. His opinion of popularity. I present him to Queen Hortense [made Duchess de St. Leu by Louis XVIII]. Soirée at house of the Duchesse de Luynes. Conversation with the Duke of Wellington before a glass door. Empressement of M. de Talleyrand towards me. Madame de Boigne stops me as I am leaving followed by the Duke of Wellington. Continuation of his visits. He writes me unmeaning notes which all resemble one another. I lend him Mademoiselle de l'Espinasse's letters which have just appeared. His opinion of these letters. He leaves Paris. I see him again after the battle of Waterloo. He calls upon me the day after his return. I did not expect him. Annoyance this visit occasions me. He returns in the evening and is denied admission. I again refuse to see him the next day. He writes to Madame de Staël to complain of my treatment of him. I do not see him again.

It is reported that he is very much impressed with a young English lady the wife of one of his aides-de-camp. Return of Madame de Staël to Paris. Dinner at the Queen of Sweden's with her and the Duke of Wellington whom I then see again. The coolness of his manner towards me. His attention to the young English lady. I am placed at dinner between him and the Duc de Broglie. He is sullen at the beginning of dinner but grows animated and finally becomes very agreeable. I observe the annoyance of the young English lady who is seated opposite to us. I cease talking to him and devote myself entirely to the Duc de Broglie [who later marries Madame de Staël's only daughter]. I see the Duke very seldom. He comes to call on me at the Abbaye-aux-Bois on his last visit to Paris.

Juliette had met Maria Edgeworth, Kitty's cousin, in Paris, so doubtless her flirtation with the Duke was made known in London.

Chapter Sixteen

FRANCES, LADY SHELLEY – REVIEWS AND BALLS

Madame, Countess, and later Princesse de Lieven was a devoted Duke-watcher, not only for her masters in St Petersburgh and for her lover Prince Metternich, but also, in a convoluted way, out of admiration and love. Writing to Metternich from Paris (16 December 1827) she said,

> I know from Frederick Lamb [one of Harriette Wilson's lovers and later to become Viscount Palmerston] that the Duke received orders recalling him to London for he wanted to stay in Paris. He was perfectly happy between the women who ran after him and the ones he ran after in his turn.

One of the women who ran after the Duke, and certainly he ran after her too, was known to her husband Sir John Shelley as 'My old Goose'. The Duke first met Lady Fanny Shelley née Winckley at Wanstead on 21 July 1814 at a party for Marshal Blücher, when the 'Goose', or the 'Country Girl' as she was christened by Lady Jersey, had been married for seven years. Her husband was a gambler, kept two packs of hounds, liked shooting, and owned horses that twice won the Derby for him; he was sixteen years older than his wife and suffered from gout. They mixed in the Jersey set with Lord Byron, Beau Brummell, Princess Charlotte and Lady Sarah Fane. Frances grew up in Preston with an eccentric, Jacobite, Port-drinking father. Her mother remarried an Irish major of most disgusting vulgarity. She was a very pretty young matron (painted by G. Sanders) when she and her husband arrived in Paris shortly after Waterloo and she was a superb rider, which especially appealed to the Duke. She also kept a remarkably interesting and well-written diary which started in 1813 when she was aged twenty-six. She was very observant, very innocent and thought the best of everybody practically all the time. Her story starts with her recollections, written as an old lady.

> I found myself in a dangerous atmosphere but I held my own like a true Englishwoman until in 1814 an influx of foreigners led to a change of

manners. In company with my lovely niece, Harriet Greville, then in her modest fresh beauty, I entered into the dissipation of that exciting period. I attended the great fêtes and balls given in honour of the Sovereign and I danced at them. It was then that my hero-worship of Wellington caused me to accept with pleasure – though shrinking from the notoriety it gave me – the attention of the Saviour of my Country, a man to whom everyone was then devoted: the intoxication of being the chosen companion – but my awe of Wellington was very great when I first saw him I was so overcome that I nearly fainted at his feet. Such was the high romance, now called Folly of those days, that even my husband felt exaltation in the notice which the Duke took of us both.

Fanny's recollections of their first meeting are vivid.

The Duke's manner is formal and at first introduction very imposing. He seldom speaks until he is well acquainted. He greeted Shelley with the utmost cordiality having known him before he went to Spain ... He retains that simplicity of character and manner which is still his distinguishing excellence. He remembers his old friends with the same interest as ever. The youngest of his subordinate officers enjoys his society and is indeed much more an object of his attention, than are those of a more exalted station in life ... From that time our acquaintance increased till it has almost become intimacy.

The Duchess Kitty was there too, and Fanny had met her the month before. Fanny's eldest son John had gone up to the Duke (the boy aged seven and the Duke aged forty-five) and declaimed 'I am so glad to see you, Duke of Wellington, I have wanted to see you such a long time.' The Duke kissed him on both cheeks. One of the surest ways to the Beau's heart was through young children. A subsequent meeting was at a ball at Carlton House given by the Prince Regent. Watching his handsome dashing ADCs dancing with the prettiest girls in London, the Beau remarked to Lady Shelley, 'How would society get on without all my boys?' At the same ball the Duke was making jokes with his nieces Priscilla Burghersh and Georgiana Fitzroy. Shortly afterwards the Duke gave away in marriage Georgiana to Henry Marquess of Worcester and Emily Wellesley-Pole to Lord Fitzroy Somerset.

Reading pretty Fanny's diary she makes it plain that her romance with the Duke was almost platonic. But to Princess Lieven and his niece Priscilla Burghersh he, perhaps surprisingly, quoted a rather different story. A year or so later Lady Shelley was in Vienna (the Shelleys made three Grand European tours) and had advances made to her either by 'a fat Austrian baron' or by Prince Metternich, or by both, and with appropriate 'pride and Indignation' fended them off saying 'Know Sir that I have resisted the Duke of Wellington and do not imagine, etc etc etc!' Wellington in the two stories made slightly different answers. 'In my own justification I must say that I was *never* aware of this resistance,' and in the second case 'Devil take me if I ever *asked* her for anything.'

Harriet, Countess Granville (youngest daughter of the 5th Duke of Devonshire) whose husband was ambassador in Paris for many years (1824–8, 1830–40), was a jolly, plain but observant lady. She wrote to her sister Lady Morpeth (30 December 1812),

> Lady Shelley is not superior or clever. Indeed she is not. Do observe pray it is all commonplace and superficial. She is not foolish and she has had an education 'tres soigné' in every respect. I see you are coming round to admire Lady Shelley. I see her with a sort of hoisted-up look in her figure, tight satin shoes, a fine thick plait of hair, bloodshot eyes, parched lips, fine teeth and an expression of conscious accomplishments in her face.

Well, that is one feminine viewpoint, but worse was to come.

> Lady Shelley pursues her pursuits with the most unremitting diligence and makes herself really ridiculous as the Duke pays her no attention, and she follows, and watches him quite laughably. There is no harm in her, I am sure, beyond inordinate vanity ... All the scandal of Paris that Sir John and Lady Shelley ran after the great Duke in a very disgusting manner, but as they were together 'sans peur et sans raproche.'

Despite the overt attractions of these elegant beauties – the English ladies and the French duchesses – the most vivid and intimate recollections of the conqueror in Paris derive from Fanny Shelley. It may have been simply that she was the only confidante, who fortunately for posterity, had the wit and intelligence to absorb Wellington's innermost and confidential thoughts and then record them with affection, and presumably accuracy.

After squiring Fanny to an opera in London, the crowd made way for them with 'the greatest respect' and the Duke turned towards Fanny and said in the gayest tone 'It's a fine thing to be a great man is not it?' In August 1814 the Duke returned to Paris, but not before Fanny wrote in her diary,

> The adoration felt for the Duke by his family, his children and above all by the Duchess are proofs of his goodness of heart and disposition. He is undoutedly the finest character that any age has produced.

The first tour made by the Shelleys ended up in Montmartre and Fanny noted that within the course of a week their hotel changed name four times from Hotel de Napoleon, to Bourbon, to Louis Dix Huit, and finally and safely to Hotel de la Paix (with which no one could quarrel). She recorded her first meeting with Wellington since Waterloo.

> W. entered the room looking as simple and unobtrusive as usual. I must admit that my enthusiasm for this great soldier was so great that I could not utter one word and with great difficulty restrained my tears. He was dressed in dark blue military great-coat, plain hat and boots. His eye had ever more of its usual fire: he looked remarkably well and was fatter than he was last year.

The Duke gave the Shelleys the free run of his boxes in all the theatres in Paris. He took them to Madame Crauford's salon. 'The D. shows no taste by going so often to her house.' The women wore large bonnets, cambric muslin gowns and looked like demure housemaids.

The Duke introduced the Shelleys to Paris society to hear, see and talk to Grassini, the pretty dancer Greslin, Biggotini, and Baptiste who was the best Buffo actor in *Le Mariage de Figaro* at the Theatre Français. They went to the Feydeau, to the Varieties with the Kinnairds (Lady K. was said to be in love with W.) 'Fanny noted that Grassini sang beautifully. The Duke enjoyed it *extremely!*'

The Beau took them to the soirées at the Duchesse de Duras' at the Tuileries, where they met Prince Talleyrand, whose niece kissed the Duke so dramatically, the French marshals, Marmont and Victor 'who were dull but addressed W. with respect', the emperor of Russia and the young princes of Prussia.

Wellington flaunted his pretty young conquest at the frequent military reviews,

> where I had the happiness of riding by his side along the line and stood by him while the troops marched past.

The Duchesse de Duras praised Fanny's riding at the review and her horsemanship, but deplored her conduct as 'indecorous'.

Meanwhile Fanny communes with her feelings in her diary

> I hope my head wont be turned. There really is some danger – my dislike, contempt for the commonplace amusements of London society. It is lucky for me that my happiness is centred in domestic life . . . encourage me to devote my sons to the service of W. and of my country.

What she wrote may have been for posterity, but to the outside world

Fanny's intimacy with the Duke was clearly very close. He encouraged her to ride Copenhagen at reviews. He lent her his mare to ride to St Cloud with Baron Tripp and Lord Edward Somerset. But above all he confided in her tête à tête some of his most famous sentiments.

> During the whole of June 18th [at Waterloo] he was exposed to the hottest fire. As he himself said to me 'The finger of God was upon me. I hope to God that I have fought my last battle. It is a bad thing to be always fighting. While in the thick of it I am too much occupied to feel anything, but it is wretched just after. It is quite impossible to think of glory. Both mind and feelings are exhausted. I am wretched even at the moment of victory and I always say next to a battle lost, the greatest misery is a battle gained. Not only do you lose those dear friends with whom you have been living but you are forced to leave the wounded behind you. To be sure one tries to do the best for them but how little that is! At such moments every feeling in your breast is deadened. I am now just beginning to regain my natural spirits but I never wish for any more fighting.' I quote the D's words just as they were spoken . . . the intensity of feeling, the face lit up straight to the listeners heart.

Wellington saved the Bridge of Jena being blown up by posting armed English sentries, and said to Fanny of Marshal Blücher 'famous old fellow – can't stop his troops from plundering.' Fanny dined with the Duke at Lord Stewart's who was 'most delightful' and sat between the wounded Prince of Orange and Prince Metternich, Talleyrand and Prince Schwartzenberg sat opposite her. She thought T. was diabolical, had a clubfoot, no marked feature, was pale, with a crafty expression and a most villainous mouth, his fiendish laugh 'still haunts me.' At dinner Metternich was very entertaining. 'I wonder if one may believe what he said?' Every day was filled with reviews, riding in the parks, visiting the duchesses, even La Grassini received the little English 'goose'. She went shopping for dresses with Lady Kinnaird and then to the Louvre and was struck by the beautiful statue of Apollo. The Duke sent a sergeant to escort them to ensure admittance. One evening the capture of Bonaparte was announced. 'All the women jumped up and almost embraced the men in an ecstasy of joy.' But Lady Kinnaird thought Napoleon had been the greatest man in the world until he ran away from his army after Waterloo not understanding that there were excellent tactical reasons for doing so in order to rally his generals and ministers in Paris.

Meanwhile the Duke was still entrusting his intimate thoughts to the little 'Old Goose'.

> It is my experience that gives me the advantage over every other officer.

Nothing now can happen to me and I always feel confident that I shall succeed. The troops feel the same confidence in me. For that reason I firmly believe that if anything had happened to me at Waterloo, the battle was lost.

Every evening she dined with the Duke since usually Shelley was elsewhere, occasionally ill with gout and is rarely mentioned in her diaries. She visited the stables to see his horses, and in her words 'back to his billet.' He talked to her '*à coeur ouvert*' of Waterloo and his own feelings and his eventual return to England.

Do you know I never anticipate. I think it will certainly be very gratifying but I am quite happy here.

Fanny told him that he would not settle into the quiet of private existence after such an exciting life.

Oh yes, I shall but I must always have my house full. For sixteen years I have always been at the head of our army and I must have these gay fellows round me.

The Duke's views on the army rankers are well known. At reviews and manoeuvers his face, Fanny noticed, would stiffen when his troops took off their hats and shouted their applause.

I hate that cheering. If once you allow soldiers to express an opinion, they may, on some other occasion hiss instead of cheering.

The Beau was leading an active life in every sense. Certainly in the summer after Waterloo, Lady Charlotte Greville and La Grassini were his mistresses. Lady Frances Wedderburn-Webster very probably was too. Several times the beautiful Annesley sisters (W-W and Lady John Somerset) were honoured guests in the Duke's box. Each time Lady Shelley made a discreet excuse to withdraw.

The D. thought me foolish for leaving his box. One ought *never* to be discrète. What happiness! I was quite right last night to leave the box . . . How I adore that great man! . . . I cut off a lock of his hair!

Soon Fanny was being introduced by the Duke to Monsieur, to the Duc de Berri, the emperor of Russia, the emperor of Austria, Pozzo di Borgo and was taken to see Madame Georges act in *Semiramus*. She noted that the Duke often went home early and appeared unwell! Fanny visited the Luxembourg museum, admired the beautiful Vernets and went to the Chamber of Peers. Every evening she went to a salon, either at Lady Castlereagh's, Madame Crauford's or Lord Stewart's (now regarded as 'so great a fool'). The Duke sent a glass coach with two outriders and two footmen behind so that in July she could attend the Allied review of 65,000 troops. The Dutch looked sloppy, the Russians very fine fellows and the Siberian cavalry had large handsome horses, but the British Guards were magnificent and so were the 18-pounder guns with twelve horses, the Royal Horse Artillery, who made a great impression on the foreign officers. The emperor of Russia and the Duke took the salute. The Duke kept his sword drawn throughout the day, 'He looked indeed the Conqueror'. After an evening at the Tivoli gardens to watch the dancing and fireworks, she met the D. at Lady Castlereagh's who reproached her, 'Well, why did not you ride? I waited at home all the morning expecting you to come.' Fanny wrote, 'How provoking. Ever since Emily Wellesley-Pole's arrival [the Duke's attractive niece] things have taken a guignon!' The Duke and the Shelleys rode several times to Malmaison where Fanny drew several sketches.

But all was not roses. The French cuisine was all the same. Having no saltspoons, the French dipped their knives into the salt. On a visit to Madame de Peysac's and to Grassini's house Fanny noticed the aroma of onions, the dirty stairs and making of mattresses in their courtyards. When she visited Benjamin Constant with Lady Kinnaird they had to walk up to the fourth floor up a dirty, narrow winding staircase!

> After all, French society is a bore unless one goes with a jolly English party to enliven them: then it is excellent fun.

Colonel Stanhope was the life and soul of every party, full of fun and mirth. She talked to Walter Scott of his poems ('the ideas and images re-occurring and carelessly expressed'). She also disliked his clubfoot, white eyelashes, and clumsy figure, but appreciated him when a chance remark would lighten up his whole countenance, and she would discover the man of genius. At Malmaison she helped herself to one of the Duke's pens from his sitting-room and walked with him in the beautiful gardens, 'when we reached the Conservatory it was quite dark.' But the romance had its sombre aspects.

> The Duke very busy. He writes all night. He is sad and looks ill. He is evidently much worried.

Now one of the Duke's characteristics was that if he ever was anxious, he never showed it to the outside world. The date was significant – 15 August 1815, when he knew that Captain Wedderburn-Webster was about to sue him for adultery and claim damages of £50,000 for 'Crim. Con.' with Lady Frances W-W. It is possible that the Duke to some extent used his mild but ostentatious flirtation with Lady Shelley as a deliberate smokescreen. In her diary she commented on 16 August,

> The Duke was at Lady Stewart's ball, charming and most kind. His manner is the most paternal of any one I ever saw and so far removed from any nonsense that I am convinced his attachment to Lady Frances W. is platonic. Of this I am certain – if there is any love in the case it is only on the lady's side.

'How I love a Review' she cried on one occasion. The emperor of Russia was particularly gracious, 'We rode home with him at full gallop.' The Duke made several sentimental comments to her. 'Don't you think I could take care of you?' on one occasion, and 'Stick close to me' as they galloped together in a cavalry review. 'The D. full of attentions and kindness to me during the charges. We galloped v. hard.' No wonder General Sir Manley Power said (to her husband as it happened) 'The Duke pays a great deal more attention to his lady than to the review!' In the evenings they danced Polonaises together until three in the morning.

After the two happiest months of her life, Fanny and her husband continued their Grand Tour towards Champagne country. Fortunately the Duke arranged to go there too to attend a grand Russian army review including 30,000 Russian cavalry. On the way by carriage the Duke talked to the little Goose about his own private affairs, his annoyances, the embassy expenses, and about his Indian campaigns. He also dwelt on 'the licentiousness of the Press re himself and Lady Fr. W-W.' Lady Shelley was worried about the dirty inn at Montmirail, a minor accident at Ferté-sous-Jouarre and the band boxes, for her hats, getting battered *en route*! The emperor of Russia was rather taken aback to see Wellington's fair companion and asked was she '*contente*'.

> The D. took great care of me, I never lost him for a moment. We were of course always in front.

She also drove seven miles to the Château Auger with the Duke in a gig.

> I began to feel sad. I could scarcely restrain my tears at the thought that I was looking at the D. for the last time and that all our pleasant intercourse would soon come to an end. And now we were riding together for the last time. [The Emperors of Austria and Russia bade her farewell.] So deeply did I feel the parting that I could not help crying but I do not think he saw me . . .

The Shelleys rode off to Belgium, stayed with the Duke and Duchess of Richmond, visited Waterloo, and returned to England in September

1815. After this separation Lady Shelley and the Duke corresponded and the little old English Goose returned to Paris in the summer of the following year. Nothing much had changed although there were no more military reviews. Madame Grassini was looking desperately ill; the young seventeen-year-old Duchesse de Berri was well dressed à la Parisienne, with a very pretty bust, a long throat and beautiful skin. The Goose was very observant. The old king waddled into his opera box very ungracefully, his second stomach more pronounced; Madame, his wife, was much improved in looks and was better dressed. At one party with the Corps Diplomatique the Duke wore his full Spanish uniform, probably out of politeness to his Spanish mistress of Madrid and Cadiz days for the Duchesse de San Carlos was there together with the Duc de Mouchy and the Prince de Poix. The Duke gave a ball for the Duchesse de Berri. Lady Shelley was escorted by the Duc de Fitzjames and the Duke contented himself with Marshal Marmont's wife, the Duchesse de Ragusa.

Fanny rode Copenhagen in the Bois de Boulogne. She saw the Duke every day 'we took a few turns in the garden until I had quite recovered from the flurry.' She went to the opera with the Beau to see Madame Mars in *Les Etourdis*; to see Talma, 'He is wonderful or a mere buffoon,'; to hear Madame Camporese, Gressling and Biggottini sing. 'B. made me cry.'

The Duke needed a change from Paris and was planning to go back to England for a short time to Cheltenham, not only to take the waters, but also to collect Kitty and the two boys. For a short time he was to be seen as a '*père de famille*.' Fanny told him how sorry she was to lose him and he answered 'You must dine with me every day until I go', which she did.

> The Duke acted as my chaperon as Shelley was bored with the heat . . .
> How grieved I was to part from the Duke – who was all Kindness to the last.

When he left, the little Goose fainted at the opera '*en pleine vue*'.

The Shelleys went on their second Grand Tour through Burgundy to Switzerland, all described superbly by Lady Shelley. The Duke wrote from Cheltenham dated 10 July 1816. He mentions Kitty and the boys and launches into a complicated gossip about Lady Caroline Lamb (who had a tendresse for the Duke) and Lady Jersey (who also had a tendresse for the Duke). General Alava, the garrulous Spanish ADC of the Duke, had been left behind in Paris and had obviously been gossiping, as was his habit, about the Duke's romantic affairs to Lady Shelley.

If he does [gossip] he is very ungrateful and as to the others, whether men or women, he cannot *know* the facts. The truth is that for fifteen or sixteen years I have been at the Head of Armies ... necessary to lay aside all *private* motives in considering publick affairs. I hope this practice does not make me cold-hearted or feel a diminished interest for those I am inclined to love. I hope you will believe so.

The Beau was back in Paris the next month and, considering his passion for La Grassini, his preoccupation with Madame de Staël, the tone of his next letter to Fanny Shelley is rather surprising;

You will see by my empressement to answer that I am not dissatisfied with the warmth of your fire. I really hope that you will write to me whenever you will have a leisure moment and I will answer you punctually and I only beg that you will not show or quote the contents of my letters and I promise you the same discretion respecting yours ... I never shew my letters to anybody and never talk of them ... I hope that you will soon come back and that you will spend some time with me at my chateau at Mont St Martin near Catelet races, hunting and shooting. The Duchess of Richmond and all her daughters [including Dearest Georgy] propose to spend the whole winter with me ... plenty of whist for Shelley ... gambols for you and the girls.

In the meantime Lady Shelley and her husband had reached Vienna where they met Prince Metternich again, Prince Esterhazy and Princesse Galatzin.

Letters received by the Duke were always destroyed immediately they had been read. Lady Shelley for some reason kept a copy of this letter which she incorporated into her private journal. It was from Vienna and was dated 25 September 1816.

My dear D, A thousand thanks for your letter. With what pleasure I sign the contract of silence which I already felt was understood between us or I should not have dared to write to you as I have done. I know you would regard my letters as for you alone, consequently I did not doubt that their contents would be sacred. Your letters are and shall be the same and when you know me better you will feel that security in my promise which I feel in yours ... I hope soon to receive an answer upon which so much happiness depends. What a tempting proposal you make that we should visit Mont St Martin. How delightful to see you daily and hourly, but alas it cannot be at present.

Could the Duke come to Vienna for the emperor's marriage?

If you were here I think we should have some excellent fun and the glass coach would be in great request, *especially if you brought Georgiana Lennox with you!* Believe me, Ever your attached Frances Shelley.

Their correspondence continued. He had news of reviews in honour of the Dukes of Kent and Cambridge. 'Queen Willis' (Lady Jersey) was on her way to Italy. The Duchess of Richmond and *all* her daughters were at Mont St Martin.

> I wished much for the company of my absent ADC during this review which I think she would have much enjoyed . . .

To which Fanny noted in her journal,

> I am naturally romantic and at Vienna I had '*beau jeu*' such as seldom falls to the lot of woman. Life was an enchantment, called the '*enigmée*'. I endeavoured to show that love of Society not inconsistent *with perfect modesty and virtue.*

To reassure herself she also wrote 'The Duke of Wellington's attentions to me in Paris last year were the result *of a pure friendship.*' The Shelleys' tour continued in November to Venice, Rome and the Vatican where they kissed hands with the Pope. They also met 'Queen Willis' who had reached Rome on the Jersey's Grand Tour.

Just before Christmas the Duke wrote,

> I am delighted to find that you are thinking of your return and I will certainly meet you at Paris I propose to go there at the end of this month and to stay till the spring: *or till you come.* There are numbers of English at Paris and still more going there. Lord and Lady Conyngham and their daughter, Sir James and Lady Erskine etc. I amuse them with bad hunting but excellent coursing of which I wish you were here to partake.

Fanny copied another letter to the Duke in her journal, dated January 1817, from Naples.

> The end of our pilgrimage henceforward every step we take will bring us nearer to you and to England. The certainty of your being at Paris delights us. Shelley has promised me three weeks of your society.

The Goose was enchanted with the beauty of Naples, her audience with Saint Père, and her fortnight in the Eternal City. Metternich had given the Shelleys letters of introduction in every city they passed through. Fanny was bored to death in Rome since the cardinals and bishops overshadowed society. The English visitors (Jerseys, Lansdownes, Cowpers) made Pauline Borghese their bosom friend. Lady Shelley entered with gusto into the breeze (quarrel) between Lady Jersey and the

Duke's niece, Lady Burghersh. Prince Metternich wrote to Lady S. from Vienna (February 1817),

> Si vous voyez Lord Wellington dites lui mille choses de ma parte. C'est l'un des hommes que j'aime le mieux au monde, et si j'étais femme, je l'aimerais plus que le reste du monde.*

Was this letter encouragement for Fanny?

The Shelleys' tour took them back via Sienna, Florence, Parma, Monza and Milan to Paris. In the spring of 1818 Fanny and the Duke saw each other frequently. In May at Lord Conyngham's

> *Il a assez bonne mine cependant il n'a pas l'air de Waterloo.*** He put off his journey to Stratfield Saye to attend my soirée which was a great success.

Later she noted in her journal,

> I enjoyed a renewal of the D. of Ws former warmth of friendship: we dined together at Lord Westmorlands. He has become as I predicted a perfect Englishman, simplicity of manner, unconscious of the honours heaped upon him.

The Duke had returned late in 1818 to live in England, either at Apsley House, purchased from his brother Richard for £42,000, or at Stratfield Saye.

Fanny faithfully kept her private journal and mentioned the frequent meetings with the Duke. In the spring of 1819 at Mrs Edward Bouverie's,

> he talked to me almost the whole evening, not only great in itself but also valuable because *it promotes the agrements of London life . . . relief from dullness and it excites attention from others. . . Alas poor human nature, such despicable vanity.*

She used to meet the Duke most days about 5 p.m. in Green Park 'at which hour he takes a gallop between the duties of his office and his attendance at the House of Lords.' They exchanged letters on the days they did not meet. In the autumn he came to visit the Shelleys at Maresfield, their home in the country near Uckfield.

> I cannot describe the mixture of joy and anxiety that I felt when I received his letter telling me that he was coming the next day. I was afraid he would be bored to death here.

* If you see Lord Wellington remember me kindly to him. He is one of the men I like best in all the world, and if I was a woman I would love him more than the rest of the world.
** He looks quite well but he doesn't look as he did at Waterloo.

The visit was a great success. The Duke talked of the battles of Toulouse and Orthez and he played with Fanny's children 'caressed them as much as the fondest mother could desire.' He also went out shooting and peppered the game keeper's garters and the arms of a washing woman at her cottage window.

> 'You have had the distinction of being shot by the great Duke of Wellington.' A gold coin changed hands.

Fanny scarcely slept all night but she woke to a heavenly morning, the fountains were playing and the birds singing and she walked with the Duke round the flower garden.

Fanny became firm friends with Harriet Arbuthnot, who was soon to displace her as the Duke's chief confidante. For the next fifteen years until Harriet's death a bizarre triangular correspondence took place. For a start the key players were given nicknames. Harriet was known as Black Cap, My Tyrant, or La Tyranna. A certain handsome Mrs Parnther, who though married was on good terms with the Duke and with General Alava, was known as the Gay Widow. The Duke was known by both women as 'the slave'. And Lady Caroline Lamb was called 'Calanthe', a role from one of her books. The Duke had many facets to his character, not only did he go along with this coy interchange but he positively encouraged it. A few examples will suffice. The Duke to Lady Shelley,

> I think you ought to be excessively obliged to La Tyranna for her excessive good nature in writing to you. I presume upon it, also in venturing to write without leave! (26 February 1820).

After the Cato Street conspiracy, Mrs A. wrote a long letter to Lady S.

> Don't be shocked at my expressing myself so warmly but really out of my own immediate family they are the two men *I love best in the world* [Lord Castlereagh and the Duke] I feel pleasure too in writing to you upon this for I know you feel towards the Duke as I do . . . and if you seduce my present slave [i.e. the Duke] I think I shall throw my chains over him, however I am not afraid of you . . . (24 February).

> I dare not do so without the permission of my Tyranna (22 March 1820).

Wrote the Duke, and Mrs A. wrote to Lady S. (20 October 1820)

> The slave (poor creature) has asked my leave to invite you to dinner next Saturday and in order to bribe me into compliance has invited me to meet

you and keep watch in order to prevent any attacks being made upon my legitimate authority.

And so it went on. In 1823, the Duke wrote to Lady Shelley,

La Tyranna will not allow you to have a better picture of me than herself. The picture not to be painted by Sir T. Lawrence . . .

Sir John Shelley had the gout but won £8,000 on Cedric winning the Derby. He also coached the Duke in the field and made him a better shot. The Duke gave the Shelleys advice about a military career for their eldest son. He was colonel of the Blues and that regiment was naturally his recommendation. During 1825 Fanny wrote,

after a riding accident which might have proved fatal a family sorrow fell upon me. I appealed for counsel to the Duke. His daily visits sometimes for minutes only on his way to the Horse Guards with his cheery 'How are ye today?' and kept up my spirits. Dear Mrs A and the Duke came together and stayed a long time telling me all the news of the day. Their intimacy may have given gossip an excuse for scandal: but I who knew them both so well am convinced that the D. was not her lover. He admired her very much – for she had a manlike sense – but Mrs A was devoid of womanly passions – was above all, a loyal and truthful woman . . . *We three together formed a perfect union where no jealousy or bitterness of feeling ever intruded to destroy its harmony* . . . One day I told her that she need never be afraid of my taking the D's friendship from her although I was far more devoted to him than she was. Mrs A used to laugh at my reverence for, and my shyness with the D. She had no such feeling. The Duke required a fireside friend and one without nerves . . .

Two years later Mrs A. wrote to Lady S. from Stratfield Saye,

You may depend upon it, I shall always be *too happy* to make my fireside agreeable to him, tho' I think it a great shame you should only propose my having him there when he is *too old* to *be agreeable elsewhere*! However I have much too good taste not to prefer him, any how or at any age to any other friend and you need not be the least afraid of my ever changing in that respect. I flatter myself that he will not change so that I am never made jealous even when you tell me to take care. You need not be afraid of being deceived in me if I am anything, I am honest.

Whilst the Shelleys were on yet another Grand Tour in Europe to France and Italy with their son Frederick and daughter Cecilia, they heard the news of Harriet Arbuthnot's sudden death of cholera (3 August 1834). Lady Shelley at once wrote to the Duke from Milan,

I am so deeply afflicted and I feel so much for your loss, for the loss of your home for such to you was her house. Neither you, nor any one except Shelley know how much I loved and with what delight I looked forward to increasing intimacy ... that *we* should survive her never entered my thoughts ... with her I could talk of you as I never could have talked to you.

The Duke wrote back to her and she replied on 22 September,

How well I understood your feelings ... no one can replace her ... I honestly think that she liked to talk to me of you, quite as much as I liked to hear her do so. We had perfect confidence in each other.

To which the Duke answered,

You regret her and lament her as everybody does. It is impossible to describe the effect produced by her death. It is felt by all.

And in November,

Alas our poor friend. I miss her more and more every day. Her poor husband has been with me these two months.

Lady Shelley and the Duke continued to see each other and write with great regularity until they had a falling-out over the Burgoyne letter. Due to over-enthusiasm Fanny leaked a letter of the Duke's at the end of 1847 about defence requirements for the country. In her memoirs she regarded the quarrel as lasting two years, but in fact, although it may have felt like that to Fanny, it was but two months. The Duke, rarely one to harbour a grievance, wrote Fanny a charming and forgiving letter.

I can think that the word (Old Goose) applies to a lady fat and fair but less than forty! However Sir John knows best. Believe me Ever Yours Affectionately W.

The husband of the 'Old Goose' and her sentimental lover both died in the same year – 1852.

Chapter Seventeen

THE THREE GRACES FROM BALTIMORE

The last surviving signatory to the Declaration of American Independence was Charles Carroll of Carrollton. In 1786, one of his daughters married Richard Caton, an Englishman who had settled in Baltimore the year before. The Catons produced four beautiful daughters, three of whom married into the English nobility. They were known as the Three Graces of Baltimore – Louisa, Elizabeth and Mary Anne (eventually anglicised to Marianne).

Sometime before the battle of Waterloo in 1814 Wellington met in London one of the Caton sisters – Mary Anne – who in company with two of her sisters was touring Europe at the end of the English-American war. Mary Anne was *the* belle of Baltimore before her eighteenth birthday. When Sir Thomas Lawrence painted her for the Duke in 1817 one can see what a beautiful woman she was. Andrew Robertson also painted her, and his miniature is now at Apsley House in Hyde Park.

She was married to an elderly and wealthy Baltimore businessman called Robert Patterson, who was described by Lady Holland as a 'boor'. At the same time she noticed how gentle and patient Mary Anne was to her husband.

Robert's sister, Betsy, married Jerome Bonaparte (the emperor's youngest brother) in 1803 whilst he was serving as a midshipman and on a fleeting visit to Baltimore. Betsy was a fair, pretty, witty girl with an airy, nonchalant and often cynical manner. Society admired her beautiful arms, but Wellington thought her to be hard and mercenary. Thomas Raikes in his journal noted in 1814,

> This American family came to Europe consisting of Mr and Mrs (Robert) Patterson and her two sisters. They were introduced to the Duke of Wellington who showed great partiality for Mrs Patterson which led to the marriage of the elder Miss Caton with his ADC Colonel Hervey. On Hervey's death she later in 1828 married the Marquess of Carmarthen, eldest son of the Duke of Leeds. Mr Patterson returned to the USA and shortly afterward, he died.

Another diarist noted,

> Three beautiful Americans, the Misses Caton and their sister a certain
> Mrs Mary Anne Patterson also formed part of the Duke's feminine train
> and with the last named he appears to have had a tolerably serious love
> affair; when it had run its course, they remained the best of friends.
> Richard Caton, their father, was a prominent citizen of Baltimore.

In the story that follows it can be seen that this American lady was the
true love of Wellington's life. The three reasons for this belief are as
follows: She was the only woman for whom the Duke, strong, brave and
stoical, was actually seen to be 'ill with love'.

She was the only woman in the whole of the Duke's long life for whom
he begged favours. Amongst others he wrote to his niece Priscilla, Lady
Burghersh, to his political friend Madame de Lieven, and to Lady
Granville, to beg of them to introduce Mrs Patterson, the American, to
their friends. Moreover, he risked *his* reputation by giving her an
introduction to the Prince Regent!

Finally, when she, in despair of coaxing the Duke to the altar (which
he would not contemplate during Kitty's lifetime), married the Duke's
brother Richard Wellesley, the Duke was beside himself with rage and
frustration.

When Mr and Mrs Patterson and the two Caton sisters arrived in
Europe during 1814 they were introduced to the Wellesley circle by Sir
Charles Bagot, who had married a daughter of William Wellesley-Pole
(now Lord Maryborough). Lady Bagot then introduced the American
party to English society. According to Hyacinthe Littleton, a niece of
Wellington's,

> *En attendant*, the Duke of Wellington fell violently in love with Mrs
> Patterson and it was the amusement of all London. Mrs Patterson was
> evidently much pleased with the éclat of the thing but always behaved
> very correctly.

According to *Harpers New Monthly Magazine*,

> the Great Soldier who had conquered the Conqueror of Europe was
> himself conquered by the irresistible charms of Mrs Patterson. The
> irreproachable conduct of the beautiful American won the everlasting
> friendship of the man who became the Iron Duke.

After Waterloo the Catons arrived by invitation at Cambray, the Duke's
HQ on the Belgium frontier, and Mary Anne asked him to show them

over the field of battle. Out of affection for them he agreed although Mary Anne noticed his reluctance to go and his deep depression, silence and 'mental anguish' at dinner that same evening. The traumatic memory of a visit to the mass graveyard of 15,000 of his best men would have disturbed the most stoical of generals. Soon, however, the Duke recovered and sponsored a match whereby Louisa Caton became engaged and soon married one of his two arm-less ADCs, Colonel Felton Hervey. The third sister, Elizabeth, married Lord Stafford in 1836. Wellington was determined that these bewitching girls should become part of his 'family' at army HQ.

One day the Duke and his ADCs, including Colonel Hervey and his wife, were out hunting near Cambray. Seeing the hounds and fox dodging in and out of the woods, Louisa asked the Duke, 'Pray, in foxhunting, do the hounds follow the fox or the fox follow the hounds?' A witticism which surely the Duke would have greeted with his deep whooping laugh!

On 6 March 1817, Wellington wrote from Paris to Priscilla, Lady Burghersh, his niece,

> I shall be very sorry to lose the poor Americans. You must *for my sake* protect them against their host of enemies when they will go to England.

He was worried by the flood of gossip that would accompany them from France to London. The ambassadress in Paris, Harriet Lady Granville noted in her journal,

> the Duke is less with one American branch, Mrs Hervey, but has neither love nor hatred to display, his wife being at Cambray and his loves dispersed over the earth so '*il se laisse admirer*' as a great hero with very simple unaffected manners. I must tell you what amuses me. I have met His Grace several times and with the weakness I have about great people treated him '*du haut de ma grandeur*'. I suppose he was pleased with the '*variéte du fait*' and today Mrs Patterson could not have seen him more devoted . . .

The Duke's love was now common knowledge. Poor Kitty on a fleeting visit to Cambray must have known all too well that she had lost him irrevocably.

Meanwhile, the Duke had commissioned Sir Thomas Lawrence in London to paint two portraits. One of himself as a present for Mary Anne; the other of her for himself, which can now be seen at Stratfield Saye. On 9 May 1817 he made a downpayment of £78-5s for his picture and £52-10s for that of Mrs Patterson. On 4 July both portraits were completed and he paid Lawrence the balance owing of £158-7s for the portraits and the gilt frames.

Mrs Betsy Patterson-Bonaparte, now a disillusioned divorced lady after Napoleon had forced his brother to agree to an annulment, was living in Paris and took her place on the fringes of the 'haut ton'. Although she was American, she spoke French fluently but most of her friends were English. To her friend, Sydney Owenson, better known as the novelist Lady Morgan, she wrote this letter on 8 May 1817. Betsy seems now to have been a hard, vindictive woman after the end of her marriage.

> Mr Tom Moore, the poet, called to show me the article of your letter which mentions the report of the Duke of Wellington's loves. I am *not* the Mrs Patterson the Great Man gives as a successor to Mme Grassini. You would be surprised if you knew how great a fool she is at the power she exercises over the Duke but I believe he has not taste '*pour les femmes d'esprit*', which is however no reason for going into extremes as in this case. He gave her an introduction to the Prince Regent and to everyone of consequence in London and Paris. She had, however, no success in France where her not speaking the language of the country was a considerable advantage to her since it prevented her nonsense from being heard. Do not tell what I have written to you of this affair, since I should pass for malicious and unfriendly towards my compatriot and relation. She writes too, all the paragraphs you may have seen in the newspapers and might revenge herself by saying some spiteful things of me through that channel.

This was a bitchy letter by a bitter woman jealous of her sister-in-law's influence with the Beau, the uncrowned king of Paris. One must admire the ease with which strings were pulled in both countries by the Duke for his loved one – although the introduction to the Prince Regent might have been fraught with danger! Mrs Calvert, the Irish friend of Kitty's noted in her journal about a grand ball that took place in Paris two weeks after Betsy's letter was written,

> The Duke of Wellington and all the beau monde of Brussels were there. The Duke of Wellington with Colonel and Mrs Felton Hervey in his train. She is not long married and was a Miss Louisa Caton of Baltimore, sister to Mrs Patterson, a genteel looking young woman. It is the fashion to make a fuss about her because the Duke of Wellington is in love with Mrs Patterson whose sister-in-law is married to Jerome Bonaparte.

There was no escaping the sharp eyes and tongues of the society-watchers in Paris, Brussels and London!

Thomas Creevey spent the summer of 1818 in Belgium and was a frequent visitor to Wellington's HQ at Cambray. He reported:

> Today I rode to see a cricket match between the garrison officers near the town and presently the Duke of Wellington rode there likewise accompanied by Mrs Hervey and her sister Miss Caton. The following evening the Duke gave a dinner party of sixteen or eighteen and the two Caton sisters were the only guests. Soon afterwards our conversation was interrupted by Mrs Hervey and Miss Caton coming up with the Duke of Wellington with a Yankee general in their hands, a relative of theirs just arrived from America – a General Harper whom they presented to the Duke. It is not amiss to see these sisters, Mrs Hervey and Miss Caton, not content with passing themselves for tip-top Yankees but playing much greater people than Lady Charlotte Greville and Lady Frances Cole – to *me*! I remember their grandfather old Caton, a captain of an Indiaman ship in Liverpool – their father an adventurer to America, and I knew their two Aunts now at Liverpool – Mrs Woodville and another – who move in about the third rate society of that town. The young ladies and I were at a Ball at the Duke's and he was very civil to us all as he always is and called out to us in going in to supper, to sup at his table.

Creevey was obviously a snob!

During the spring, on 27 March 1818, Lady William Russell wrote to Miss Berry (indefatigable travellers and observers),

> Lord Kinnaird is here '*fra mille quai*' and the Duke of Wellington looks horribly ill, *si dice* that it is not the present *combinazione*, but love – that he *declares he never knew the* meaning of the word until he *saw Mrs Paterson* and her departure for America *decire son tendre coeur* in a terrible manner. He really looks mighty sick.

This is the only occasion in Wellington's long life when he has been *seen* to be in love. Never in moments of great danger on the battlefield in India, Portugal, Spain, France or Belgium did he display emotion although after the battle as the death rolls were called out he was seen to suffer grievously. But to suffer on the field of love was unheard of!

The Duke wrote regularly to Mrs Patterson. His letter of 27 February 1820 was very long concerning many subjects. To 'My dear Mrs Patterson', he mentioned the dreadful assassination of the Duc de Berri at Paris and told her details of the Cato Street plot.

> We have had a good deal of trouble with our Master K.G.IV about his wife. But I think we have settled that point in a very satisfactory manner. Your sisters are well – Louisa is still in the same state. God bless you my dear Mrs Patterson. Remember me kindly to Mr Patterson your father

and mother and to her and Mrs Harper and Believe me. Yours most affectionately, Wellington.

The Lievens went to Stratfield Saye in April and found the house ugly and the park rather barren. The Duke took Madame de Lieven into his study and showed her the two portraits there – one of Lady Charlotte Greville and one of Mrs Patterson, the American. She noted, 'How can one have two passions at the same time and how can one bear to parade them before the world at large?' The Duke was a rare man in that he could deeply love several women at the same time without embarrassing them or society too much and still act with the greatest discretion. In July Madame de Lieven was conscripted by the Duke to look after Marianne.

> Yesterday Wellington wrote to tell me of the arrival of Mrs Patterson the American and to ask me to introduce her to the pleasures of London. The style of his letter radiates happiness. I know Mrs Patterson only by sight and certainly that is the best way to know her, she is superb. W. does not bother himself much about the rest.

Madame de Lieven was one of the shrewdest observers of the London and Brighton court and in a curious way was half in love with the Duke herself.

The romance continued for all of 1821 until the ailing Robert Patterson insisted on his dazzling wife accompanying him home to Baltimore. 1822 was a difficult year for the Duke, although it got off to a good start with the death of his old adversary on St Helena, leaving him now without question as Europe's finest soldier. In the summer the pointless and painful operation to his ear took place (an eminent specialist had treated his ear with a strong caustic solution), followed by the shattering news of Lord Castlereagh's suicide. Mary Anne was in Baltimore and, in default, his relationship with Harriet Arbuthnot was increasing in tempo.

In the autumn he travelled – deaf, frustrated and with a heavy cold – as Britain's representative to the Congress of Vienna and Verona. There he found two emperors, three kings, a cardinal, three grand-dukes, twenty ambassadors, and twelve foreign ministers including Prince Metternich. The Duke was noticed in splendid finery and profile moving through a line of bowing gentlemen in stars *en route* to greet Napoleon's ex-empress and widow, Dorothea Lieven, Metternich's niece and Madame Récamier. His own niece Priscilla, Lady Burghersh was as usual adoring, but scarcely an effective chaperone.

He returned home, having written many letters to Harriet Arbuthnot in the two months he was away, to be greeted by the news of the death of Mary Anne's elderly husband in Baltimore just before Christmas. She and her unmarried sister Elizabeth were soon on a ship to England and according to *Harpers New Monthly Magazine* were shortly at Stratfield Saye as the Duke's guests. Richard Wellesley was also there which was unusual since there was little love lost between the brothers. Richard was a widower after his French wife's death six years previously. He knew that his brother was besotted with Mary Anne – after all it was common knowledge in London and Paris. Richard himself was now noticeably struck by Mrs Patterson's 'extraordinary personal attractions'. There is no record of what Kitty thought of this bizarre situation. Her husband's contempt for Richard's lecheries were well-known.

The Duke was now confronted for the first time by the fact that his well-beloved mistress was free to marry him which he could not, or would not do, to protect Kitty and the proprieties. He was also faced with the fact that Richard was displaying too much interest in the lady.

Mary Anne enlisted the support of her grandfather 'Old Caton', who on 4 October 1824 despatched to Wellington four barrels of American apples to speed his convalescence from his usual autumnal cold and fever.

During the next two years the affaire continued. Mary Anne was in Paris just before Christmas 1824, and Wellington asked the ambassadress, Harriet Lady Granville a favour.

> I called yesterday in obedience to the Duke of Wellington's entreaties, upon Mrs Patterson. She seems a very charming person, very handsome with *l'air noble* and not a shade of her mother country. She shook all over when I went into the room, but if for grief at the loss of Mr Patterson, sentiment at the recollection of the Duke, or the coldness of the room she received me in, I do not presume to judge.

Mary Anne was staying with her sister Louisa, now a widow since her first husband, Colonel Hervey (Wellington's ex-ADC) had recently died.

Richard Wellesley's natural daughter Hyacinthe Littleton reported that,

> Mary Anne was no sooner a widow than she came back hoping to establish herself in England again – and some said she went over to Ireland with a determination to become the Lady Lieutenant [i.e. Richard Wellesley's wife] as there was no chance of the Duchess's demise at present.

Certainly, there was no question of the Duke divorcing Kitty and he would have made this quite clear to Mary Anne. Divorce in the early nineteenth century carried a considerable social stigma. The Wedderburn-Webster affair in 1815–16 had been 'a damned serious business' indeed, and other scandals in the Wellesley family (Richard and his mistress Gabrielle Hyacinthe Rolland, Henry deserted by his wife Charlotte, and Gerald also abandoned by his wife Emily) must have had a profound effect on the Duke. His natural caution and his undoubted protectiveness for Kitty and their two young sons would have inhibited thoughts of divorce and remarriage with Marianne Patterson – despite his passion for her. Had Kitty died before 1825, the year when Marianne decided she could not catch the Duke, then it is possible he would have married her, despite Mrs Arbuthnot's strong feelings.

In the spring of 1825 the two widowed sisters were staying in Rylands Hotel, Sackville Street in Dublin. The Marquess Wellesley, lord lieutenant, was a matrimonial catch in name only, although he still displayed a modicum of charm. He was then a man of small stature, three inches shorter than the Duke, inordinately vain, who spent several hours a day on his toilette. He was extremely lazy, but beautiful in a mildly evil way. His body was well-proportioned, with an intelligent face, large deep-set eyes, and still topped by dark hair. His relationship in and out of wedlock with Hyacinthe had lasted eleven years. Since her death this highly sexed man took his pleasures in quite notorious fashion which adversely affected his political career. He had squandered the various fortunes he had earned in India and was – all round – a high-class profligate.

To Richard that spring Mary Anne wrote a series of loving letters, as she must have done for ten years previously to his younger, now more famous brother.

My dear Lord Wellesley, I believe I am as frank and as unaffected and I will cordially tell you what I had not an opportunity of saying this morning. After the conversation of Saturday evening I was fully convinced of the feelings of my own heart and the conflict of giving you up, and of leaving my own family for ever who are inexpressibly dear to me, was too much for my health. You have triumphed and I confess all that you wish. Let me entreat you to keep this a profound secret as my situation is one of peculiar delicacy. I am convinced there cannot be a more feeling and honourable heart than yours and in making you the guardian of my happiness I feel that I have secured it. Ever Devotedly Yours, M.A.P.

Marianne (she anglicised her name in England) had written to the king about her engagement to Richard.

> He was so good as to give me frequent opportunities of seeing him at Brighton and I do not know which made the greatest impression, the Princely elegance of his manners, variety and animation of his conversations or the warm benevolence of his feelings.

It was ironical that Marianne's success with the king and court was the direct result of the Duke's support in 1816/17.

On 26 October 1825 the Duke at Stratfield Saye received an account of his brother's intention to marry. Harriet Arbuthnot, who was there at the time, records the drama in her journal.

> Lord Wellesley's intention to marry Mrs Patterson an American who was some years ago supposed to be the Duke's mistress and with whom he was certainly very much in love. I have never seen the Duke more annoyed. His love for her has long been at an end, but he had a great interest for her and he told me he had given her credit for more real good sense than to make such a preposterous match. I told him I was not the least surprised for that she had come to this country on matrimonial speculation; that it was pretty well for the widow of an American shopkeeper to marry a Marquis, the Lord Lieutenant of Ireland, and a Knight of the Garter, and that I was not at all surprised. The Duke said that the honours were all empty ones and that the real facts were that Lord Wellesley was a man totally ruined. When he quitted Ireland, which he must soon do, he would not have a house to take her to, or money to keep a carriage – that he had not a shilling in the world and moreover was of a most jealous disposition, a violent temper, that he had entirely worn out his constitution by the profligate habits of his life. He says he is sure Lord Wellesley will never allow her to associate with him from feelings of jealousy and that he considers all intercourse with her at an end. Mrs Patterson wrote to him to inform him of her intentions and in his answer he stated all these objections. I told him I thought he was very indiscreet for that Lord Wellesley would be sure to know it. He admitted the indiscretion and said that in his letter he had remarked that a wise man would hold his tongue, but he said he could not help pointing out to her the fatal consequences of the marriage to her happiness as well as to her real respectability. I think he wrote his letter with a faint hope that it might induce her to change, but it has not had that effect.

The letter had no effect and the marriage took place on 29 October at the royal lodge, Phoenix Park, first by the Protestant Primate of All Ireland, the Bishop of Armagh and then by the Roman Catholic Archbishop of Dublin, since Marianne was a devout Roman Catholic.

Harriet continued later,

Lord Wellesley is married: he had a most extraordinary set of low people present at the ceremony which does not look as though his lady had cured him of his love for inferiors. He had the Catholic Archbishop of Dublin to perform the ceremony which I think a scandal as his assuming that title is contrary to law. To be sure the marriages of 1825 among the old men and women are quite curious. Mr Cholmondeley at 73 has married Miss Townsend, Lord Sidney's daughter. He is 13 years older than her *father*! Sir Harry Featherstone 76 has married his kitchen maid aged 18. Lord Wellesley 66 has married a lady under 40.

On 3 November the Duke wrote to Sir Robert Peel.

You see that the marriage in Dublin has been celebrated. Allow me to ask you – is not the appearance of the Roman Catholic Archbishop in pontifications contrary to law? It is at all events very improper!!

Even Marianne's sister-in-law Betsy Patterson-Bonaparte was outraged. 'I married the brother of Napoleon the Conqueror of Europe,' she cried out, 'Mary has married the brother of Napoleon's conqueror.' To Lady Morgan she wrote from Paris,

I hope the gloves fitted – wedding gloves sent by the Lord Lieutenant of the Marchioness of Wellesley? Was the Duke, Great Bolingbroke, at the wedding?

But when the Duke calmed down he had, as ever, the good sense and decorum to make his peace, and wrote to his brother to send him his good wishes for the marriage.

I don't think I have been blinded by my partiality for her when I state that in disposition, temper, sense, acquirements and manners she is equal if not superior to any woman of any country with whom I have ever been in Society.

Having studied most of the Duke's letters, this was the grandest accolade of them all. Never had he put his feelings of love and admiration as unequivocally as that before. George IV was irritated by a *Catholic Mass* taking place in the viceregal lodge in the midst of the Catholic problems in Ireland. Richard's eldest son, of the same name, joined in the fray four days before the wedding took place. He wrote to Edward Littleton, Richard's son-in-law,

I have not received one word from the Marquess regarding the Marriage and for many reasons. His conduct is not to be judged by the ordinary rules of mankind. I do know Mrs Patterson quite well, and I do not think that in point of sense, personal attractions, manners and age he could have made a better choice. If it in any way affects *our* interests I think it is likely to be useful to them [she was a wealthy lady]. He can take no property where there is none and she would probably think that in a *worldly* vein, if in no other, it would be of service to Lord Wellesley to treat his children with something like Christian regard . . . .

And on the 6 January 1826 he wrote,

The report of Brighton is that the Marchioness has announced officially her pregnancy, losing no time, as the malicious declare. Whatever be the fact, it is a '*coup de maitresse*' on her part and will probably secure her victory over the Parasites.

This was a reference to Richard's camp followers, the Johnstone family and others. Marianne confided to her sister Louisa who told the Duke who wrote her long letters of advice. She was not pregnant and the marriage was not happy. When Lord Canning became prime minister he manoeuvered Richard's resignation and the rift between the brothers was complete.

The Duke hoped that Marianne would leave his brother, and wrote to her sister Louisa Hervey on New Year's Day 1826 knowing full well that the contents would be passed on,

The first of all wordly duties for a wife and her connections is to endeavour to raise her husband in the eyes of the World. . . . I certainly hoped for the sake of your sister, but more for that of Lord Wellesley, that she would have been able to banish from His Presence for ever all the Parasites [Edward Johnstone, Richard's illegitimate son and his dissolute friends] . . . but they only deprive her of sound comfort. They totally destroy him in fortune, reputation and everything which renders life desirable to a man like him. But, bad and noxious as they are, the time is past at which it was possible for her to get rid of them . . .

Let this example never be forgotten, your sister must make up her mind to do the best she can.

Harriet Arbuthnot also wrote in her journal,

The Duke has had one letter from Lady Wellesley saying that all the evils he had predicted had come upon her even to a greater degree than he expected, although she thought that if she had Lord Wellesley to herself, she could go on very well with him. She described herself as very unhappy and only anxious to die.

Richard wrote to a friend of his wife,

As his dearest soul ... but looked more wondrous than ever and is adored, impossible to describe how much.

But the 'worsting of Lady Wellesley was the talk of Dublin.' Richard and Marianne left Dublin in December 1827. George Canning wrote rather tactlessly to the marquess 'But Lady Wellesley sees the Duke of Wellington (as it is natural that she should do) almost daily.' In the next year Wellington became prime minister and refrained from offering his elder brother any appointment in his government. Initially Arthur, the dunce of the family, admired his clever eldest brother, who secured him his two early military appointments. In India Arthur Wellesley had achieved military fame, title and some wealth, but Lord Mornington (as Richard was then) was governor-general of India from 1797, and therefore his civilian 'boss'. Richard continued to be protective during the Iberian campaign but by 1814 their roles had completely changed. Arthur had grown contemptuous of Richard's scandals, debts and fumbled political career. After Waterloo the brothers, never close, drifted apart. As Lord Lieutenant of Ireland, Richard's influence paled in contrast to his brother's dukedom and premiership. By 1828 the Duke, as Prime Minister, had the opportunity of re-instating Richard as Lord Lieutenant of Ireland but failed to do so.

The rift caused by Marianne's marriage to Richard in 1825 was deep and continued until the last few months before his death in 1842. Their reconciliation was thanks entirely to Marianne's efforts.

At Windsor in September 1832 King Billy paid Mary Anne a compliment, when she was 'in waiting' at his court. Some one said of Mrs Trollope's new book to Lady Wellesley,

> Do *you* come from the part of America where they 'guess' or where they 'calculate'? The King interrupted and said 'Lady Wellesley comes from where they fascinate'.

That might well have been the end of this extraordinary saga. The Wellesleys had moved to a villa in Hurlingham, and thirteen years after the ill-fated marriage in 1838, Marianne engineered a reconciliation between the man she truly loved and her second husband. By then the Duke was aged 69 and Richard was 78, and she wrote to her husband (Kitty had died in 1831 and Harriet Arbuthnot in 1834),

> I write to tell you that the Duke of Wellington called upon me an hour ago and you would have been amazed to hear the manner in which he spoke of you. He was proud of belonging to you. We went through many subjects all of which you will be surprised how they have been perverted.

He ended in saying 'I wish to call upon him' [i.e. Richard]. I said he might but that you have not been very well. 'I will go tomorrow or next day, if he will see me I shall be glad, and if not I will leave my card.' There have been some terrible mischief makers busy. I write this to prepare you to do as you may like, but I am sure, peace with him is the wisest thing. He is most anxious for it! [And later], I have just seen the Duke, he says nothing could be more gratifying than your reception of him, that he was delighted to see you looking so remarkably well. That you were the most brilliant and wonderful person in the world. I gave him your letter to read and he has kept it. He was much affected and evidently highly pleased and in high spirits. He says you are the most eloquent person in the world. Thank God that you are now on good terms and that nothing will ever change it

William Wellesley also wrote to Richard,

Nothing could give me the greater pleasure than to hear that you and Arthur had renewed the affectionate intercourse which had subsisted for so many years and which from my heart I pray may continue for the rest of your lives.

Queen Adelaide, the queen mother, saw the Duke and told him how happy she was to hear of the reconciliation.

The indomitable Richard asked Lord Melbourne for a dukedom with a lengthy memorandum. This was refused, and he died in 1842, still good friends with his younger brother, the only duke in the family. Wellington went to his brother's funeral to comfort the widow. Lady Holland commented that Lady Wellesley had only a pension of £300 a year plus a salary of £500 as lady-in-waiting to the queen dowager. 'Her health and habits make this but a sorry pittance for her.'

Chapter Eighteen

THE GREVILLE
FAMILY

Lady Charlotte Bentinck was the eldest daughter of William Henry, 3rd Duke of Portland. In 1793 she married an undistinguished young man called Charles Greville (1762–1832) who was the grandson of the 5th Lord Warwick. Greville soldiered under Wellington in Spain as a colonel and fought at the siege of San Sebastian in October 1813. Lady Charlotte was a woman of outstanding beauty and was the mother of three sons and a daughter. She was also the Duke of Wellington's mistress for many years.

Her eldest son was Charles Cavendish Fulke Greville (1794–1865) who went to Eton and Christchurch and then became private secretary to Lord Bathhurst, then Secretary for War and Colonies. After that he had a series of minor political appointments before finding his true *métier*, which was not to be discovered until his death when his diaries were revealed. They are full of brilliant political and social observations and cover the period 1815–65. Although he had several love affairs with Harriet Lady Ashburton, Georgiana Lennox and others, he never married. Because of his surly temperament he was nicknamed Punch or the Gruncher and he, in turn, nicknamed many of his friends. The Duke, of course, was 'the Beau', Charles Arbuthnot was known as 'Gosh' and Lady Jersey as 'Sally'. His perceptions of the characters of both men and women were shrewd, penetrating and probably accurate. Greville had access to all the salons of London and his sources of gossip were blended with his natural malice. He lived in Hanover Square and then in Grosvenor Place.

Algernon Frederick Greville (1798–1864) was Lady Charlotte's youngest son who fought at Waterloo as an ensign in the Grenadier Guards, became ADC to the Duke in Paris and was his private secretary for the next thirty-four years (1818–52). Since the Duke was so often away from 'home', Algy soon became a confidante of Kitty and often gave her good advice. Once he cautioned her to improve her sartorial attire before the Duke's visit since he was a stickler for 'la mode', which he expected and found from his other ladies.

Lady Stafford wrote on 3 February 1792 of,

> Lady C. Bentinck who was presented, and they tell me is vastly pretty. She looks good humoured, natural and cheerful, and not ill-looking *selon moi*, but not a Beauty.

As a 'Lady of Quality' she was painted that year by Sir Thomas Lawrence and it was hung as No. 225 in the Royal Academy. Hoppner painted her in 1795, also hung at the Royal Academy. After her marriage she was again painted by Lawrence and in her old age by Lord Leighton. In 1793 she married the younger son of Fulke Grenville of Wilbury, Wiltshire. The Duchess of Devonshire, who knew her well, described her at Longleat as being 'pretty, *caressante et un peu languissante.*' Her husband Charles was 'A little bilious and a little sarcastic' – like father, like son!

In her brilliant youth Lady Charlotte was known as *La Coquette Gentille* or the Chrysolite (a semi-precious golden green stone) and in the early years of the Peninsular campaign she and her husband were friendly to Kitty at Tunbridge Wells. At the beginning of the century the Grevilles were seen at Spa in Belgium taking the fashionable waters along with Lord and Lady Conyngham and the Duchess of Gordon. After Napoleon's initial downfall in 1814 they made Brussels their home, possibly with a view to economise.

Arthur had met Lady Charlotte in London when he returned from India after 1805 It is clear that they were lovers before Waterloo. Lady Caroline Capel (sister to one of Wellington's favourite cavalry officers Lord Henry Paget – the famous eloper) wrote in the summer of 1814 of that 'Gossiping Place', Brussels that Lady Charlotte Greville 'has adopted all the Foreign fashions and you cannot distinguish her from one of the most *outré* of the natives.' There is little doubt that this ravishing well-dressed creature was very popular, not only with Wellington but also with all the itinerant journal-keepers such as Thomas Creevey and the Misses Ord, who attended many of her balls given in Brussels. It was difficult to assess which of the young beauties enraptured the Duke most – 'Dearest Georgie', the pale elegant Lady W-W, or Lady Charlotte. Certainly her house in the Hôtel d'Angleterre was *the* focal point of all the news – social and military – before, during and after Quatre Bras and Waterloo.

The Duke arrived from Vienna and reached Brussels on 5 April. Amongst several comments, Creevey wrote (22 April 1815) that at Lady Greville's the Duke told him that Carnot and Lucien Bonaparte were forming a new republic in Paris. On Easter Monday in the same place the Duc de Berri called upon her and was astonished that the English were still there since Bonaparte was at Lille. His panic was luckily not contagious. Lady Charlotte, during the weeks of crisis gave a party *every* evening to all the 'principal persons' then in Brussels including the Duke. So, to a lesser extent did the Duchess of Richmond and Lady Conyngham.

After Waterloo followed the exhilarating year in Paris followed by the move of the Allied army HQ to Cambray. The Duke was a frequent visitor to Brussels to see Lady Charlotte and in the summer of 1817 they were strolling home accompanied by Lord Kinnarid when an amateurish attempt to assassinate him was made by two Jacobin journalists. The same pair tried again in the streets of Paris in June 1818 with an equal lack of success. Creevey continued to see the Duke at Cambray and in midsummer dined at HQ.

> Lady Charlotte and Lady Frances Cole were the only ladies present, both very good looking, excellent manner and most agreeable.

Around Mont-Saint-Martin the hunting was good, the shooting was indifferent, cricket was played in the summer and rousing Mess nights were held where the Duke's young men, his ADCs, frolicked. Harry Smith and Juanita were there and the American Catons turned up too. Lady Charlotte was also a frequent visitor. Lord William Russell encountered the Grevilles on several occasions. One occasion was at Fontainbleau in June 1818. His father the Duke of Bedford was to meet Wellington,

> those two forming a partie carré with the Duchess [of Bedford] and Lady Charlotte Greville, have been in a vortex of pleasure and amusement. The Duchess proposed to end it by giving a dinner to the Duke and Lady Charlotte at Versailles. The Duke said, 'No', that he would give the dinner and ask for the Petit Trianon. On asking for it Louis Le Gros Tyran [the King] said 'No', he would give the dinner, which he did. Wellington plucked red roses in the gardens for the two elegant ladies, at which they called out to him through the grille *'qu'il savait cueiller des lauriers mieux que les roses!'*

At the end of that year the Duke returned to England as the army of occupation was disbanded. The Grevilles followed shortly afterwards. Quite soon Lady Charlotte's sons Charles and Algernon realised that their mother was the Beau's mistress. After all, Algernon was his ADC and Charles was a professional 'Duke-watcher' and was no fool. He therefore alerted his father Sir Charles, now a retired colonel, to a possible scandal.

The Wellington Manuscripts have two curious undated letters between Colonel Charles Greville and his wife Lady Charlotte, deriving from the Duke's love affair with Lady Charlotte in the period 1814–1820.

> I am extremely sorry to find that the information I gave you has caused you so much agitation. . . . with respect to Charles [i.e. the son], living in the world as he does and quick and clear sighted as he is, if you had reflected but a moment it would have occurred to you that he could not be blind to your conduct with the Duke of Wellington. But it did not follow that he must know or even suspect, the degree of intimacy which had subsisted. . . . For God's sake awake from the dream which seems to have taken possession of your mind and look to, as other women do, for your happiness and interest in this world, the affection, the respect and the welfare of your children . . .

The colonel was in a state of great anxiety and was equally worried about *his* honour and his wife's good name. Presumably husband and wife were living apart, hence the need for letters. Lady Charlotte then wrote on 'Friday 17th' to her son Charles,

> It is true that I prize highly the friendship and confidence of the Duke of Wellington and should extremely regret to be obliged to renounce altogether his Society. . . . but I have no desire to cultivate it in a *clandestine manner*. . . the *fascination* which you do not comprehend is *the having for years experienced* from him a thousand acts of kindness, *friendship* and attention with professions of regard and affection for me and all belonging to me which I believe to be very sincere . . . I need not, therefore, repeat that I put myself entirely under your guidance and shall, if you desire it, make the immediate and unqualified relinquishment of all intimacy and correspondence with the Duke of Wellington. [But she went on,] Was this final break, and great sacrifice really necessary?

It was a bizarre situation – the beautiful matron bargaining with her son about her future relationship with her lover. Charles later endeavoured to obtain some revenge for his own satisfaction, but as it turned out with little success.

During the Duke's long political career he continued to see Lady Charlotte but with less passionate intensity. He was deeply in love with Mary Ann Patterson and the Greville's, father and son, had warned the lady of the family 'off the turf'. Thomas Creevey saw them both outside the House of Lords (August 1819). She was furious with Mr Henry

Brougham, the MP who was heavily involved in the Queen Caroline trial. The Duke was of the 'anti-Queen' faction and most of the political ladies were 'pro-Queen'. The lovers met several times in the Court Pavilion in Brighton (September 1822 and in 1823).

Charles Arbuthnot, Harriet's husband, in July 1822, received a series of threatening letters signed by a 'Mr Jennings'.

> A vulgar placard evidently printed for the purpose, threatening to accuse me, [wrote Harriet] of a love affair with the Duke of Wellington. This naturally annoyed us both most excessively and we agreed to consult Lord Londonderry on what steps to take.

Londonderry came to see the Arbuthnots on 7 August and Harriet records in her diary a strong presentiment of evil. Almost immediately after this meeting Lord Londonderry had a brain storm, developed a persecution mania and shortly after committed suicide. This disaster may have been indirectly caused by Charles Greville since 'Mr Jennings' was almost certainly his pseudonym. The handsome Lord Castlereagh who had become the 2nd Marquess of Londonderry the year before, was an extremely good friend of Harriet's and had worked closely with the Duke in Paris. There were several reasons for the suicide, including fear of blackmail and acute depression, but the Arbuthnots thought that the anonymous letters were a contributing factor.

The Arbuthnots again started to receive anonymous letters in April 1824, accusing Harriet of being in love with the Duke and always being in 'holes and corners' with him, and also of being so jealous of him that she could never bear him to speak to any other woman. She showed the second letter to the Duke who told her that Mrs Georgiana Henrietta Lane-Fox had about two weeks previously also received a similar style of letter, in the same handwriting and with the same seal, abusing her too about her relations with the Duke. He said that he was positive from the handwriting and 'other circumstances' that the writer was Charles Greville. Harriet added,

> I know he is the most unprincipled reprobate in the Kingdom. I used to be very intimate with him but got disgusted with his entire want of principle. . . . . The anonymous writer would be surprised if he knew how amicably we three had discussed his amiable letter.

Reading her journal and her letters it does seem clear that Harriet did love her older husband deeply, that she did love the Duke *equally* deeply and that she was jealous of his other friends particularly Lady Jersey.

Charles Greville was trying to take revenge for his mother's affair with the Duke. The letters appear to have stopped for some time, although later on the Duke and his lady friends received another batch.

At the end of that year Harriet noted in her diary a conversation with the Duke,

> Lady Charlotte Greville's house was where all the society of Brussels met every night. She herself the daughter of the Minister, Duke of Portland, full of grace and talent and the charm of every society she went into, was afterwards supposed to have conquered the Conqueror of France. For a long time he appeared to be devoted to her and though the passion has subsided (December 1824) they are still great friends.

Two years later (on 10 December 1826) Harriet, Lady Charlotte and the Duke were guests at the same house party. Harriet's journal recounts,

> The Duke who has never missed being here for my birthday since the year he was at Verona. Lady Charlotte Greville had been an old and intimate friend of his youth and he was delighted at having her under this roof [at the Arbuthnots]. I was rather in hot water while she was here. I was so afraid the Duke should pay *me* more attention than he did *her* and as he was formerly said to be in love with her. I was afraid of her being mortified by neglect from him. I thought her rather cross one day when he drove me out in the Curricle, but he drove her two or three times and that set it all right.

All the courtesies were observed by the two beautiful matrons circling round their prey.

There are many mentions by the various diarists of meetings in the years that followed. Lady Charlotte wrote to her son Charles expressing concern in 1827 that the Duke was about to lose his appointment as army C-in-C. Lord William Russell in May 1828 described her husband, 'Old Greville sour gossiping, ill-natured, *il foglio piano*, blasé, spoilt, out of humour with himself and the world'. He died four years later and his son describes him candidly and quite warmly in his diary. In July the Duke obtained, at her request, an appointment for her son-in-law Lord Francis Leveson-Gower of the post of Secretary of State in Ireland, which Creevey solemnly noted as being 'prejudicial to the Beau'.

When the Duke was prime minister he visited Lady Charlotte at Shepperton and discussed with her his visits and meetings with the king. When in July 1829 the Beau threw a large party for two of his Parisienne ladies – the Duchesse d'Escars and Madame du Cayla (mistress of Louis XVII) he also asked Lady Charlotte. Charles noted in his diaries that the Duke visited his parents several times during 1831. The Grevilles moved in high society and were to be seen at country houses dining with the Prince de Talleyrand, his ravishing niece the Duchesse de Dino, with the Esterhazies and the garrulous Spanish General Alava. The Duke was often at the same party. Leighton painted Lady Charlotte when she was a handsome old lady and it can be seen at Bridgewater House. She lived to a ripe old age and died in 1862. Undeterred by snide attacks on him by her son, Charles, the Duke remained all his life on the best of terms with Lady Charlotte. Her youngest son Algernon served him as private secretary until the Beau died in 1852.

Along with Mary Anne Patterson and Harriet Arbuthnot, Lady Charlotte was undoubtedly one of his three great romantic loves.

Autumn

Chapter Nineteen

HARRIET ARBUTHNOT – LA TYRANNA

During Henry Wellesley's messy divorce his closest ally was the then Secretary of the Treasury, Charles Arbuthnot. Arbuthnot was born in 1767 in County Mayo, and thanks to two legacies idled away his time in fashionable London as a young man about town. He was too lazy to become a lawyer and at the age of twenty-six became a précis-writer in the Foreign Office. Two years later he became MP for East Looe and continued to drift into his career at the Foreign Office. From Stockholm and Stuttgart he moved to Lisbon and eventually became ambassador in Turkey. His first wife died in childbirth in 1806. He re-entered the House of Commons and served under Perceval and Lord Liverpool. Castlereagh soon became a warm friend, as did Liverpool, Bathhurst and Peel. After serving under Canning until 1809 he became indispensable to Lord Liverpool, who was head of Treasury until 1812. Arbuthnot was a charming, inoffensive, lightweight politician who was the *real* patronage secretary for many years. He was the man behind the scenes who knew everybody, was liked by everybody, and his judgement of appointees was generally very sound. In modern parlance he might be called a 'fixer', with little thought of advantage to himself.

Charles Greville's profile of Arbuthnot is,

> He had no shining parts and never could have been conspicuous in public life, but in a subordinate and unostentatious character he was more largely mixed up with the principal people and events of history than any other man.

He was a slim, timid, retiring man the complete opposite to the Duke – gentle, almost pensive, with a good memory, a walking almanac, who could quote precedents and was very trustworthy. On 31 January 1814 he married Harriet Fane, daughter of the Hon. Henry Fane of Fulbeck, Lincolnshire, second son of the Earl of Westmorland. He first met her in 1807 when she was a schoolgirl and he in mourning for his first wife. Although Harriet fell in love with Captain (afterwards Admiral)

Thomas Capel, she decided early on in life that a political 'career' was what she wanted. She was a very beautiful, fair-complexioned young woman with brown silky hair, an elegant, graceful figure, soft brown eyes, regular expression and features. Her conversation was described as agreeable and often brilliant. She was also of a very jealous nature. She never bore any children, but was a good stepmother to the four children she 'inherited'. At her marriage she was twenty-six years younger than her husband, and as we see, obviously preferred mature men.

A lithograph dated 1831 entitled 'A Sketch in the Park' is a charming sketch of the Duke of Wellington walking in Hyde Park with Harriet on his arm. She has turned her face to look at the handsome profile, the strong nose and chin of the sixty-two-year-old Duke, as erect as a young subaltern!

Lady Bury saw her shortly after the wedding and wrote (February 1814):

> At Mrs Villiers I saw Mr Arbuthnot and his bride she is very pretty, but has what is vulgarly called pig beauty in English, in French *La Beauté du Diable* i.e. Youth. He is all fire and flames and love, *selon son ordinaire* and so very proud of her. It is rather agreeable to see any person so completely happy.

This is the young matron to whom the Duke wrote at least 1500 letters from 1816 to her death in August 1834. He also wrote nearly 150 letters to her husband, one of the earliest being from Elvas in Portugal in the spring of 1811 when he declared that he would 'make Boney's situation in Spain, not a bed of roses.' Richard Wellesley had earlier recognised Arbuthnot's ability as a 'fixer' and in the autumn of 1809 had asked Charles to secure a place in parliament for his son who became MP for Queensborough in 1810.

Harriet's brothers were named Henry, Edward, Mildmay and Robert Cecil, but her favourite brother had been killed and buried at the battle of Vittoria. Her cousin, Lord Burghersh, had married the Duke's niece Lady Priscilla Wellesley-Pole in 1811. The Fane and the Wellesley families had known each other for many years so that it was inevitable that the Duke should in 1814 meet the Arbuthnots briefly in London before he became ambassador in Paris. For most of his life Charles Arbuthnot wrote almost daily to the Duke with political news.

Thanks to the immense amount of material in the Duke's letters – about a hundred a year, plus the superb political and social diary that Mrs Arbuthnot kept, their fifteen-year relationship is absorbingly portraited. Moreover, after 1815 they became the cynosure of all eyes!

'You are all Syrens. You the Principal and want to keep me from where I ought to be,' wrote the Duke on 20 July 1816.

The Countesse de Boigne recalled the Parisian society scene a year or two after Waterloo,

> It is usual for women of doubtful reputation to behave perfectly in society. I do not know whether morality gains anything but society is certainly more agreeable. The English women on the contrary, appeared to have thrown propriety to the winds. I remember in M. de Talleyrand's drawing room – a certain little Mrs Arbuthnot, a young and pretty woman who had set up a claim to the affections of the Duke of Wellington, left the ladies' circle, joined the group exclusively of men, leaned against a little side table, put her two thumbs on it, sprang lightly on to it and remained there with her legs swinging, her very short skirts scarcely lower than her knees. An entire colony of English ladies soon came and proved to us that Mrs Arbuthnot's customs were not exclusively reserved to herself. The ten years that had passed without any communication with the Continent had made them borrow their fashions from their own Colonies – the easy going manners and customs of the tropics – those great square divans on which they inclined rather than sat, men and women indiscriminately.

Harriet had a brother who was a clergyman and her diary indicates that she was prudish, so that this Parisian scene seems a trifle unlikely. It is clear that she possessed a strong character, dominated her sweet retiring husband and sought (and sometimes succeeded) to influence the Duke. She certainly preferred the society of men to women and took little part in the Almacks scene, the fashionable club in St James, run by a committee of elegant ladies. She, like the Duke, strongly disapproved of Lord Byron and Charles Greville and was biased against Canning. She liked the works of Walter Scott and admired Lord Castlereagh immensely. She was a high Tory, loving stability, hating change and experiment, sharing identical views with the Duke. She also rode to hounds.

Lady Shelley was a loyal friend of Harriet's and about the only person in society who did not believe that Harriet and the Duke were lovers. 'Mrs Arbuthnot was devoid of womanly passions and was above all a loyal and truthful woman.' If one reads Harriet's own journal, the love for her husband is paramount, but, so too, is that for the Duke. She would have been unlikely to put clues into her diary about the extent of their intimacy.

Wellington first started writing to Harriet in 1818, but by the summer of 1819 he still did not know where the Arbuthnots lived.

I should be delighted to go to see you and will obey your commands whenever you will call me. But I really don't know in what part of England your house is and I direct this letter to London.

The Arbuthnots had a small house in Carlton Gardens and a country house in the Midlands.

Her diary was started in 1820 and continued until 1832. The first mention of the Duke is dated 9 February of that year. The Arbuthnots were usually impecunious. Charles had a salary of £4000, of which half was a pension for diplomatic services. Despite the expenses of the upkeep of his four young children, he had always lived extravagantly. Harriet had little money of her own and in any case had eight surviving brothers and sisters. Charles purchased an estate at Woodford in Northants when land prices were high, 'a great ruin for him', and was thus a rather keen but inefficient gentleman farmer in his spare time. In 1823 his finances were so bad that the Arbuthnots contemplated flight to Europe to avoid his creditors and face a debtors' prison. King George IV baled him out, made him a loan of £15,000 and provided a civil list pension of £1,200 per annum for his beautiful wife – 'The King was angelic,' she commented. Charles' health deteriorated and he frequently suffered from gout.

Sir Thomas Lawrence had been commissioned by the Duke to paint a portrait of himself as a present to the Arbuthnots. Lawrence, of course, had just completed a portrait of the Duke for Mary Ann Patterson, as well as a portrait of himself for the same lady. He was a good client of Lawrence's as can be seen. For instance, he commissioned a portrait of another beautiful woman, Lady Lyndhurst, from Lawrence, but hastily made disclaimers as to his feelings for Lady Lyndhurst! In Apsley House there is a miniature of Mrs Arbuthnot which the Duke wore round his neck, suspended by a chain of her dark brown hair.

In her diary of July 1825 Harriet reminded herself of the breakfast she and Wellington had had together at the Duke of Rutland's,

we had there three years ago which was almost the beginning of my great intimacy and friendship with him. He is greatly improved in looks lately and I trust is getting really better.

There is little doubt that their close relationship started about 1819. Lord Castlereagh at that stage was even more involved and certainly devoted for he wrote to the lady's husband,

If Mrs Arbuthnot had come to Aix (for the Congress) she would have had the whole of Europe at her feet. There never was such a dearth known of female society, Madame Lieven reigned with absolute sway, but Mrs Arbuthnot was better employed in the freshness of the farm [at Woodford] instead of wasting her bloom upon us old diplomats!

After his suicide in July 1822 Harriet wrote,

After the funeral the Duke promised to take the place of Lord C. as my closest friend, nothing could exceed the Duke's kindness and attention to me.

During 1820 the Duke discovered Woodford and spent a weekend there, sometimes riding up to twenty-five miles a day, and noted that Mr Arbuthnot had 'a farming mania'. They later spent some time at Stratfield Saye which Harriet declared to be 'not a nice place, seems damp and low, and the house an indifferent one for him.' She also recorded her frank views on their relationship (23 September):

Nothing could be more amiable and delightful than the Duke was during his visit to us. It is quite refreshing to be in constant and habitual intercourse with a mind so enlightened and so superior as his is, which is familiar with every subject and whim at the same time, can find amusement in the most ordinary occupations of life. He remained four days with us and I only wish I could remember and note down every word that he uttered for there was not one that was not well worth remembering. He talked of his political and military life after each successive battle when all ideas of triumph and gratified pride were lost in his regrets for the friends and companions that those triumphs had cost him. He is as excellent in heart as in mind and may God preserve him to us for without him we should all go to ruin!

Wellington secured promotion for Harriet's brother Mildmay Fane, initially a majority and later an exchange from a West India regiment into the 33rd Foot, the Duke's old regiment. Now this was very unusual. The Duke never, or very rarely, procured favours for his friends. So there is the initial loving gift of a painting, a chestnut foal, son of Copenhagen, patronage for a brother to be followed by a series of expensive presents – an Indian bracelet with strung emeralds and pearls of great value; a diamond button, a clock and a pensée (seal holder).

He cannot employ them better than in sending them to me as tokens of his regard and affection.

In the Duke's correspondence to other people, Harriet was now known half in jest as 'La Tyranna' and he referred to himself as the slave ('La Tyranna and I have been beating the Duke of York at whist').

Like half-a-dozen other society beauties Lady Emily Cowper was half in love with the Duke herself. She wrote on 14 July 1825,

> The D of W is to dinner with us on the 22nd and to toad him out I have invited Mrs Arbuthnot. There is nothing I would not do to please him, he is such a love.

When the Duke resigned as commander-in-chief in April 1827 Lady Emily Cowper wrote to her brother Frederick Lamb,

> I am so fond of him [the D of W] but he has not acted wisely on this occasion and if I had been at his elbow I should have prevented him. What a pity that he was not in love with me instead of Mrs A. The moral of this story is that no man should be in love with a foolish woman if he is ever so clever himself he is sure to be ruined by it . . .

Harriet was a sharp, shrewd lady and describes many of the personalities of the day very clearly. Of the Duke's brother, now Sir Henry Wellesley,

> Charles Arbuthnot's best friend, excellent charming person, he has not the same brilliant talents that the Duke has but he is a remarkably sensible, well judging man and very agreeable.

Of Richard Wellesley, Harriet wrote,

> he is notorious for a degree of laziness and sloth which prevents his ever doing any business. Ten years ago he had the Foreign Department and literally *did nothing!*

At Belvoir, Harriet opened the ball with the Lord Chancellor and the Duke danced with the mysterious, beautiful Lady Lyndhurst 'who is a most absurd would-be fine lady'. Later,

> It is always amusing to be with the two Princesses, Lieven and Esterhazy, they hate each other like poison, with all the affection of great fondness. The Lieven is the cleverest, *pétillante d'ésprit et de grace*. The other is gay, lively, coquette d'exces but good humoured and amiable.

Of Lady Georgiana Wellesley she wrote,

> some people call her handsome, I do not and her husband is detestable. He is said to pick his teeth with his fork and his ears with his tooth pick!!

Harriet was the confidante of the Duke on important subjects. King George IV made the Duke the executor of the Royal Will. She recounts the Duke's description of his sovereign,

The Duke of Wellington. 'He rarely wore a sash except on occasions of reviews and balls when he wore his full red uniform with decorations. He preferred to wear the Order of the Garter under his left knee, the Golden Fleece suspended round his neck and seldom wore his full collection of ribbons, medals and orders'.

Mary Anne Caton, Belle of Baltimore, Mrs Patterson and finally the Marchioness Wellesley. A raving beauty in her youth and Wellington was seen to be 'ill with love' of her.

Mrs Harriet Arbuthnot, née Fane. 'You are all Syrens. You the Principal and want to keep me from where I ought to be' wrote the Duke who called her 'La Tyranna'. A beautiful woman who loved the Duke wholeheartedly and often dominated him.

Dorothea, Princess Lieven. Her husband was Russian ambassador in London and her brother was head of state security in St Petersburg. Her lover was Prince Metternich, Austrian Premier. Of Wellington she wrote, 'he is a most excellent resource for us and is quite happy if one will pet him'.

The most extraordinary compound of talent, wit, buffoonery, obstinacy and good feeling – in short a medley of the most opposite qualities with a great preponderance of good – that I ever saw in any character in my life.

He talked to her of his old generals 'Lord William Beresford far superior to all in talents'; and of his troops he had much to say. He disliked the subversive 'union' activities in the Horse Guards. Harriet then recalled,

He would like to begin his campaigning again – it was such an active and merry life, all in high spirits and always confident of victory. It is quite delightful to hear him talk of his campaigns which he seldom does. His countenance lightens up, his eyes flash fire, and his whole appearance is as if he was inspired.

When Lord Goderich was made premier unexpectedly (most people estimated the Duke was the favourite) the Arbuthnots were very unhappy when the old war horse accepted to serve again as army C.-in-C. Harriet wrote in August 1827,

We had a desperate scene for he was excessively angry, swore (which he never does) and said he would do as he liked. I thought that he had shown more eagerness to resume the Command than was consistent with his character as a politician. He said the Army had shed their blood for him and looked to him as their protector and that he could not sacrifice them for any party purpose.

The Duke and Harriet often had strong arguments, even altercations together since Wellington disliked criticism. Although he was frequently at risk in the streets, he scorned a guard, and when Harriet reproached him for this, he turned sharply on her:

We had *une scene très vive* . . . I had sent him a letter from the Duke of Rutland expressing the fears of the Tory party, lest he yield the Catholic question. . .

The Duke was livid.

In May 1829, we had a grand dispute about the mode of treating those who have voted against the Government . . . I was for filling up their places and I told the Duke. I thought it would shew great want of power and dignity if he did not . . . He was considerably annoyed . . .

They agreed on many topics. Queen Caroline's infidelities angered them so much that the Duke said to Harriet he would resign if she was 'whitewashed of guilt.' Harriet was very puritanical, and so in some ways was the Duke. They both adored music, went to concerts, several times to Kitty's music evenings, to the opera together, 'where we had beautiful music. Madame de Lieven played to us in the evening, quite beautifully.' They went to plays together such as *Virginius* or the *Liberation of Rose* and Miss Kemble in *Mrs Beverley*.

Some of the Duke's biographers state that he was not interested in cards. Not a bit of it, he played whist, piquet and several other card games. Harriet recalled how at Lord Bridgewater's house party at Ashridge she played whist with the Duke of York against Wellington,

> whose luck at cards is quite extraordinary. It seems as if his good genius accompanied him in every, the most trivial, concern of life.

The Duke often expressed some of his 'bon mots' to her. After Napoleon's death on St Helena on 4 July 1821 he said, 'Now I think I may say I am the most successful General alive!' Of Metternich he thought him 'a sharp clever man but overrated!' and Pozzo, the Russian ambassador in Paris, was the 'greatest rogue in Europe and bribed everyone.'

He wrote of his relations with the king which were particularly difficult in 1825–6,

> The King tried to talk to him about the new Peers but that he maintained a dead silence and that in consequence the King became cold and distant in his manner. . . . moreover, the Duke did all he could to be gay and galant with the ladies of the Court, till the King became quite in a rage for he can't bear that anybody should hold a conversation to which he is not a party.

The Duke complained bitterly to Harriet about his poor duchess in great detail and on several occasions:

> The parties at his house are certainly spoilt by the Duchess for she is the most abominably, stupid woman that was ever born but I told the Duke I thought he was to blame too, for that all would go on much better if he would be *civil* to her but he is not. He never speaks to her and carefully avoids ever going near her. He protested he was always very civil to her and never said a harsh word to her in his life. I dare say he *thinks* this is true but he is not aware that his manner is abrupt to the greatest degree to everybody, particularly to her as she is frightened to death at him (a thing he detests). She always seems *consternée* when he comes near her. Then she will talk and complain of him to everybody which enrages him to the greatest degree; he says he should not care if she abused him to his face, but he cannot bear that his affairs should be talked over with anybody she can get near. Poor woman!

Wellington also was bitter about his sons' neglect of him, and Harriet took the same view,

> if his sons have not the sense to feel what advantages they would derive from constant and intimate intercourse with one whose mind and talents are so superior to anyone else's, *they* will be the sufferers and not he.

Growing up in a great man's shadow is proverbially difficult and since their father was rarely at Stratfield Saye it was even more difficult for his boys to get to know him. When he did come there it was usually with his political and social friends, so family meetings were rare. Harriet even manipulated the duchess. Once she wrote to her husband Charles (1824),

> writing the enclosed to the Duchess of W. *After all it is very* desirable for us to be well with her though she is odious and if *you approve what I have written*, pray send it on to her.

Harriet Arbuthnot according to her husband,

> had the religious devotion of an angel. She made no parade of it, but into her closet she retired (as I used to find her) to prepare herself for the Heaven which under the blessing of God she now enjoys. She devoured every book from the most profound to the most trifling. In London it seemed that the society alone could suit her. Here and elsewhere in the Country she was as if she could take interest in nothing but Trees and Flowers . . .

This eulogy was written shortly after her death in 1834. She was naturally prim. At the opera with the Duke and Lady Charlotte Greville they saw M. Albert and Mme. Noblet the two best dancers from Paris.

> It is certainly very graceful but I confess the gross indelicacy of their dress took away all the pleasure I had in seeing them. They might just as well have had no clothes on and I was astonished they were not hissed off the stage.

She disapproved of old men marrying young ladies 'disgusted at the marriage of my old friend Mr Coke of Norfolk aged 69 to Lady Ann Keppel, a girl of 19.' The fact that she was twenty-six years younger than her husband (and twenty-five years younger than the Duke) did not matter! Curiously enough despite her puritanical attitudes Harriet was a gambler, not only at cards but in stocks and shares. The Duke heartily disapproved of the speculating mania in Mexican, Peruvian, Brazilian mining; 'companies are bubbles for stock jobbing purposes and there will be a general crash'. *Au contraire*, Harriet wrote,

> I am very fond of these speculations and should gamble greatly in them if I could, but Mr Arbuthnot does not like them. We have ten shares apiece at £3 each in the new London and Manchester Railway.

In her journal she writes quite uninhibitedly of her efforts to influence the Duke to *her* point of view,

> I wanted very much to see him before he saw the King and *urge upon him the good* policy *of being conciliatory and kind in his manner and* expressions about the Duke of Clarence [who had resigned as head of the Navy], the Lord High Admiral.

On another occasion:

> *I am not altogether satisfied with the Duke's management of Ireland on this Catholic question.*

She could be very possessive indeed. When the Duke was prime minister, on 25 January 1829 she wrote,

> I cannot say I am satisfied and I wrote to the Duke this day *urging him not to give up too much* and not to take any plan to the King which he could object to and refuse to sanction.

On another occasion,

> *I have urged the Duke* to get on with the business as quick as possible and adjourn as early as he can . . . [and later] As soon as Sir William Knighton had gone *we sent for the Duke* and told him all that had passed . . .

So it continued,

> The Duke, who seems never to do anything without communicating with Mr Arbuthnot and me, shewed us some memoranda he had written and sent to Canning of the consequence of war with Spain

she wrote in a matter-of-fact style in her diary.

The Duke's letters and Harriet's diary (and presumably her letters destroyed each day on arrival by the recipient) are crammed full of political news, of court news, of the Beau's travels in the autumn of 1821 and 1822 (partly in diplomatic journeys but perhaps to meet Mary Ann Patterson), of his mission to Russia and the gossip of the day. Sometimes he wrote about his health, and her health (with remedies), about books (suggestions for Harriet to read), and music listened to. There were many little jokes and anecdotes and occasionally a harsh letter of reproof (but not very often). There is no doubt that the Duke was very happy chez Harriet. Once in the autumn of 1829 when the Duke was still prime minister she wrote,

> He is a wonderful man! With such simplicity, having finished his post, he passed half an hour in laughing heartily with me at some caricatures of himself which he had brought me down, particularly one in which he is represented reading *The Times* to the King 'We have to announce on undoubted authority that a serious difference has arisen between a great personage and his Prime Minister.' The likeness is very good, he enjoyed it as much as anyone could.

Of their deep love there can be no doubt. When the Beau was very ill in the winter of 1824 and was very giddy from his ear 'operation', thin, and did not sleep, Harriet wrote,

> His life is so precious and he is so inexpressively dear to me that I cannot look on his pale face and wasted form without the deepest sorrow.

She was intensely jealous of his relationships with other women, particularly Lady Jersey, Lady Georgina Fane and several others. Of Lady Conyngham the king's favourite (Elizabeth Denison), she noted in her diary in February 1826 that the Duke of York had told her that the king was very jealous of the Duke who is, 'much too civil to her and kisses her hand and pays her a great deal of attention.'

Of Madame de Lieven she wrote on the Duke's departure for Russia on 10 February 1826,

> He was well but out of spirits, told me I was the last person he came to see and should be the first on his return. He told me not to forget him (which is not likely) and to write to him twice a week. I could scarcely speak to him. I was so unhappy at parting from him and he told me that everybody was sorry and that Madame de Lieven had cried and kissed him at parting from him and told him that there was nobody in the world she loved so much as him. He asked me if I was not glad that everybody regretted him so much departing. I *was* very glad, very glad, that he should be appreciated as he deserves, but it is impossible to *know him well without loving* him, *he is so kind to everybody*, so affectionate and so good natured and I must say I never did know any man so universally beloved. Our prayers will be all for him.

But two months later she wrote,

> At Verona when Madame de Lieven used to get information as much as

she could from the Duke and then went and betrayed him to Metternich. They affect great friendship for the Duke, I dare say they do admire and like him very much, but they would give him up any day if their interests required it.

The Beau and Harriet behaved in every way like a happily married couple.

He said I told him always the most disagreeable things in the most invidious manner and that he would take care never to tell me anything again or ask my opinion – and I, on the other hand, got at last into a passion, too, assured him I would never tell him the truth again and that if that was his way of behaving, he would neither deserve a friend nor have one. In short, we had what he calls a grand breeze and I thought the people on the Mall would have thought he was mad, he talked so loud *but we ended as we always do*. We made up our quarrel and were very good friends and I must do the Duke the justice to say that though he gets into a passion for a moment, he never likes one a bit the less for telling him unpleasant truths.

She wrote that in November 1828 and she had been arguing for an hour in the Mall with the prime minister. What usually happens after lover's quarrels?

Exactly two years later she was noting down,

I sometimes think it is most unfortunate but it is quite true, that excepting my husband (and his children), I have no feeling of warm interest for any human being but the Duke. *There is something about him that fascinates me to a degree that is silly, but which I cannot resist.* He is so amiable, so kind hearted with a great appearance of roughness and so frank *that I always feel I would die for him. . . .*

Just before the Christmas of 1830, the Duke's 100 Days as premier had just come to an end, and Harriet writes about the 'married' couple,

If I thought only of him, of his own comfort and my own pleasure I never would desire to see him again at the head of affairs. I have not for years enjoyed so much of his society and seen him in so much repose and comfort as I have in these three weeks that he has been out of office. He has come some times and sat two hours at a time in my armchair, enjoying his idleness and the power of sitting in the '*dolce far niente*' and he will never be bored, for he reads a great deal, is never tired of it, has bought hunters, occupies himself in setting his country to rights and Time does not hang the least upon his hands.

During his premiership the Duke refused to give Charles Arbuthnot a *better* job than his department of woods and forests. Harriet predictably was up in arms,

> It has annoyed me most terribly – I cannot think but that Mr Arbuthnot is right [Charles wanted a job in the Cabinet after his long services] and that the Duke ought to, and might have, done it. *He is the dearest and most intimate friend we have* and a separation would I am certain make him as unhappy as it would us. I shall hope for the best but it makes me very uncomfortable. Now that the Duke is head of the Government every trifle is interesting to me!

Harriet boasted frequently to Lady Shelley of her conquest of the Duke,

> with the exception of ten days I have been in his company ever since the 27th December [letter dated 20th July 1828], he has hunted and shot with the youngest. The last two days we were *'en trio'* with him which I enjoyed very much. What do you think of his having dined with me *tête à tête* yesterday? I was going to dine alone and he also, so he came down here, *est-ce que cela blesse les convenances?* I don't care, I think we are old enough now!

Harriet was perfectly prepared to break the conventions for her lover. Their time together was relatively short. Harriet died suddenly of cholera at Woodford on 2 August 1834. Not too long afterwards her elderly bereaved husband went to live with her elderly bereaved lover.

But what did their friends and enemies have to say about their relationship?

Their closest friend Fanny, Lady Shelley, had no doubts at all 'We three formed a perfect union where no jealousy or bitterness of feeling ever intruded its harmony.' To show how the trio worked together here is Harriet's diary for 1 April 1828:

> We dined at Lady Shelley's. She has got a medallion of the Duke's framed with a Garter he has worn for some years, and she wanted some of his hair. So she had him for dinner, the first of the month as he said that was his day for having his hair cut and I cut off two pieces for her, one quite brown and the other as white as silver, with which she was quite overjoyed and meant to to put into the frame and keep as an heirloom in the family for ever.

In Fanny's own diary she wrote after Harriet's death,

> Their intimacy may have given gossips an excuse for scandal but I who

knew them both so well am convinced that the Duke was *not* her lover. He
only asked for repose from the turmoil of public affairs, for absolute
truth and the absence of little-mindedness.

Henry Greville, younger son of Lady Charlotte, wrote of Harriet's
death,

> – a very heavy blow to the Duke of Wellington to whom the intimacy
> with the Arbuthnots for the last 20 years has been his greatest resource
> affording him an agreeable and comfortable 'interieur' such as he can
> never meet with again. I believe him to be equally attached to husband
> and wife and there was no manner personal or political in which he was
> concerned or interested that he did not freely discuss with them in the
> most unreserved manner.

Thomas Raikes noted:

> Mrs Arbuthnot was a very clever agreeable woman and from her great
> intimacy with the Duke, a prominent feature in the Tory party. Her death
> was awfully sudden, a sister to Sir Henry Fane.

Sir Robert Peel (to whose youngest son, Arthur Wellesley Peel born 3
August 1829, the Duke stood godfather), was under no delusions over
the relationship between Mrs Arbuthnot and the Duke. On one
occasion early in 1827 Peel was discussing the Duke with Kitty at
Stratfield Saye. The Arbuthnots were staying there too.

> She burst out a-crying and such things make me still more hate the sight
> of those who can find it in their heart even if they have no sense of virtue
> to usurp her place. What wickedness, what folly, to undervalue and to be
> insensible to the affection of a wife.

To Mrs Peel he wrote:

> Do not my love, whisper to anyone ever the gossip I send you. I see no
> signs of the influence of Mrs Arbuthnot having abated. She takes her
> place next to him at dinner as if it were a matter of course . . . but let us
> leave alone these odious things.

Charles Greville was in no doubt either:

> I heard of another death – Mrs Arbuthnot after a short illness. As the
> Duke of Wellington's mistress, she was rather remarkable. The Duke
> evinced a good deal of feeling but is accused of insensibility because he
> had the good taste and sense to smooth his brow and go to the House of
> Lords with a cheerful aspect. She was not a clever woman but she was
> neither dull nor deficient but very prudent and silent! [A little later he

wrote] only think of the Beau's flirt Mrs Arbuthnot being dead!

Greville was always caustic about their relationship. At the Doncaster races in September 1829 he wrote,

> The Duke was with Lord Chesterfield who was to have had a large party of women, Mrs Lane Fox and Mrs Arbuthnot in the number. I think the Duke very like advised Mrs Arbuthnot not to go. *It would have been rather indecent after all to have exhibited these ladies, notorious as they are* before the whole county of York.

The two ladies subsequently received anonymous letters (clearly in Greville's handwriting) accusing them of being the Duke's mistresses.

The Spanish General Alava had his own viewpoints, although as he was quite dependent on the Duke's patronage he had to watch his words.

> Alava told me [Harriet] he was sure I must always have had *la conduite la plus parfaite* and have established the best reputation that anybody ever had, for that in this most 'medisant' country in the world though everybody saw how intimate I was with the Duke and how much he admired and liked me, and though *he had the reputation of always being 'faisant les grimaces aux femmes'*, no creature ever even imagined the possibility of an impropriety in it.

Fanny, Lady Salisbury, at whose home the Duke heard of Harriet's death and noted his initial despair and total loss, thought on balance that the Duke and Harriet were merely good, intimate friends,

> It is a dreadful loss to him for whether there is any foundation or not for the stories believed about the early part of their liaison she was certainly now become to him no more than a tried and valued friend to whom he was sincerely attached. Her house was his home and with all his glory and greatness he never had a house. His nature is domestic and as he advances in years, some female society and some fireside to which he can always resort becomes necessary to him.

To the outside world, to society, and to many of the Duke's biographers Harriet was indeed at one stage his mistress. The circumstancial evidence is very strong as Peel and Charles Greville quite strongly felt.

For twenty years the Duke had this warm attractive young woman on his arm, proudly proclaiming to the world that he was her property. She had a weak, amiable, compliant, older husband. She and the Duke saw each other almost everyday from the time she was twenty until her death aged forty. They laughed together, fought each other, and respected each other's views and intelligence.

Let the reader look at 'A Sketch in the Park' in Stratfield Saye and examine the cool confident look on the beautiful lady's face, La Tyranna, as she looks at her slave.

Chapter Twenty

PRINCESS LIEVEN – THE RUSSIAN SPY

The Russian Bear at the beginning of the nineteenth century was much as the Russian Bear in the mid twentieth century. Intense distrust and suspicion of the West was founded on fear. The French conqueror had burned half of Moscow in 1812, and a German conqueror did exactly the same in 1942. Information gathering for the tsar at the Court of St Petersburg was as vital after Waterloo as it is for the Kremlin today. The jovial visits by the emperor of Russia to Paris and London to take part in the Allied victory celebrations encouraged statements from the East and West to regard each other with temporary bonhomie. The tsar's ambassador in Paris was Pozzo di Borgo, with whom Wellington was on friendly terms. In London the Russian ambassador was Count Christopher Lieven, who was an amiable shrewd diplomat and an excellent husband. His wife was born on 17 December 1785 at Riga as Dorothea von Benckendorff. She married Lieven in 1800 when she was fifteen and was to be unfaithful to him on many occasions. Her intimacy with King George IV and with Earl Grey caused much concern. She was a close friend of two Foreign Secretaries, Lord Castlereagh and Canning; of three prime ministers, Wellington, Lord Grey and Lord Aberdeen; and of three royal dukes, Clarence, Cumberland and York. She became the mistress of Prince Metternich and ended her life in Paris as the mistress of François Guizot, French ambassador in London and later premier of France under Louis Phillippe.

Countess (she was made a Princess in 1826) Lieven was of German extraction. Her father was a general and her mother, a baroness, was a close friend of Tsar Paul I's wife. The Lievens had the embassy in Berlin from 1810–12, and came to the London embassy at the end of that year. She became and remained a leading light of English society for twenty years until her voluntary exile to Paris in 1834.

Sir Thomas Lawrence painted Dorothea in 1805 when she was twenty and rather later so did F. F. Watts RA. She had a long reddish nose, large ears, a long slender neck, a large irregular face with sharp features, grey eyes, dark curly hair, and a graceful and sinuous walk. Countess Lieven dressed superbly as money was never a problem for her, she also played the pianoforte and harp – all of which endeared her to the Duke. She was ambitious, attractive, charming, totally ruthless, loved power, was a dedicated snob, loved royalty, suffered from ennui, and her political friendships were often passionate in intensity and sexuality. She admired Shakespeare's works and Walter Scott's novels.

The countess was a bold, dangerous and fascinating woman. The Duke of Wellington wrote a minimum of 166 letters, and probably many more, in French to her between March 1819 and September 1840. She kept an intimate journal and wrote almost daily to Tsar Alexander's foreign office, to her brother Alexander and, after autumn 1818, to her lover Prince Metternich. In effect she became the second *Austrian* ambassador in London (Prince Esterhazy was the official ambassador) and she fed her lover all the political and social news of England. King George and the Prince Regent were natural targets for the attractive Russian spy. Charles Greville, that shrewd judge of human nature, wrote of Madame de Lieven,

> She is excessively clever, and when she chooses brilliantly agreeable, fastidious, conscious of her own superiority and inferiority of other people for whom she had contempt. She is dignified, graceful, accomplished, charming on the pianoforte. She endeavours to assume popular and gracious manners but this is done languidly and awkwardly. She suffers from ennui, but at the same time is so clever, imaginative and has keen penetration. She talks with extra ease and gracefulness, her letters and conversation are to the point. Because of her dignity, little bonhomie, stately and reserved manners, she is not liked and has hardly any friends.

In her family and to her husband, she was known as 'Darja' and she called the count, 'Bonsi'. Her brother became a major-general and head of the tsar's secret police. Altogether she had six children; her daughter died in infancy but her sons Constantine, Alexander, Paul, George and Arthur survived. The Duke was godfather to her youngest son.

She became one of the patron ladies of Almacks and was extremely fashionable in dress, dance and music. From their embassy at 36 Harley

Street the Lievens entertained lavishly. Later on they rented Mrs Pozzi's house in Streatham which had more space for their large family and retinue of servants. There were only four embassies in London. The Austrians were the poorest and the Russians the richest. Until the battle of Borodino, the Tsar had hoped to appease Napoleon by not maintaining friendly relations with England (i.e. no Russian embassy) but Wellington's success in Portugal and Spain made England a desirable ally.

Prince Talleyrand's niece, Dorothea, Duchesse de Dino, who knew Wellington well, and Countess Lieven even better noted:

> Madame de Lieven is the woman to be most feared, respected, cultivated and courted. Her political importance which was founded on her intelligence and her experience was accompanied by an authority which no one dared question. Her house was the most exclusive in London. It was inevitable that the two embassies – that is the two women who reigned over them [Princess Esterhazy being the second] would enter into competition with each other, and the contest was highly publicised and a favourite diversion of London society.

Thomas Creevey on the sidelines also wrote,

> The female Lieven and the Dino were the people for sport. They are both professional talkers – artists, in that department. We had them both quite at ease, and perpetually at work with each other.

Madame Lieven's loyalties were primarily to her tsar who gave the Lievens permission to come or to go. He was in total command all the time as his millions of serfs and slaves knew only too well. Although Dorothea was a supreme patriot she was above all a passionate woman and gave some of her loyalty to her lovers, and particularly to Prince Metternich, the Austrian premier, who had 'the good fortune to know His Imperial Majesty's mind.'

A scrutiny of her many comments about the Duke in her journal and her letters to Russia and Austria would indicate that she is the spider in the centre of the web, and the Duke a semi-willing fly. On several occasions Wellington confided in his friends about the Russian spy. To Lord Aberdeen he wrote in the summer of 1829,

> To attain this object [to upset his government] all is fish that comes to her net. She wants to attain this not from any personal dislike to me or any of its [the government's] members, not because we entertain any notions hostile to the Russian Government, but because we are an English administration. They – the Lievens – have played an English party game

instead of doing the business of their sovereign's, since I have been in office. I have the best authority that both have been engaged as principles in intrigues to deprive my colleagues and me of power since Jan 1828, that they have misrepresented our conduct and views to their Sovereign . . . In another country, in Russia itself or France, or with another Sovereign or in a different state of society, would amply justify our interference to have Prince Lieven recalled. But it is my opinion that this measure would do us more harm than good . . .

To Lord Heytesbury at the same time, the Duke wrote,

I have known since the year 1826 Prince and Princess Lieven have taken pains to represent my conduct whether in or out of Government in the most unfortunate manner in St Petersburgh.

The Duke was in France until the end of 1818, but Madame de Lieven was writing of him to Alexander from the summer of 1817 'We still have the Duke of Wellington here who enjoys himself very much and is very agreeable.' She has more comments about him the next year, and was writing to him from 24 March 1819. In the next years the relationship is more intimate. On 8 February 1820,

A few days after my confinement Wellington came to see me. I told him he must stand sponsor for my boy (and the Prince Regent too). W. is the only one who laughs at everything and above all talks of everything . . . He is charming, agreeable and accommodating in the highest degree: *he is a most excellent resource for us and is quite happy if one will pet him.* The truth is that *London bores him and* that *he is never so much at ease as in our house* [in Harley Street].

Wellington told her all about the Cato Street Conspiracy organised by Arthur Thistlewood. 'What a horrible thing, a general massacre of the entire cabinet. What a monstrous idea!' Thistlewood had chosen Wellington as his victim. There had been a long fight over Castlereagh as everybody wanted the honour of cutting his throat. Two of the gang were to cut off the heads, a third held the bag in which the heads were to be carried . . .

Our friend Wellington takes no precautions. He shows himself too much and everybody knows that he is always followed . . . I have been obliged to promise the Duke to visit him in the country tomorrow. You have no idea how much it bores me and puts me out. He has unfortunately taken it into his head that his house is the most comfortable in the world. Well there are two very definite drawbacks to that comfort. It is always cold there and his wife is stupid. What's to be done?

The Beau was now writing her long gossipy letters, certainly from 1824, full of news about Lady Jersey, and Dorothea's friend Harriet Granville, about Lady Conyngham (the king's mistress, known as La Regnante), about the king and the coronation on 19 July 1821. He also wrote to her of his political views about Turkey and about Metternich who was not then her lover. In her journal she notes on 21 July 1821,

> The Duke was sitting beside me yesterday evening. He seemed to be almost asleep. Suddenly he woke up and observed 'Devil take me, Prince Metternich must march. He must advance all his troops against Naples . . . but he must come out of it with clean hands, do you understand. He can play a splendid part.'

She wrote to Alexander that Wellington behaved in very bad taste by keeping his hat on during Queen Caroline's trial, in her presence. She played picquet with the Duke at Wherstead.

> He knows as little about it as I do and the only difference between us is that I play badly and know it and he plays badly and thinks he plays well. It is incredible how his pride has a share in everything that he does. It plunges him into despair not to be able to do something or to do it badly. It is a strange vanity. Men have a great deal of it, a hundred times more than we have.

On one of her earlier visits to Stratfield Saye she persuaded Wellington to tell her the full story of his military career. A challenge from an intriguing sophisticated woman hard to resist.

> He began in India where he spent seven years. After that he was in Hanover with the English army in 1805. Later he bombarded Copenhagen. He was appointed Secretary for Ireland, then despatched to Portugal where he was in command of the Army and then he did what all the world knows and admires. He has never been wounded. He has never lost a battle. He considers Waterloo the most difficult battle he has fought. His first feat of arms was as follows. He was sent out on an expedition near Calcutta. He mistook the direction and let a fortress be captured which he ought to have defended. He shut himself up in despair and what do you think he did? He fell asleep. I suppose that it was in his sleep that he made up his mind to be a great man. He said to your Ambassador who declared that all would end well in the Neapolitan campaign 'But my dear Prince (Esterhazy) I have always noted that in order to end, you have to begin. We all laughed!'

All her letters to Metternich and her brother have been preserved. To the former she wrote,

How, mon Prince, did you come to think of using my letters in a report? I am overwhelmed by the honour you do them. Did I give you any news? I never know what I write to you. I tell you everything at random. They must make an odd collection, my letters to you and the relationship between us is in itself odd. As a result of seeing one another for a week two years ago, here we are engaged in an intimate correspondence which ought to imply a whole lifetime of daily contacts. Some day if our letters are read, people will wonder what we were about, whether it was love or politics.

She reported to 'Mon Prince' that the king was a dangerous madman, his new passion for the Marchioness of Conyngham had turned his head, and that she was a malicious fool who might do a great deal of harm. The Duke dined with the Lievens once a week and told them about the Cabinet's quarrel with the king.

Really I have no more pleasure in Society for I have not one in whom to confide what strikes me as ridiculous in our best of all possible worlds

was a phrase he wrote to Dorothea. He was writing to Mrs Patterson, to Lady Shelley, to Lady Jersey and to Harriet Arbuthnot in the summer of 1821, so that he could not complain of a dearth of intelligent and feminine audiences! Dorothea's position in society was so strong that she could boast to her lover,

The position in England is indeed extraordinary. I know a great deal *more* than the interested parties: for I am treated so much as an Englishwoman by both sides that nobody minds talking in front of me. The English, silent and cold about everything else are particularly talkative and frank about their own affairs. They have not got the knack of ordinary conversation and do not take the trouble to talk to you if you want to talk of trivial things, but boldly propose the most intimate questions and they are on their own ground.

The intimacy grew apace. The Duke had told the king that he had to leave the court to attend a Council of Ministers. 'Damn the Council' was all the king said. Dorothea undertook to write a letter for the Duke to his colleagues. She wrote on a card 'By His Majesty's Command, damn the Council, signed "Wellington".' And the Duke sent the letter off.

The countess knew all about Lady Frances Wedderburn-Webster and the Duke. She also knew all about Mrs Mary Anne Patterson since the Duke asked her to introduce Mrs Patterson into society. She knew about Lady Charlotte Greville and the Duke, having seen her portrait in his private study at Stratfield Saye. They were both in Brighton in the spring of 1822. It was the Duke's first visit to the Royal Pavilion.

> You cannot imagine how astonished the D. of W. is. He had not been here before. I do not believe since the days of Heliogabulos there have been such magnificence and such luxury. There is something effeminate in it which is disgusting.
>
> One spends the evening half lying on cushions: the lights are dazzling, there are perfumes, music, liqueurs. W. said 'Devil take me, I think I must have got into bad company!' I succeeded in getting the Duke invited and he is as pleased as a child. The King is ill and anxious, he talks of nothing but his approaching end.

Emily Cowper, who later married Lord Palmerston, was a great favourite at court. She admired the Duke and was quite prepared to take a hand in his 'amours'. In her diaries and letters to her brother she wrote on many occasions of the intrigues of the day.

> Madame de Lieven is grown rather tiresome with her perpetual trips to Richmond. She cut us upon the Water Party last Friday and I have not forgiven her yet as we had the D. of W. *on purpose for her* and it would have been awkward, if fortunately, when we were all prepared and going to start I had not bethought myself of sending off for Mrs Arbuthnot – who instantly put on her bonnet, tucked up her petticoats and came off to us in Earl Clanwilliam's cabriolet.

That was on 30 June 1822, but the matchmaking continued as she wrote on 16 January 1823.

> *I wished the D of W to come to meet Mme Lieven* next week but he says he cannot, he's to be in Town. He sent an excuse here for this time but people say he is more in love than ever with Mrs Arbuthnot, I wish Lady Jersey would make a diversion for she (Mrs A) is an odious little woman.

That spring Lady Emily wrote,

> The King is in better health and going very soon to the Cottage. He cannot stand on his leg but the D of W is very much against the idea of his marriage, he says it is a loss of Caste. I cannot express how fond I am of that Man. There is always something honest and straightforward in all he does and says.

That autumn the Duke was very ill with inflammation and congestion and the countess was genuinely worried for his life. He also had a 'breeze' with the king, but the Duke resolved it peacefully and diplomatically. By now Dorothea was an experienced Duke-watcher. The Lievens took the Duke to a royal performance of the opera at Drury Lane. The moment he appeared he was cheered to the echo. At first he did not want to take any notice but when he was compelled to go forward to satisfy the audience, he gave two little nods as if to say 'How do you do' and then left them to clap their hands sore without giving them another look. They went with him to Richmond Park on a wet and cold May day.

> On these occasions nobody is more amusing than our friend Wellington. He cannot understand things being other than he wishes: that it should rain when he is counting on good weather or that I should not want to accompany him when he is setting out for a walk!

The Duke wrote to Dorothea expounding this philosophy:

> You have judged me correctly: it is true that I never encounter difficulties and the reason is I believe, *because I always put myself on the high road to Fortune.* You will admit that is the way to meet it!

During 1822 they heard of the death of Napoleon; in the summer Wellington's ear operation was bungled and he became deaf in one ear, and their friend Lord Castlereagh committed suicide. Wellington and the Lievens then attended the Congress of Vienna, which transferred to Verona.

> I shall be on the Rhine towards the 15th [July] and I shall see you for certain. I want to be in Paris on the 24th [To see Mrs Patterson]. For the rest I am at your orders, he wrote.

Dorothea wrote to Metternich from Paris on 26 December 1822,

> Pozzo calls you the Grand Inquisitor of Europe. He is very much incensed with the D. of W. who everyone says behaved like an intriguer while he was here.

One wonders whether the highly intelligent woman who wrote that comment realised the irony! She, her lover Metternich and Pozzo, the Russian ambassador in Paris, were supreme examples of political intriguers.

At Verona she wrote that the Duke 'is the best and the firmest of my English acquaintances', but it was Metternich that she wanted to see. She saw a great deal of these 'two stars who have deprived me of the society of my fellow countrymen.' On her return from Congress to the London court, the countess spent half a day with the king and reported his comments back to her lover.

All my ministers are fools. Canning has just started. Wellington was the only one who had followed affairs and who knew the Sovereigns personally at the Congress and the heads of their cabinets. He had the great, great disadvantage of being incapable of flexibility or of making a diplomatic approach. He sets about a question like a battery of cannon that was bound to do harm at Verona where conciliation was essential: it was very unfortunate . . .

It is difficult to understand a ruling monarch openly criticising his own ministers in a private situation *tête à tête* with a beautiful foreign agent! Dorothea had bearded the Duke about becoming Minister for Foreign Affairs.

No, I dont want to be: that would mean deviating from my position and my career . . . if the King's service demand that I should assume this post, I will take it but only if the worst comes to the worst. I have no ambition . . .

In her journals she makes scathing comments about the Duke 'he counts for nothing in affairs' and 'the D. of W. grows stupider every day.' Despite this in 1823 their relationship became closer, flirtatious and loving, although they were not lovers. His 'coqueterie' was noticed on several occasions and his letters to her in Florence, where she had stayed after the Congress of Verona, were intimate.

You can be assured that you are wanted in this country as the Messiah by the Jews or the King Sebastian by the Portuguese and above all by those connected with Ashburnham House and by me. [She was given careful advice about travelling in Europe] start late and stop early. In my opinion it is of no consequence whether the Inn is good or bad . . . [The Duke went on] I have plenty to tell you, but I dare not. I must find myself one morning by your fire at Ashburnham House before I can give you my Budget which is however quite enough to amuse you.

The curious thing was that his relationship with Mrs Arbuthnot was also at its most passionate in 1823 and the succeeding years. Dorothea wrote on 2 October 1823, 'The D. of W. deserted the Scottish marches, Mrs Arbuthnot and the partridges to spend the last few days with me.'

In his letters Wellington adopts the same skittish tone he uses to Lady Shelley and Harriet Arbuthnot. Much talk of 'love affairs', everything is '*couleur de Rose*', gossip about the king 'better terms with his Friend than ever.' Dorothea stayed abroad for seven months until late spring in 1824 and the Duke was in ecstacies when she came back.

To begin with I assure you that everyone is delighted at your return. This begins with Monsieur de Lieven who is completely radiant. I have not met anyone who does not congratulate himself upon it. Even Lady Jersey . . . Here they dream of you: and the King speaks of your return with a pleasure that one sees in him very rarely. Who knows if he has not received *news of those rounded arms of which you tell me!*

On several occasions the king was noticeably jealous of the Duke's intimacy with Countess Lieven.

The next year, 1825, she was in Berlin and Wellington wrote to her with news of her children. 'I did not see my godson because he was dressing but the Nurse assured me that he was very well.'

This was a difficult time for Wellington who was losing his beloved Mrs Patterson to his brother Richard and he was in mental agony, especially as there was little he could do to stop their marriage. Dorothea spent four weeks in Russia captivating the tsar – who nevertheless was to die on Christmas Day. On her return her influence with the 'Cottage Coterie' surrounding the king at Windsor and Brighton was greater than ever. She could hold her own against Lady Conyngham, Sir William Knighton and the other favourites. With diamonds linked across her creamy satin gown, bracelets, and pearl necklaces '*la grande mondaine*' manipulated Wellington as well. He stood godfather again to a boy called Arthur who died in early childhood.

Forget the W. of Verona. *He is the only check we have on Mr Canning's follies. The latter hates him, but he fears him.* W. is utterly without fear. Our friend W. has a difficult part to play but his reputation for honesty and sincerity and above all his lucky star help him to carry it off.

In the spring of the following year, 1826, Wellington was deputed to visit St Petersburg and present English alliance credentials to the new tsar, Nicholas on his accession. Dorothea wrote to Alexander,

I am sending you a line, dear A, by the D. of W. I am delighted that he is going to see our country, and I am sure that his visit will be greeted with much satisfaction by the Emperor and our people. I rejoice in anticipation both in his success and in the impressions of our country which he will bring back. He is the finest and noblest character of the day and he is probably even more distinguished by his feelings than even by his high military reputation. The visit he is paying to our country is a genuine pleasure to him and England could not send an Ambassador more worthy of the great occasion. Like all the world he is full of admiration for the splendid conduct of our Emperor. What events! What character our Emperor displays. I agree with what the Duke says 'Where Kings can ride on horseback and can inflict punishment, revolution is impossible.' So on this point I am at ease. The D is taking with him his nephew Lord Fitzroy Somerset – a man of great ability and of the highest character.

Before he went on his long journey through the Low Countries, Germany and Poland to the Muscovy Court, Dorothea kissed the Duke passionately with tears in her eyes, as though she might never see him again. He wrote to her several times from St Petersburg during March 1826 and visited her mother-in-law. He attended the funeral of Tsar Alexander, a terrible ceremony since the corpse was over four months 'old'. In the meantime Prince Metternich and Dorothea broke up their long-distance love affair.

Early the next year the Duke of York died. He was the army commander and Wellington was given the appointment. Complications followed when Lord Liverpool, the prime minister, died a few weeks later on 17 February. The king invited Wellington to recommend the new head of government and suggested either Peel or Canning. It was a very dramatic period. The Tories resigned and the Duke resigned command of the army a few weeks after accepting the role. In August Canning died, Goderich became premier and once again the Duke took command of the army – all within a space of six months.

Dorothea had now changed political sides and had openly backed Canning and made known her views to society and to Wellington's friends. For once she had made a major mistake and had backed the wrong horse!

During a stay at the royal lodge on 2 August 1826 the Duke was a victim of the king's paranoid jealousy. He was not allowed to drive Madame de Lieven in his carriage. In his letter to Harriet Arbuthnot he described the scene.

> The fact is that H.M. is a petit or rather Gros Infidele. He is making love to Mde de Lieven and supposes I am His Rival. When she arrived at home, I happened to follow her into the House. H.M. having got rid of Lady Conyngham was at the door to meet her and he said to her '*Que fait it donc içi pour nous Interrompre?*' Observe that Lieven [the lady's husband] was there likewise! I was afterwards with Lord Conyngham in the Drawing Room when H.M. and Madame de Lieven came in together, by accident I suppose. He said again '*Encore ici pour nous Interrompre*' so that I pass here for a Jealous lover ... but the love making to Madame de Lieven and his voting me a Rival are capital!

Harriet was sure that the Duke had been very graciously received at court. She herself was present at Windsor on the Duke's birthday and noted that Madame de Lieven was there saying to the Duke that she loved him better than any man in England. Wellington only laughed and said that at least 'she *ought* to love him!' That strange Slav mind probably did genuinely love Wellington – from time to time. Seven months before the king handed over his government to Wellington. Dorothea was writing in June 1827 to St Petersburg:

> The Duke continues his policy of hostility towards us even in the matter of the corn duties. A Bill introduced during his Ministry has been thrown out by himself because he is no longer in the cabinet. However this explosion of temper will hurt only himself for I hope his amendment will be defeated. In any case he has seriously compromised his reputation. *His conduct is bad, perfidious and injurious to the country* [That autumn the cold war was still intense]. D of W still looks very coldly on me. I can wait for it really is of no consequence. He cannot forgive me for having preferred the Minister friendly to the Greeks, to the Minister friendly to the Turks [Russia's old foe]. The King has restored him to office but not to favour.

On 9 January 1828 Wellington was made prime minister much to the delight of the Arbuthnots, Lady Shelley, Lady Jersey and the new Lady Wellesley. In April Lord Palmerston wrote to his brother William Temple, then charge d'affaires at St Petersburg,

> The D. is very anxious to break with Russia. He has a strong personal dislike to Russia. He has had violent quarrels with the Lievens. A great many things have contributed to set him against the Lievens . . . she was foolish last year when Canning came in and too openly expressed her joy at the Duke's retirement and was to a certain degree uncivil to him.

Initially Dorothea tried to laugh off her misjudgement when writing to Alexander, the direct pipeline of course to the tsar.

> Everything will now once more be topsy turvy here . . . The Duke prefers the trickiness of M. de Metternich to the straightforwardness of the Emperor Nicholas. Very well so be it . . . *we can count too upon other friends in the Cabinet* but they are over-awed by that despot Wellington. He makes it understood that he is the master . . . The King does not like Wellington, the nation which expected mountains and marvels from his firmness in the absence of talent is beginning to see that he temporises on every question.

Dorothea knew what she had to do to keep her 'balance of power'. 'At the same time the D. of W. and I are on good terms.' Wellington as prime minister of England came to the fireside of this strange woman to have political discussions, often quite violent. 'If I were to break out some day I am sure we would come to blows'.

Towards the end of that summer, during the Russian-Turkish war, she wrote,

> He reverted to some of his former coquetries with me during our recent stay with the King at Windsor. He was most attentive and we talked on every subject except Turkey. He complained that I treated him badly, that I did not invite him to come to see me: but I preserved my dignity and most certainly *I shall not again become the dupe of his sagacious demeanour which is all he possesses.*

In the autumn the Duke was back to his 'former ill-will', but two weeks later,

> I found in him a remarkable change much gentleness and great friendliness. The D. of W. with his usual boastfulness said to me 'I am the most popular Minister that England has ever seen – take my word for it. I am very strong.'

Then followed the unnecessary duel with the earl of Winchelsea at Battersea on 21 March (the latter imputed support for the Catholics by the Duke), on which Dorothea commented, 'It is the first he has ever fought in his life and blame and approval are about equally divided.' A week later she was on tenterhooks,

> The D may be thrown out in the next 24 hours. The King is furious against the Catholic Bill, the D of Cumberland is egging him on. If the King could show but a spark of courage the D might be upset – if not he becomes the dictator and the saying of the King is fulfilled 'Arthur is King of England, O'Connel King of Ireland and myself Canon of Windsor'.

Dorothea's soirées and those of Lady Jersey were the most brilliant and the most agreeable in town. They ruled at Almacks, where the men *had* to dance with skill and grace wearing knee breeches, white cravats and the correct coats. Once a week the ball and supper were attended by the 'ton' and gossip blended with domestic politics and international diplomacy. The court stories by and about the king were told to Lady Conyngham, who passed them on to Lady Emily Cowper, thence to Madame de Lieven, to the Duke and finally to Harriet Arbuthnot!

The Duke and Dorothea met and wrote to each other every week. She mentioned him and his political status in every letter that she wrote to her brother in St Petersburg, although she covered her bets with Lords Grey and Aberdeen. The latter, lays bare to me with the greatest simplicity his innermost thoughts. They are mean and cowardly but they are thoroughly in conformity with our interest as it is possible to desire. [And on 27 August 1829,] We are hated but feared. The Duke must be mad with rage, for he hates us and will not cease to do so.

George IV died in June 1830 and was succeeded by William IV.

There's the King! a great King, indeed! a bon enfant with a weak head! At times I think he is likely to lose it, so great is his pleasure at being King.

This is what the Russian spy was writing to her masters in February 1830 when the Iron Duke was firmly in the saddle.

There is no longer any idea of conciliating the good will of the English. Russia will never be able to gain this from them but must adopt a firm attitude *and enforce it by cold but polite language. Inspire them with fear and all will go well* . . .

Four years later the Lievens were recalled to Russia. Lady Elizabeth Holland who much admired Mme Lieven bade farewell to her in July 1833.

Poor Mme de Lieven made me quite unhappy at taking leave. She is quite affected at going. She is a very great coward and the voyage in the steam vessel frightens her a great deal. She is to spend 3 weeks with the Imperial family at Peterhof. The return tho' apparently certain is never quite sure with such Russian despots, [and later] But those barbarian princes have a volonte fute and she is wretched . . .

Dorothea had sadly just lost two of her sons. Possibly she was temporarily unbalanced for she not only left her husband but also defied the tsar by settling in Paris. There her salon quickly became famous, but lacked the influence that she had built up so carefully in London over a twenty-two year period. *The London Times* – the *Thunderer* – wrote of her,

There never figured on the courtly stage a female intriguer more restless, more arrogant, more mischievous. She fancied herself a 'power'. She was however more frequently a dupe. The dupe of her own artifices reacted upon by those of others.

The Duke often discussed Dorothea with his friends. To Fanny Lady Salisbury he said, the year after the Lievens left England,

She is not a clever woman. I am a tolerably good judge and I tell you that she is not a clever woman. She is an '*intriguante*'. She is now writing to people of all parties here in England except to me for I would not answer her letters. Her house at Paris is a foyer d'intrigues and Pozzo [the Russian Minister] is very much annoyed at her intriguing here and the end will be that she will be recalled to Russia. She is under the greatest obligation to me that a woman can be to a man, I mean an obligation of society, as a preux chevalier and I once said to her 'Well at least your conduct proves that you think me the most honourable man in Europe'.

A few years later on 23 November 1840 the Duke talked to Thomas Raikes,

I do not doubt the inclination of the Lady [Princess de Lieven] to do this country all the mischief in her power in return for much kindness and good will with which she was treated during the long residence here. Nobody knows better than I do, the Lady whom you mention. She can and will betray everybody in turn, if it should suit her purpose.

The last word on this extraordinary woman comes from Harriet Arbuthnot, who was not only possessive where the Duke was concerned, but also disliked Princess de Lieven.

It is curious that the loves and intrigues of 'une femme galante' should have such influence over the affairs of Europe . . . she disgusted all parties by her uncalled for interference in our internal concerns, behaved with base ingratitude to the Duke because he has put her back into her proper place viz. Ambassadress from Russia . . . The whole society of London are in the greatest anxiety for fear that the Duke whose good nature is proverbial should forgive her past conduct and *become again her dupe.* However I am certain he will never do that, he never forgives cold heartedness and ingratitude.

So who in reality was the spider and who the fly? 'Lieven in velvet and diamonds and the Beau basking by her'!

Chapter Twenty-One

FANNY, LADY SALISBURY – THE GASCOYNE HEIRESS

Before he was married, young Arthur Wesley hunted from Hatfield House, the home of the Cecil family. At the birth of his first son and heir in 1807, Emelia Mary, Lady Salisbury accompanied by her daughters visited Kitty to see the new arrival and asked the father to spend the weekend with them hunting. He accepted the invitation with alacrity. During the Peninsular campaigns he always wore the sky-blue Hatfield House colours during his own fox-hunts in Portugal, Spain and southern France. There is little doubt that the first Lady Salisbury had a soft spot for Arthur Wesley. She was Irish born, a Hill, and knew Lord and Lady Mornington in Dublin as cousins.

Hatfield House is in Hertfordshire near St Albans. On Saturday nights there were card parties and over the six-week Christmas period, on every Tuesday and Friday, there were places for 500 people, eating and drinking all day long. Lady Emelia Mary Salisbury 'goes a fox-hunting in the morning, or in her open carriage, and to all the balls in the county at night.' The assemblies at Hatfield were certainly 'the best of their class in London.'

Hatfield House was once a royal palace but the main building is a large redbrick E-shaped house surrounded by a large park with woods, a lake, a maze and long avenues. It has a great hall, a long gallery, a great staircase – an Adam and Eve staircase – and in the minstrel gallery in the dining hall were some of the spoils of war sent back to his cousins by Wellington from Spain and France. One description of a Hatfield House weekend party describes the mélange of diplomats, cabinet ministers, pretty women, jealous husbands, perfumed dandies, long dark corridors, chapels, towers, bats in the bed, curtained alcoves – everything one needed for a romance – or at any rate an affair! Arthur would undoubtedly have visited the Salisbury family before and after Napoleon's 100 Days, so it is no surprise that in February 1816 Arthur's brother Sir Henry Wellesley had made a second marriage with Lady Georgiana Cecil, daughter of the 1st Marquess and Lady Emelia Mary.

James Brownlow Cecil was Viscount Cranborne, the only son of the Marquess of Salisbury. He had been born in 1791 and to his eternal regret had been forbidden to join Wellington's army on campaign, although he commanded a regiment in the Hertfordshire Militia. He longed for active service either in the military field or in the political arena. All his life he sought for useful employment; being MP for Hertford was simply not enough for his talents and energies. On 2 February 1821 he married Frances Mary Gascoyne, a tall, graceful dark girl, who danced well, a considerable heiress from Lancashire. She was musical, keen on amateur dramatics and rode reasonably well.

The marriage was performed by Gerald Wellesley and the Duke gave the bride away. Lord Arthur Hill, who was a nephew of the dowager Lady Salisbury, and Wellington's ADC at Waterloo, was also present.

At the time of this wedding the Duke was in the amiable clutches of Harriet Arbuthnot, who noted in her journal that Wellington spent the evening with the Arbuthnots after the Salisbury wedding, 'Miss Gascoyne a very pretty girl who has £12,000 a year. They say he has married her for her money.' Young 'Fanny' Gascoyne-Cecil produced five children in her first six years of marriage. One child, Arthur George Villiers to whom Wellington stood godfather, died aged sixteen months. They then lived in St James at 21 Hanover Square and in 1827 Fanny decided to start a diary which she kept up until her early death from dropsy twelve years later.

Her smart London society friends included Lady Charlotte Greville, Lady Frances Shelley, Madame de Lieven – all great admirers of the Duke; but she had little time for Harriet Arbuthnot. In her diaries she refers to her husband as Ld. S. and to Wellington simply as 'the Duke' – her husband always called her 'dear Fanny' and after her death 'poor Fanny'. Although the young Salisburys had their social round in London and Hertfordshire – Ascot in June, a cricket festival in August at St Albans, autumn shooting, as well as three grand tours of Europe – they, and particularly, Fanny managed to see the Duke on many occasions. Once Kitty sent her a sepia sketch of La Gitana and El Jovenato of Spanish origin. The Duke became prime minister in January 1828 and Fanny's diary became more politically aware, particularly after their first grand tour which lasted six months and covered many of Europe's capital cities.

The Duke stood godfather to her sixth child, Robert Arthur Talbot born on 3 February 1830. The young couple made their second

European tour that year and the Duke himself showed them the field at Waterloo after he had been defeated in the House of Commons and resigned as prime minister.

Fanny was a beauty, even after the birth of six children, and in 1829 was painted by Sir Thomas Lawrence. A lovely pastel portrait by C. Bartonford, now in the Hatfield House collection, was painted in the same year.

The Duke watched Fanny acting a key role in her amateur dramatics at Hatfield, and visited and stayed at the Gascoyne house at Childwall after the ill-fated opening of the Liverpool and Manchester Railway. From time-to-time he showed her his confidential papers, one about coalition, and which was addressed to the king.

The Duke had now started confiding to Fanny many of his political problems and she wrote them down in some considerable detail in her diary. They lent each other books, 'Have you read Ward on Mexico? and Blaquière's visit to Greece.' They agreed that J.J. Rousseau was a terrible fellow.

A few months after his dismissal from parliament, Kitty died on 24 April 1831 at Apsley House and the London mob stoned and broke the Duke's windows whilst her corpse was lying in the house (discussed fully in Chapter 23). In Hertfordshire the Salisbury's coaches had been pelted with mud and stones and the Duke wrote to Fanny, 'I heard of the row at Hertford, but I did not know that you had been assailed. The miscreants ought to be swept from the face of the earth.'

Certainly, as the Duke had predicted 1831 and 1832 would be gloomy years. The farming workers were desperate and in the north, new industrial machinery was smashed. Riot Acts were read up and down the country.

In the last six years of her short life Fanny moved in far more interesting circles than hitherto. In 1833 she dined at Talleyrand's, now the first ambassador from the citizen-king in Paris. He was now seventy-eight and had turned his coat many times, not only to stay in power, but to save his life. Wellington, of course, had known him well since 1814 although he thought the Princesse de Talleyrand was 'a most silly woman'. Talleyrand had brought with him to London as ambassadress, Dorothea Duchesse de Dino, his nephew's wife, whom Wellington had met at the Congress of Vienna and had commended to King William IV. At dinner Talleyrand spoke to her of the Duke, who was sitting opposite them!

Voila votre Ministre assis à cette table. C'est l'homme du monde qui a le plus

*de droiture dans les sentiments et dans la conduite: j'ai souvent eu des affaires
à conduire avec lui, et je peut l'attester.**

The Duke later told Fanny some amusing anecdotes of Talleyrand's
views about King Charles X and another of the news of Napoleon's
death *'ce n'est plus un evenement – c'est une nouvelle'*.** Wellington always
had a soft spot for Talleyrand, wily, corrupt old rascal that he had always
been. He said to Lady Salisbury that Wellington was *'le seul homme qui
a jamais dit du bien de moi!'**** Wellington always had a caustic tongue
but he recognised brilliant turncoat diplomacy when he saw it!

From 1830 to 1852 each 18 June the Duke held an annual Waterloo
banquet for his senior veteran officers. Fanny made frequent visits to
Apsley House to see the ceremonial plate used for that occasion and to
admire the porcelain, and pictures looted by Joseph Bonaparte, which
the king of Spain asked the Duke to retain. He showed her pictures of
the Duke of Marlborough on horseback, one of Napoleon by Le Fevre,
another of General Schomberg. One room was devoted to portraits of
the Duke's contemporaries painted in the post-Waterloo era including
Lord Beresford and Field Marshal Sir Henry Hardinge.

Many of his campaigns and victories were discussed with the
Salisburys and their friends. He thought that Massena was the best
tactician of Napoleon's generals, that Marmont was clever but not equal
to Massena. 'We thought great things of Suchet and others employed in
the East of Spain.' Other anecdotes concerned the battle of Assaye and
the incapacity of the Spaniards 'No Spaniard ever could learn anything'.

He had many observations to make about his own generals,
particularly Sir Thomas Picton who was 'a very violent vulgar fellow
who blackguarded and abused his troops, but he was a very brave man
and a good soldier', who used to go into battle wearing a top hat under
a spread umbrella! Sir George Murray was an excellent subordinate
officer but not fit to be entrusted with a great command.

He talked to Fanny about his feelings after Assaye 'a confused notion'
that *all* his officers had been killed. Many times he talked to her and her
husband about Waterloo and it was written down in considerable detail
in her journal, often in question and answer form. There is little doubt
that Fanny would have made an excellent wife for a field marshal.

---

* There is your minister sitting at this table. He is the most correct man in the world in
   his feeling and in his conduct: I have often done business with him and I can vouch
   for it.
** It is no longer an event – it is news.
*** The only man who has never spoken well of me.

The Prussians were decidedly beat at Ligny and he could distinctly see their field of battle from the Quatre Bras which was about eight miles off. Napoleon committed a big mistake in not moving his forces by the great road from Mons to Brussels . . . but Napoleon committed mistakes just like other people. The great thing in military affairs is never to make a false step, or to go farther than you ought, especially when you are moving in parallel lines with such a man as Napoleon.

A sentiment with which Bonaparte would have agreed since he greatly admired the Duke's prudence and patience.

On leadership the Duke told Fanny that nothing is so true as the proverb, 'Better an army of stags commanded by a lion, than an army of lions commanded by a stag!' He was talking of the pathetic surrender of good quality British troops in Buenos Aires under the command of General John Whitelocke.

Fanny and her husband stayed frequently at Walmer Castle, one of the Duke's houses after he was made warden of the Cinque Ports in 1829. Often in their walks together she would take the initiative and ask him questions about his campaigns and his views on specific individuals. He told her frankly that he thought the king was parsimonious and the whole of the present royal family more or less tinctured with insanity. The late Duke of York was the best of them, but with much to condemn.

Cumberland was a spendthrift but had lost £25,000 to the late Mr Villiers whose wife he fancied. Lord Londonderry was not to be trusted, he was wicked and deceitful in the highest degree. Lord Holland was one of the worst of the Whigs. Wellington hated meeting the Dukes of Cumberland and Gloucester and Fanny never asked either of them when her favourite Duke was a guest.

He told her that he reckoned men to be generally inferior to women, 'In real and useful information, young men read so as to be fit for the society of women!' Wellington adored her four small, surviving children, and played and talked to them – one of the best ways to a woman's heart. He talked freely to her about some of the other women in his life – Madame de Lieven, Miss Jenkins, Madame de Staël, Lady Jersey, Miss Mary Anne Jervis, Lady Wilton. After the deaths of Harriet Arbuthnot and his wife Kitty, Wellington really unburdened himself; with grief and sorrow about the former and with clinical and remote accuracy about the latter. He talked to her about his sons and his disappointment with them. She did not tell him that Lord Douro had made her a declaration, i.e. a proposal, not however, of marriage. Fanny was consistently critical of Mrs Arbuthnot. She suspected Harriet and Charles of colouring the

Duke's views against Peel. She thought that Charles was 'a very prejudiced though honest man and she received his statements with some allowance' i.e. she did not believe him!

On 9 August 1837 she wrote with glee in her diary 'I told the Duke his marriage was announced *both* with Miss Mary Ann Jervis and with Lady Georgiana Fane to his great amusement.' Fanny noted with dismay the constant efforts of certain ladies to seduce the Duke,

> Provoked at hearing that Maria Tollemache Lady Aylesbury has set about a report that she refused the Duke, before she took her present juvenile spouse . . . It is really too absurd. The Duke scarcely ever spoke to her! Lady Georgiana Fane [Lady Jersey's half-sister] never ceased pouring her eloquence into his ear but it won't do.

The point being that after Kitty's death and then Harriet Arbuthnot's in 1834, the Duke, although aged sixty-five, was the most eligible widower in the country. Famous, wealthy, a well-known lover of the ladies, and free. That summer at Oxford, homage was paid to the 'Deliverer of Europe'. 'I am convinced that if he were to set up his horse like Caligula, the whole town would pay obeisance to it,' wrote Fanny.

On their return from their third grand tour of Europe the Salisbury's dined at Apsley House on the following night, 20 November 1834. He had missed them, particularly Fanny, and six days later he told her so to her face.

> I cannot repeat word for word his kind expressions but they will never be erased from my remembrance. He called me his friend, twice over, with emphasis, as if he would have said 'my first and best friend' and expressed a confidence in me which I feel a gratitude and pleasure I cannot express. 'With you,' he said, 'I think aloud!'

David Wilkie was painting the Duke for the Salisburys, which when finished, Lord Aberdeen thought looked like a Spanish beggarman!

The fund of anecdotes continued. On Portugal, using his inimitable simplicity and bonhomie,

> I found Craddock doing nothing when I came, so I went to Oporto immediately and set things in a train and in a week the French were out of Portugal.

Of George III, Wellington told her,

> he was the best King England ever had, and understood *Kingcraft* the most thoroughly – a far superior man in real ability to his son, though he had not the same quickness and talent. George III, however, had no

scruple in throwing over his friends or his instruments whenever it suited his purpose – in this he resembles Queen Elizabeth.

He spoke of Mrs Fitzherbert to Fanny,

> She was the most impudent devil that ever lived, never handsome in my remembrance and doing everything with an effrontery that supplied the place of cleverness. The Dowager Lady Jersey made the marriage simply because she wished to put Mrs Fitzherbert on the same footing as herself and deprive her of the claim to the title of *lawful* wife to the Prince.

In the summer of 1835 the Duke showed Fanny the laid out table before the Waterloo Dinner and she wrote,

> Very gratifying to see that great man in his advanced age, his white hair and strongly lined features marking indeed his time of life but his eagle eye and commanding aspect still showing all the vigour of youth.

The following day, 19 June at Sion the Duke sat between Fanny and the queen on a beautiful midsummer day at the magnificent fête. She wrote that she had never enjoyed herself more than at that delightful breakfast.

> I had a long walk with the Duke after dinner from about eight till past eleven when we came away with him. His kindness, his expressions of friendship, of real and *friendly* attachment I can never forget. I sometimes think how can I be worthy of the friendship of such a man, what have I done to deserve the highest honour a woman can attain to be *his* friend?

Face to face he called her 'Lady Salisbury' – this was a very friendly and respectable relationship! Fanny was insistent on chaperones on her visits to Walmer or Stratfield Saye.

Fanny met the Wordsworths,

> Look like patterns of patriarchal old age with their simple dress and manners, no pretension to what they are not. No attempt to disguise their age, or to make effect.

She met Pozzo di Borgo, the Russian ambassador, Prince Paul Esterhazy, the Austrian ambassador Comte François Sebastiani, the French ambassador Marshal Soult. Her elevation into the very top ranks of society was entirely due to her friendship with the Duke. During the period after Harriet Arbuthnot's death, 1834 to late August 1839 she saw the Duke at least three times a week and for longer when she stayed at Walmer and Stratfield Saye with her children.

She described the Duke's daily life in the country,

Nothing can be more quiet or less exciting than his life here. He gets up early, breakfasts before ten, goes to his room to read and answer letters till luncheontime, never eats more than a jelly or a biscuit, often nothing. I walk or ride with him for an hour or two. We dined at 7 and sat until half past eleven. Twice a week he is out with the harriers. He never seems absent or bored, always gay, cheerful, extracts amusement from everything even the most absolute trifles. His mind is always energetic, never feels low spirits or ennui.

Each year on 10 February the Duke bought Fanny a gift, once it was an elaborate gold charm.

After a long stay in summer at Walmer in 1837, Fanny received an anonymous letter, and shortly afterwards the Duke also received one written in the same hand. Both implied that their friendship was not a proper relationship. One possibility was that the author of the letters was Mary Ann Jervis, daughter of Lord St Vincent, nicknamed by the Duke 'The Syren' who was evidently besotted with him. Another more likely candidate was Charles Greville the diarist who had definitely sent unpleasant anonymous letters to Harriet Arbuthnot and the Duke as far back as 1824. As a result, Wellington warned Lady Salisbury,

> I shall be delighted to see you at Walmer with all your children. But I strongly recommend you not to come without Lord Salisbury. One would suppose that you might hope to go through the world without giving reason for scandal, and that I am beyond the age to afford any ground for it, but it is not so. There was plenty of it last year.

Fanny's diary continues into the late summer of 1837. Her life was one of undiminished gaiety. She hosted parties for 600 guests. She went to the grand dinner ball and assembly at Count Stroganoff's, to a ball given by the Duchess of Gloucester, another in honour of Marshal Soult. She visited the House of Lords to hear the Duke speak. Fanny dined at Lord Londonderry's with four ambassadors, the Duke *and* Peel together. She danced at the queen's ball, at the Duchess of Cambridge's Ball, at the Duchess of Buccleuch's breakfast and went to see the National Gallery. On most of these occasions she went with the Duke, or else he was there already. She saw him practically every day now, perhaps prescient, for she fell ill in August and died on 14 October.

The Duke went into mourning and sealed his letters with black wax. Three weeks later he was found speechless and temporarily blind on the floor of his study at Walmer Castle.

Fanny was only thirty-seven and it was inconceivable that his best friend should be wafted away so quickly and cruelly. But the Duke's

Fanny, Lady Salisbury – the Gascoyne heiress who wrote 'what have I done to deserve the highest honour a woman can attain – to be his friend?'

Lady Sarah Sophia Villiers, née Fane, Countess of Jersey, a beautiful, rich, garrulous lady, nicknamed 'Silence', 'our Sally', 'the Jewel', 'Queen Mab', 'Queen Willis of Almacks', who adored the Duke and pursued him all her adult life, perhaps with some success.

Mary Egerton, née Stanley, Countess of Wilton, a cold beauty, and the Duke's confidante for nearly 20 years. 'I hope that you consider me as your best friend,' he wrote.

Angela Burdett-Coutts, handsome rich philanthropist, known as the 'Queen of the Poor'. She was 45 years younger than the Duke and proposed marriage to him. He regarded himself as 'her Friend, Guardian and Protector' which made Charles Dickens very jealous.

involvement with the Salisbury family was not ended in the autumn of 1839.

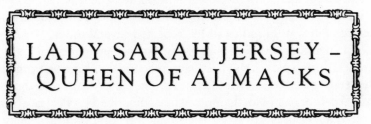

Chapter Twenty-Two

LADY SARAH JERSEY – QUEEN OF ALMACKS

One family in particular – the Fanes – appear and re-appear in the Duke's life. John Fane, 10th Earl of Westmorland, Harriet Arbuthnot, née Fane, Lady Sarah Sophia Villiers, née Fane and Lady Georgiana Fane were integral members of the Duke's circle. The three ladies (the last two were half-sisters) were unanimous in their love and admiration for the Duke. Lady Georgiana pursued him remorselessly all her life and preferred to die a spinster if she could not marry him. The other two were almost certainly more successful in their pursuit, although marriage was never on the cards for a variety of reasons.

Lady Sarah Sophia Fane was born in 1785, a daughter of John Fane, Lord Westmorland, and Anne Child (daughter and sole heiress of Robert Child, the banker), and she married George Villiers in 1804, who became the Earl of Jersey, and lived at Osterley Park. She was a beautiful woman courted by many men and she might well have married Lord Granville, afterwards ambassador in Paris. George Villiers was a roué and had many love affairs, particularly with Lady Foley and Princess Pauline Borghese. Lady Jersey put on a brave face in the situation and boasted 'I am proud of being the only woman whose husband has a great many female friends.' To which Emily, Lady Cowper, riposted, 'Lady J was being dangerous and perhaps ill-judged in her speech.' She was a strong Tory, always garrulous, and a very rich woman who controlled Child's Bank.

Lady Sarah Fane in February 1802 was described by Lady Bessborough as, looking in great Beauty this year but I am more inclined than ever to believe that she has a strong Partiality for Villiers which he endeavours to confirm by much attention. She is not yet presented but she is generally at the Opera with Lady Westmoreland.

She was nicknamed 'our Sally' by the Devonshire family, who thought their son Granville Leveson-Gower fancied her; she was also known as 'The Jewel'. Her chatterbox habits were soon noticed by society. One pet expression was 'Goodness Me!' repeated several times.

She and her husband were in Paris during the Occupation of 1814 and in Brussels during part of the 100 Days, meeting the Duke on both visits.

The Jersey's seat was at Middleton Park in Oxfordshire and the Fanes lived at Apethorpe in Northamptonshire, described by Peel as absolute misery. Both houses attracted the 'haut ton' of London society for weekend parties and the hunting and shooting. Lady Duncannon of Roehampton was one of Lady Jersey's sisters. Thomas Creevey stayed often at Middleton.

> Shall I tell you what Lady Jersey is like? [he noted in 1829] She is like one of her numerous gold and silver musical dickey birds that are in all the shew [sic] rooms of this house. She begins to sing at eleven o'clock and then she retires to her cage to rest. She sings till 12 at night without a moments interruption. [One of her nicknames was SILENCE!] She changes her feathers for dinner and her plumage both morning and evening, and is the happiest and most beautiful bird I ever saw.

She was described as a tragedy queen, sometimes rude, sometimes ill-bred. Henry Brougham MP, later Baron Brougham and Vaux, who knew her well, described her great influence in society as 'always honestly and heartily exerted with her usual excellence of disposition.'

She was one of the most controversial ladies in society. Her nicknames included that of Sally (by Greville and Creevey, both of whom referred to the Duke in the same breath as the Beau), Queen Mab and Queen Willis (Mr Willis was the guardian of Almacks club). By unanimous choice Lady Jersey was the most powerful patron of Almacks in St James. During 1814 as peace was declared the 'beau ton' celebrated by forming a more or less exclusive club, where admission was by special ticket. There were twelve subscription balls during the season and tickets for those allowed to enter cost ten guineas each. There were very strict rules for dress and etiquette, once the Duke was forbidden entry because he was wearing black 'trowsers', and men could only wear knee-breeches. He several times tried to get the wild young Lady Caroline Lamb elected but each time she was blackballed by 'Queen Mab'. The other patrons were

Corisande, Countess of Tankerville; Mary Isabel, Duchess of Rutland; Emily, Lady Castlereagh (wife of the then Foreign Secretary); and Emily, Lady Cowper. Eventually other patron ladies elected included Lady Willoughby and Lady Sefton and the two celebrated foreigners, Countess Lieven and Princess Esterhazy.

All the prettiest girls in England came to Almacks, provided they had tickets and were not blackballed. Baron Decker wrote after a visit, 'What beautiful womens! I have not see such fine things in all my life. I shall not *sleep* tonight!'

The fashions of the moment were to be seen there. After Wellington's victories the so-called Vittoria bodice was worn made of Sierra Leone blue satin, piped and slashed with white. After Waterloo the girls were dressed in caps and flowers with a chip straw hat at the back of the head, scarlet bodices and white petticoats trimmed with scarlet ribbons and flowers – quite entrancing. When Sarah Sophia's father was Lord Lieutenant of Ireland in 1790–5 she met his ADC George Villiers and subsequently married him. She also met Captain, then Major, then Colonel Arthur Wesley when she was a child and subsequently on his return as a Sepoy General, wished she had married *him*! For over twenty years they saw each other frequently and wrote to each other. She did not keep a diary or journal and the Duke, as was his custom, destroyed all her letters to him. Two batches of his letters to Lady Jersey still exist. At first glance one might imagine that their relationship was similar to that of several other elegant married ladies – distant and discreet. But there are a number of remarkable viewpoints and vignettes which indicate a more passionate attachment.

Lady Jersey entertained every week – usually a big dinner, perhaps a ball, often on a Thursday. There one might find the emperor of Russia who would waltz with her, or old Marshal Blücher 'a very nice old man' talking gutterally to her in fractured French. One of her many controversial friends was Lord Byron, whom the Duke could not stand (it was mutual). Lady Jersey had been a great favourite of the Prince of Wales until the time she met the young Lord Byron and encouraged him to come to her weekly routs, and was seen to favour him. She stood by him loyally during the scandal in 1816 of his marriage separation. Byron first met Madame de Staël at Lady Jersey's whose wit and kindness to both of them was well known in society. He wrote of his patron,

The veriest Tyrant that ever governed Fashions fools and compelled them to shake their caps and bells as she willed it.

From time to time the Duke wrote of Lady Jersey to his friends. Since they rarely liked Queen Mab he was usually on the defensive!

> Lady Jersey is a foolish, vain selfish woman but she has one merit and that
> in my eyes is a very great one – attachment to her children. I never go to
> see her unless she sends for me – I am always good friends with her in
> public. I always have some joke with which I attack her and never give her
> an opportunity to begin her grievances.

Sarah Sophia had two sons, both pages to the king, and two daughters.
The Duke was a godfather to one daughter.

On the other hand Charles Greville, that shrewd observer, noted that
she told Lord Granville (Harriet's husband) that 'she made it a rule
never to talk to the Duke about affairs in publick'. He went on to say that
'she contrives to make the D. see a great deal of her for he calls on her
and writes to her perpetually, but I doubt whether he tells her much of
anything.'

In correspondence with Mrs Arbuthnot, and indeed with Lady
Shelley, the Duke's nickname for Lady Jersey was either Queen Mab or
Queen Willis. He was known to both ladies as the 'Slave' and he was
amused by these beautiful ladies wrangling and sometimes squabbling
over him. He once wrote, 'I hope that Lady Shelley and Queen Willis
may not meet in a *small* town. I should like to witness the first meeting.
Certainly in 1816 he considered them both as prime contenders for his
favours.

Greville has the best description of the 'Silence'.

> Lady Jersey is an extraordinary woman and has many good qualities:
> surrounded as she is by flatterers and admirers she is neither proud, vain
> or conceited. She is full of vivacity spirit and good nature, but the wide
> range of her sympathies and affections, proves that she has more general
> benevolence than particular sensibility in her character. She is deficient in
> passion and softness (which constitutes the greatest charm in women) so
> that she excites more of admiration than of interest in conversation. She
> is lively and pleasant without being remarkable for she has neither wit,
> nor imagination nor humour. She has a retentive memory, restless mind
> and judgement warped by prejudice!

But Charles Greville was a great troublemaker and cynic. Later on in his
diaries he plays one attractive woman off against another.

> Lady Sarah Sophia Jersey makes herself supremely ridiculous by affecting
> great intimacy with the Duke and insinuating that he tells her everything,
> whereas I believe he tells her nothing at all. I have taken care to prejudice
> Mrs Arbuthnot against her (Lady Jersey) by representing her imprudence

and vanity in such strong terms as will be sure to make her for every reason do all she can to keep the Duke from telling her anything: The fact is she is very false and dangerous and to enhance her own merit with the Duke she tells him all sorts of lies of other people.

Queen Mab was described by Harriet Granville as,

> a noble, innocent unsuspecting creature and I love her quite. She gives life to society and everything is more sprack and we are all much better for her presence – it says 'up and doing' she shocks and revives us with her black hair and coral beads.

An amusing anecdote sums up their relationship. Letters were exchanged daily:

> 'My dear Arthur, The Emperor Nicholas is coming to visit me. How shall I receive him? S. Jersey.'
> 'My dear Sarah, Receive him as you do your other visitors. Wn.'
> 'My dear Arthur, But he loves me! S. Jersey'
> 'My dear Sarah, Receive him as you do your other lovers. Wn.'

All society was in Brighton in March 1823. Clever Emily Cowper and pushy Sarah Sophia were friends but at the same time rivals in society – both being patrons of Almacks. Lady Cowper wrote,

> . . . Lady Jersey thinks no more of politics – all her thoughts are how to catch the Duke – all ambition and yet as eager as if it were love. He gave her a fine diamond ring which she wears constantly on her finger or neck. He is delighted and laughs at it and at her. She is always saying 'Not at Home' to others when he calls; '*pardi cette femme, elle m'affiche*'. We call her La Comtesse Silence behind her back.

The love of children by 'Silence' and the Duke was noticed in July 1829 when the two of them plus Lady Grey took a party of thirty small children to Astleys Theatre to see a performance of the *Battle of Waterloo*.

Fanny Lady Salisbury once reproached the Duke thus 'The Whigs always accuse you that you used to tell Lady Jersey everything and show her State Papers', to which the Duke answered 'I never told her anything!' Philipp von Neumann, an Austrian diplomat, saw a good deal of the Duke and Lady Jersey together in the period 1820–1830. He commented how, by a great effort, she abstained from discussing politics at table with the Duke 'and this was a victory for the Duke not less honourable than many others.' (October 1820). She asked him in 1828 about Madame de Lieven's influence on the Duke and the next year she talked a great deal about the Duke who saw her frequently 'which gave rise to much conversation.'

When the Jerseys toured Europe after Waterloo they came back via Paris where the Duke met them in June 1817. Harriet Granville described them.

> Lady Jersey is very kind, cordial and amiable, looks very handsome, though she is tanned almost purple (her nickname is Indefatigable Silence). She is all over Paris, at all les petites soirées and great routes. They return to London tomorrow. If I was handsome [Harriet was plain, jolly and intelligent] and he not frivolous we should certainly have a little affair together.

Lady Jersey took back the favourite European quadrille to London for the members of Brooks and Boodles to dance at Almacks.

Like most of the Duke's lady friends Lady Jersey had strong political viewpoints. Here is a description of her after a violent discussion in 1818,

> She sits netting and raving, is too absorbed to think who is for or who is against. Her countenance is become so stern and political that it effects her beauty.

Philipp von Neumann said that she was the only woman in England who could cry and still remain beautiful.

The affair of the disreputable Queen Caroline divided London. She had returned to England in 1820 and the Duke was violently against her. Lady Jersey incurred the king's and the Duke's displeasure by openly visiting and welcoming the queen back. A commission had been sent to Milan in 1818 to collect evidence of the queen's infidelity and the report was published in the summer of 1819.

The next year, although the Duke's passion for Mrs Patterson was still very strong, he confided to Madame Lieven on 1 July 1821, 'It is true that I *have a sort of tenderness for Lady Jersey*. So that I am not an impartial judge where she is concerned.'

Fortunately a dozen letters exist of the Duke's to Lady Jersey in the year 1821 in which he sent her daily news bulletins of the illness of Georgina, Marchioness of Worcester, who was dying. He several times asked if he could come and see Lady Jersey and the Duke sent her four tickets for a box to see King George IV being crowned on 19 July. He apologised for his tactless remarks about Queen Caroline's 'ticket' to the coronation. The Duke called to see her new portrait by Thomas Lawrence (27 July).

In September the Duke was in Brussels and who should be there, on the 27th, but Lady Jersey being 'outrageous about a Mr Wilson' (who caused a disturbance at the Queen's funeral) as indeed was Lady Charlotte Greville. They all dined with the king on the evening of the 28th, 'he was very blackguard and entertaining.'

Madame de Lieven was accepted by Lady Jersey as a patroness at Almacks. She wrote in her secret diary on 16 July 1821,

> When Madame de Staël came here, I saw Lady Jersey *and* Lady Hertford get up on their chairs to applaud her. A similar honour has been accorded to me too: but that was because they thought a Russian partook somewhat of the Bear!

But the next month on 19 August at the queen's trial,

> Lady Jersey has become so violent that she is at daggers drawn even with the Holland family. Poor woman she is quite frenzied – she ought to go out and cool herself off in the rain!

Dorothea Lieven had been made a princess that year at the coronation of the new Tsar. It was reported by Harriet Arbuthnot with glee that Lady Jersey was beside herself with rage at this promotion. On the Almacks' committee she had been outranked by Princess Esterhazy, but now there was a second foreign princess to contend with.

Once the Duke borrowed from Lady Jersey a recommended reading list prepared by her son's tutor which he could then apply for the benefit of his two growing sons, Lord Douro and Charles. In the same year Lady Jersey, a frequent visitor to Stratfield Saye, bribed the groom to procure for her some of Copenhagen's hair (the Duke's elderly, but famous charger) in order to have a special bracelet made for herself. Fanny Salisbury went on to say that,

> Queen Mab set the bracelet with jewels lying at some jewellers and professing to be given to her [Lady J] by the Duke. I hope this woman will not succeed in throwing ridicule upon him by persuading the world he is at her feet.

He kept her informed of his political activities, particularly of his support for Prince Polignac in France, which was considered in England to be a plot 'by Wellington and Metternich.' When the Duke fought his dual with Lord Winchelsea a cruel diarist noted that, 'Lady Jersey had been very ridiculous affecting nervousness and fine feelings in case he had been injured.' At least half-a-dozen handsome matrons were equally distraught!

The influence that Lady Jersey had with the Duke is evident when Madame de Coigny wrote from Aix-la-Chapelle to Lady Jersey asking her to persuade the Duke to visit her on his way to the Congress of Vienna. She was always an outspoken lady and frequently unpopular at court. 'Why should we have Germans to rule over us?' she cried out at a party attended by many courtiers on the accession of George IV. She had been an intimate friend of Princess Charlotte, Queen Caroline's only child, born in April 1795.

Wellington had many strange alliances. Lady Jersey, Lady Cowper, Madame Lieven and Lady Granville were a group of influential ladies who not only admired him but were more or less unanimous in their hostility to Harriet Arbuthnot and her close supporter Lady Shelley. Mrs Arbuthnot's private diary for 25 June 1826 is quite specific,

> The Duke dined with me yesterday at 5 o'clock and we went afterwards and rowed about on the lake til half past nine at night. It was quite delightful and I enjoyed it excessively. General Alava called on me this morning and I told him I had been on the water with the Duke. He said, '*Voila, ce qui enrage toutes les dames: il ne veut aller qu'avec vous.*'* He then told me that Lady Jersey was always questioning him as to whether the Duke came here much and whether the Duke was in *love with me*! Alava told me he always assured her that it was, '*la liaison la plus pure au monde, car je connois l'homme et je sais qui s'étoit son amant, il là quitteroit au bout de trois mois: c'est l'amitie toute pure, et j'en suis enchanté, car cela le rend parfaitement heureux*'.** I told Alava I was delighted that he did me justice, but I do think it is a great scandal that Lady Jersey should go and pump Alava in this matter. He is the merest *sieve* in all London and would certainly tell anything he knew, but it is no concern of hers. The Duke's friendship for me and Mr A. has just been what it now is for the last ten years and unless she wants the Duke as a lover herself (which I suspect she does) it can be no concern of hers. It makes me most uncommonly angry. I am going with the Duke to dine at Greenwich on Wednesday with a large party which I suppose will be another offence for I shall certainly *not* ask *her*.

Lady Elizabeth Holland was a noted observer of Lady Jersey's idiosyncracies and her diaries have many comments.

> Lady Jersey is in Town (1823) more agreeable than she had been for years, *talkative* as you might suppose, but not tedious in her politics. She

* That is what makes all the ladies furious: he only wants to go with you.
** ... the purest relationship in the world, for I know the man and I know who is his love, he will leave her after three months: it's pure friendship and I'm delighted with it for it makes him perfectly happy.

took a turn at the Tithes and Corn Bills but she was soon turned from those to some more feminine topics. She is by way of being in devotion on Sundays, only dining out but not going to Assemblies, but receiving at her house.

After the Newmarket race meeting Lady Jersey tried to get the Sunday racing stopped which was an unpopular move, but she never courted popularity. Lady Holland called her 'a Virago in these political tribes.' The Hollands thought that they were *above* politics! She noticed after Wellington's grave illness, on 9 March 1832,

> the Duke has never recovered his temper since his illness, so that even his warmest private friends are less at their ease with him than formerly. You know that he never goes near Lady Jersey now, a complete alienation.

Harriet Arbuthnot in 1825 described Lady Jersey,

> She is the vainest and most arrogant woman in London, thinks everybody who speaks to her is in love with her and is furious because she has never been able to get the Duke of Wellington into her clutches. He does not care a pin about her and she is continually crying and making complaints of his cruelty to her and writing notes to him which put her completely in his power if he really cared for her and chose to make love to her. She sets up for being the most virtuous woman in England, whereas she has only the good luck to have set her heart on the only man in the Kingdom probably who would reject her advances. She has told him repeatedly, if she had made half the advances to any other man, they would have been at her feet. I do not really believe she means harm by all her nonsense but her vanity is so excessive she cannot bear that any body should be able to resist her.

In fact Lady Jersey flirted nearly as much with Lord Palmerston (Henry John Temple) as she did with Arthur Wellesley.

During his long life the Duke kept several intimate relationships in play at the same time without embarrassment and apart from the sad event when Mary Ann Patterson married his brother in 1825, his record was extraordinary. But in the summer of 1827 he was caught out! Mrs A. wrote to her friend Lady S.

> I did not know the Duke had been so sly about his visit to Lady Jersey, but I am greatly amused at your not daring to quiz him. I did not think you have been so shy! especially with him!

Mrs A. was a bold Tyrant who was confident of her 'slave'. 'We had the Jerseys, she always makes up prodigiously to the Duke and more than ever now that she is on the same side in politics.' Her next comment in the diary demonstrates her power. 'I was very forbearing or rash to let Lady Jersey have *"champ libre"* for two whole days.' That was at Stratfield Saye on 20 November 1827, but then she adds rather sadly,

> I do not know that any of the ladies make love to his Grace. I think he makes more love now to his letters and the newspapers than to anyone else. [And the next year] He goes to the Treasury at noon, doing business till five, going to the House of Lords, dining – generally at dull places he don't care about, then reading and writing papers till he goes to bed: What a life!

There is little doubt that Harriet's strange hold on the Duke was not as complete as she considered it to be. Viscount Palmerston wrote to his brother William Temple then charge d'affaires at St Petersburgh, two years after the Duke's mission to see the new tsar,

> The Duke now is very anxious to break with Russia. A great many things have contributed to set him against the Lievens. Mrs Arbuthnot *and* Lady Jersey (*who both have influence over him*) hate Princess Lieven . . .

In the same month of April 1828, Lord William Russell wrote to his wife,

> Lady Jersey has another girl which she wanted and the Duke of Wellington *will be the first person to see her as soon as she sees anybody*. With premiers and pretty children at command what else can she desire?

But that summer Harriet noted rather smugly 'Lady Jersey did not make her usual set at the Duke.' Occasionally the Duke was provoked by La Tyranna into a rage – a real Irish paddy. In November she recorded,

> I alluded to Lady Jersey. He fancies that he picks her brains, gets everything about her party out of her and gives her nothing in return: while on the contrary, she is sharp enough to tell him only what she chooses and she catches at every indiscreet word he utters and repeats it to all her Whig friends. My alluding to it however put him into a great fury . . .

After he had been premier for nearly a hundred days both Mrs Arbuthnot and Lady Jersey (separately) asked him in 1830 anxiously whether he would have to resign. He had just made a strong conservative but provocative speech in parliament. Ever an optimist he replied to Lady Jersey's question 'Lord, I shall not go out, you will see, we shall go on very well!' But to no avail, he and his ministers were forced out a week or so later.

Many times in the thirties the Duke met Lady Jersey at dinners and balls. Once they both dined at Lady Warwick's and she told him that the king had asked her about her social life. Did she go out much to balls and parties? She told the king in June 1831 that 'people were so alarmed and displeased with the new Measures and Laws that they did not give Parties any longer', which of course was not true. About this time many people including Mrs Arbuthnot, Lady Shelley and Creevey noticed how ill the Duke appeared to be.

> I thought the Beau looked horridly at the Levée but his uniform of the Blues plays the devil with him, he should be always in red.

There is a story that he attended her birthday party and had forgotten to buy her a present. At the last moment he collected one of her Meissen figures from her ante-room and presented it to her with aplomb. 'My dear Duke,' she exclaimed, 'how charming! *Exactly* matches one I've got in the outer drawing room.'

Letters still exist of their correspondence in 1832 – about the gloomy political prospects ahead. There is also a batch for 1835 from the Duke commenting about the Irish representative peer's advice to her for Lord Villiers, her son, over the Weymouth parliamentary seat; and he promises to ask Sir Robert Peel for help on behalf of the young man; there is also a long letter surmising the causes of the fire that killed the dowager Lady Salisbury and destroyed half of Hatfield House.

1834 was an eventful year for the Duke. He was made chancellor of Oxford University, a splendid occasion attended by most of his admirers, each anxious to prevent Mrs Arbuthnot or Madame de Lieven from taking too much of the limelight. In the summer Lord Grey resigned and Melbourne came in. At the end of the year King William IV invited Wellington to form his second government. One weekend at Belvoir, seat of the Dukes of Rutland and the cabal of Lady Brownlow, Mrs Arbuthnot, Mademoiselle Este and Lady Manners were gathered together in Fanny Salisbury's room to discuss the latest scandal.

> According to their separate accounts there must be an amusing 'carte du pays' to examine here. Queen Mab's visit to Stratfield Saye has evidently excited great conjectures and hopes appear to be universally entertained of the downfall of the Regnante who is not popular. I do not believe in a change of dynasty – besides the Duke told me Queen Mab's coming to S-S entirely at her own invitation.

This gossip can be interpreted either that Lady Jersey was supplanting

Mrs Arbuthnot as the Duke's favourite, or telling him of her plans to supplant Lady Conyngham as the king's favourite! The conspirators all agreed that Lady Jersey, given half a chance, haunted Stratfield Saye to see the Duke. Certainly the Duke attended a party at Lady Jersey's on 11 July of that year.

> Every creature that had a possibility of coming there in the hopes of hearing some news of a new government. Lady Jersey and Harriet Arbuthnot were devoted to political intrigue, but the latter died tragically and quickly late in July.

During the autumn of 1835 the Duke had rather cautiously invited Queen Adelaide to Stratfield Saye. He knew that his friends considered it an inadequate house by their standards. Peel was scathing.

> The house is a wretched one, wretchedly furnished but warm and not uncomfortable. The drawing room very small and very low, but a handsome library.

There was a billiard room, a tennis court and white violets growing in the park. Fanny Salisbury and the Jerseys were present,

> Lady Jersey never left [the Queen] for a single moment when she could avoid it and talked incessantly. I wonder if the Queen liked it: they say she is jealous of her.

At night Lady Jersey talked all dinner time and all the evening, but Fanny was the only permanent listener. The four men [the Duke, Salisbury, Jersey and Lord Rosslyn] took it in turns to go to sleep.

At the end of 1845 there was a scandal in the Jersey family. The Duke wrote a letter on 17 November to Lady Wilton.

> Horrible Event in the Jersey family, elopement of Lady Corisande Child-Villiers from Brighton [Jersey's youngest daughter]. Eloped with a Captain Ibbetson of the 11th Hussars, married at Gretna Green. The Father, Mother and whole Family are in Despair and very reasonably. I think it is altogether the worst Affair of the kind that has ever come under my observation. I asked if he had danced with her at Almacks or anywhere? They all answer No. He lived in a house near Lady Jersey's – through a Sea Spying Glass fixed on it he made Signals from His Window and Verandah, etc

At one of her weekend parties the Duke came to dine looking well but thin. One of Lady Jersey's guests complained that she tried to make him talk on military discipline on which, he had clear, sound but peculiar notions, but he preferred telling gossiping stories to the ladies, probably as a délassement after his political labours.

On another occasion at a large formal dinner given by the Duke of Beaufort for the visit of the king of Holland on 2 August 1845, according to precedence Wellington was to take Lady Coddington (a duke's daughter) to dinner. As he held her by the arm, up rushed Lady Jersey, shoved the unfortunate Lady Coddington aside and grabbed the Duke's arm, saying, 'Which will you like to take in?' Very gravely he unhanded Lady J and kept to his 'destined' lady without saying a word. As Lady Holland said as she witnessed this little scene 'Lady J is really too impudent and gushing'.

At the Great Exhibition in 1851 the Duke made a point of showing Lady Jersey round and gave her dinner afterwards. Just before his death he was present at the wedding of his godchild, Lady Jersey's youngest daughter, Lady Clementina Augusta *Wellington* Villiers on 13 July 1852. This was a fitting end to almost sixty years of love and friendship.

Perhaps they were lovers in their younger days and there are many clues to suggest they were. It is a pity that the hundreds of letters that the Beau wrote to her have not survived. She was one of the great eccentrics of the age, with dazzling beauty and character. She made no secret of the fact, nor tried to dissimulate her love for Wellington.

Chapter Twenty-Three

KITTY –
THE MARRIAGE
THAT FAILED

A grateful nation had voted funds to the conqueror of Europe in order to purchase a *suitable* residence. An architect Benjamin Wyatt, once Wellington's clerk in India, had been hired and briefed to find and then negotiate for an appropriate country house. Wyatt started work in 1816 when his master was with his army HQ at Mont-St-Martin, attended by the Caton girls, Lady Charlotte Greville and Lady Shelley. In July 1817 Stratfield Saye House in Hampshire was approved and the nation purchased it for £263,000 and presented it to Wellington at the end of 1817.

Kitty made it her home for the rest of her life. There she brought up the two sons Arthur Wellesley, Lord Douro and Charles the younger son. Mrs Elizabeth Apostles was the faithful housekeeper and Algernon Greville, the Duke's secretary, was based there. Samuel Briscall was the domestic chaplain, one of nine at Waterloo and who, as local curate, preached until 1836. Mr John Payne (a rascal) was the estate manager. A fat man called Philips was the Duke's butler. Philipp von Neumann, the Austrian diplomat, who knew Wellington well and visited the house wrote of it,

> The house is not comfortable, the park ugly, the living mediocre, the whole indicating the lack of sympathy existing between the Duke and Duchess. Wellington a man of most simple amiable character and one possessing all the qualities which contrast so vividly with those that have rendered him immortal.

To do Kitty justice, by her standards she tried very hard. From 4 Hamilton Place, she wrote to her husband on 13 June 1814. The boys were now seven and six, their absent father nearly forty-six and Kitty's hair was getting grey. (Subsequently her husband advised her to buy a wig.)

> My dearest Arthur. I have received your letter of the 26th from Madrid in which you permit me to decide for myself with respect to accompanying you to Paris, or not, from the moment I heard of your acceptance of the appointment I had no other thought than that of going with you . . . I have no hesitation in deciding to go, no other wish than to go. I think, with you, that *your* task is a most arduous one attended with, what to many people would appear extreme difficulties, but to an Ambassador's Wife there are no difficulties which I do not feel myself equal to overcome, no duties which I am not willing to perform and I may venture to add that you shall *never* have reason to regret having allowed me on this subject to decide for myself!

Despite these fine words she was desolate at leaving her boys behind.

That October she went to Paris and tried her best to be wife to the gadding ambassador. In early October 1814, Lady Elizabeth York wrote,

The Duchess of Wellington has arrived to take her station here. Her appearance unfortunately does not correspond with one's notion of an Ambassadress or the wife of a hero but she succeeds uncommonly well in her part and takes all proper pains to make herself and her parties agreeable.

In November she took guests to the opera, gave a ball on the 18th and a concert on the 24th. She did try hard to be a duchess! She wore instead of her little-girl muslin dresses, fashions more appropriate to her new station. Maria Edgeworth, her cousin and closest friend, was dowdy by nature, and to the pair of them clothes were not important – it was the mind that counted. A verse in doggerel composed by Kitty survived on the subject.

> The French petits-maîtres who the spectacle throng
> Say of Wellington's dress, *Qu'il fait Vilain ton?*
> But at Waterloo Wellington made the French stare
> When their army he dressed *à la mode d'Angleterre!*

Kitty was introduced to Madame de Staël, she was presented to the tsar of Russia, not by her husband, but by the Prince of Orange. Wellington had already presented his pretty ADC Lady Shelley to the tsar! Kitty was not too short-sighted to see La Grassini on her husband's arm, as well as a duchesse or two. At the beginning of the 100 Days she was back in England while her husband left Vienna for Brussels to prepare for his final battle. Meanwhile Kitty had to face up to the loss of her favourite brother, Sir Edward Packenham, killed at the pointless battle of New Orleans. His loss was felt just as deeply by the Duke. 'Ned' had been a close friend and one of his most reliable and bravest divisional commanders.

Kitty confided in Walter Scott; 'she was impressed with a presentiment almost to superstition that whenever her husband met Buonaporte he would destroy him at ONE blow!'

It was not till 17 October 1815 that the Duke wrote to Kitty to tell her that he could now receive her in Paris. Wellington was enjoying himself to the hilt. Problems were for solving. The problems of Napoleon, of King Louis XVIII, of Fouché, of his old colleague-in-arms Marshal Blücher (and his marauding freebooters) and finally of his old adversary, now turncoat, Marshal Ney. The galaxy of glorious women – the spoils of war – quite overawed the delicate little Irish lady with pink round cheeks, no make-up and unsoignée hair.

The Wedderburn-Webster 'crim. con' case was in the news that autumn and Maria Edgeworth wrote of Kitty,

She is not a woman who delights in titles or rank, but she does enjoy her husband's glory and therefore I hope it will not, like Nelson's, be tarnished.

Kitty was reportedly seen at the opera in a gown shimmering with humming-birds' feathers. This was such an unlikely event that Kitty wrote to Maria:

I do not possess any orna-ments of feathers – Do you recollect on a former occasion your telling me of my having appeared (in the newspaper) blazing with diamonds – my diamonds are yet in the mine and my humming-birds wear their own feathers!

Wellington expected his beautiful women to take pains over their toilette. Kitty's view was the opposite. She was once asked:

'My dear Lady Wellington, how many times a day do you think of changing your dress?'

'Why three times, morning, evening and night besides *casualties*.'

During the summer of 1816 Wellington left Paris to visit Cheltenham to take the waters and was joined there by Kitty and the two boys. For a week or so they were a united happy family. As they sipped spa water at the Well Walk, Kitty wrote to the two ladies at Llangollen (Lady Eleanor Butler and Miss Sarah Ponsonby, the 'most celebrated virgins in Europe'.)

He for whom all the world is so justly anxious is considerably better, both in looks and spirits since his arrival in England. I think I perceive an amendment every day. This happens to be the time of the holidays of our Boys and I say with delight they are as fond of and as familiar with their noble and beloved Father as if they had never been separated from him. They accompany him in his walks, chat with him, play with him, in short they are the chosen companions of each other.

It must have been one of the happiest times in Kitty's life since family reunions were to become very rare from now on.

Kitty visited her husband at Cambray during the autumn of 1817 for a few weeks and she returned for the move into Stratfield Saye. After the attempt on his life in Paris in February 1818 Kitty had written to her brother-in-law Richard,

Thank God, thank God, my dear Lord Wellesley, my Husband is perfectly safe but his life has been attempted as he returned home at his own door, a pistol was fired at him . . . he still continued the special charge of Heaven tho' so close he was not touched.

The next month the superb London mansion at Apsley House overlooking Hyde Park was purchased from Richard Wellesley by his brother for £42,000. It soon became more of a museum than anything else, crammed full of glorious portraits (from Spain), a silver dinner service (from Portugal) Canova's statue of Napoleon (from the Prince Regent), Berlin china (from Prussia) and hundreds of other trophies.

Kitty called for the first time at Apsley House on St Patrick's Day 1819. Lord William Lennox described her as 'amiable, unaffected and simple minded, also generous and charitable'. More or less as Arthur Wesley had seen her in Dublin many years ago. Those qualities may have been desirable to a naïve young army captain, but they were certainly totally inadequate for the middle-aged field marshal.

For the next few years their relationship, tenuous at best, deteriorated rapidly. He was unable to accept criticism, well-founded or not;

> You and your family have complained of my conduct towards you without Reason – your whole conduct is one of watching and spying on me, you have employed my own Servants in doing so. I really don't believe you have any Good Intention. But every day's experience convinces me that you do more foolish things – which you must regret – upon the first moment of Reflection than any woman in the world (19 April 1830).

Kitty then accused him of lack of charity and sent him a list of people for his alms. In fact the Duke was very generous indeed, but this was the last straw 'If it goes on I must live somewhere else.' In fact he now rarely lived at Stratfield Saye. He had Apsley House at the centre of London, with society, the Horse Guards and parliament on his doorstep and by now he had a wide range of country houses where he went at weekends to hunt, shoot, flirt and discuss politics. He was welcome at the Salisbury's, the Shelley's, the Arbuthnot's, at the Lieven's and many others. Lady Charlotte Greville, Lady Jersey and occasionally Mrs Patterson made him welcome. There was little *need* for him to visit Kitty. Occasionally he brought house parties to Stratfield Saye and Lady Shelley wrote of one:

> The Duchess of Wellington sat apart from her guests, dressed even in winter in white muslin, without any ornaments when everyone else was in full dress. She seldom spoke but looked through her eyeglass lovingly upon the Duke, who sat opposite her.

The Reverend G. R. Gleig, the Duke's first biographer, wrote in his reminiscences of Kitty, very amiable, very religious, entertaining for her husband unbounded admiration, she could not bring herself to take the slightest interest in the subjects which mainly engrossed his attention. Even in the smallest matters their tastes seldom agreed.

That was the rub. The Duke's elegant lady friends had good minds, and not only refused to be overawed by him, but often dominated him with their logic either expressed in conversation or correspondence. Harriet Arbuthnot, Countess Lieven and Lady Jersey 'counter-attacked' him. Lady Shelley had enough wit to ask him questions on subjects about which the Duke relished giving a detailed opinion, particularly of his campaign days. Early in 1822 Kitty wrote to her husband asking for her *personal* allowance to be increased from £500 to £670 per annum. Arthur bluntly refused and investigation revealed that half that amount she disbursed to her charitable works (she listed a dozen of them), and that she could stick within the £500 budget, but meanwhile was £200 in debt. The little Irish leopard could not change its spots and before she was married Kitty had her little flock of dependents. During the early days of marriage before the Iberian campaign, she had got into a muddle over the household bills, and now things were even worse. 'I believe I may have given away money very injudiciously, perhaps sometimes (often) to spare *myself* the pain of refusing. . . .'

Forgiven once again, debts paid, her grey locks now demanded a wig and her pale wan cheeks some rouge, although the year before she had written to her sister, 'all the world of fashion is reconciled to my white, white hair . . . I never conceal it, for the present.'

Wellington was now beginning to despair of his marriage and confessed to Harriet Arbuthnot in June 1822 of its failure. He complained bitterly of the distress it was to him to be united to a person with whom he could not possibly live on any terms of confidential intercourse, that Kitty had a mind of a child, it was like talking Hebrew to her . . . that she had so high an opinion of herself and thought herself so excessively clever that she never accommodated herself to him. When their opinions differed she never supposed for a moment that she might be the one in the wrong. Her mind was trivial and narrow and he had tried to live with her *on affectionate terms* – but all in vain. As a consequence he was forced to seek elsewhere that comfort and happiness denied him at home. One further crime was that Kitty made his house so dull that nobody would go to it whereas at Apsley House or in France, he could not keep people out.

An example of Kitty's efforts to keep the Duke's friends happy was a letter dated 11 June 1821 to Fanny, Lady Shelley.

> I am quite sorry we are deprived of your company – the last year has been one of agitation – all our pleasure for the different seasons has been destroyed, *our friends have tired and annoyed us*, we must try to make them what amends we can by cheerful society at home. Our bonny black hen died one day, left a multitude of eggs, a family of black pullets. . . .

No wonder Fanny noted 'It seemed to be the one object of her life to pose as a cruelly neglected wife;' and four years later was writing in her journal,

> Alas the Duchess had precisely those faults which annoyed the Duke most; lack of common sense, ignorance of the world, obstinacy about trifles, Calvinistic and strong religious feelings – under the mistaken impression that she was smoothing family difficulties. She made the Duke's children as afraid of speaking openly to him as she was herself. The words 'Don't tell your Father' were ever on her lips – she even tried to induce her visitors to share in this folly. She has often said to me 'Don't tell the Duke – now mind don't tell the Duke'. In such small details as – the fire had been allowed to burn itself out – that the bread had a bitter taste – that somebody had called. Lord Douro had been warned by his mother never to speak to his father about his debts. The poor Duchess who managed the household and paid the bills could never make up her mind to ask the Duke for the full amount required lest her management be called in question.

The Duke always required the greatest respect to be shown towards her by everyone who went to Stratfield Saye. He sent her a list of the company in advance and directed where they were to be lodged. She considered this unkind. She always called the guests 'the Duke's company' and sat apart from the guests talking principally to the tutor, Reverend Henry Wagner or to one of the country neighbours. She was uneasy at being taken to dinner by a royal person or an ambassador and when the ladies went into the drawing room, she retired to her own room.

The year 1825 was particularly difficult for the Duke. His son Charles was rusticated from Oxford. Mary Anne Patterson's second marriage to his brother Richard Wellesley was a bitter blow. He had been working very hard on his own peace policy for Ireland, where as now, Catholics and Protestants were in deadly combat. There was a banking crisis with speculative bubbles breaking. He took Lord Douro, his son, to the Continent which was another disappointment. The dozy boy, aged eighteen, showed no curiosity or eagerness about anything except for falling in love with every woman he got near to and 'slept almost the whole way in the carriage.' Harriet Arbuthnot, that shrewd lady with no children of her own, thought that the Duke's unfortunate marriage,

> had pursued him even in his relations with his children. He dreads their inheriting their mother's narrow mind and he says, instead of directing them to useful pursuits or urging them to read or to occupy their time, she is continually seeking out for them the most trivial and childish amusements. She certainly is the silliest woman I have ever met with and I must own she *now* does not appear to have the slightest desire to please him. She does not comply with any of his fancies in the arrangement of his house and in truth, it is so bad a ménage it is quite disagreeable to be in the house. It is hopeless, too; if she had good sense all would now be right for what he now wants is a comfortable home, but she is totally unfit for her situation. She is like the housekeeper and dresses herself exactly like a shepherdess with an old hat made by herself stuck at the back of her head and a dirty basket under her arm. The Duke says he is sure she is mad!

The following spring the Duke was in Russia. On his return the Arbuthnots spent ten days in July with him at Stratfield Saye with two other members of the Fane family, Lord Westmoreland and his sister Lady Georgiana (who was permanently in love with the Duke). Harriet noted in her diary that the duchess was in London at Apsley House taking care of Priscilla, Lady Burghersh (Wellington's niece) who was very ill.

> Certainly we were all much more gay without her. The Duke imagines that the Duchess has set his son, Lord Douro against him which only makes him the more irritated against her and mortifies him to the greatest degree.

Occasionally Kitty would go up to town. At the end of April 1826 she was a patroness for a large ball given in aid of Spanish refugees at the Opera House. She was so short-sighted but was reluctant to use her eyeglasses, so she saw little of the performance.

The following year saw the Duke become the army commander again after the Duke of York's death, this despite a rather serious illness which had Kitty in despair. 'I am so short-sighted I cannot remark his features, I can only judge them by the colour, and when I look at that precious face, it seems to be very pale.' Unfortunately Kitty had run up astronomical debts of £10,000 and her husband was predictably outraged.

In the spring Kitty wrote to Harriet Arbuthnot (whose husband

Charles was trying to keep the peace between Arthur and Kitty):

> The agitation of this time is almost more than I can bear . . . God help us
> all. Pray for me Mrs A. it will be praying for me to wish everything good
> for him on his birthday.

Kitty also wrote to Lady Shelley about her sons,

> None of them have fallen in love just now. Neither have I anybody here
> to amuse them, poor fellows, they must be content like their mother with
> NOTHING AT ALL.

Mrs Arbuthnot wrote to Lady Shelley,

> The Poor Duchess is as foolish as ever, if not more so and provokes me
> to a degree I am sorry for her too and still more so for him for every year
> he must suffer more and more from it.

Charles Greville naturally noticed the Wellington ménage in permanent
disarray. Not only was his brother Algernon, the resident private
secretary, trying to bring Kitty's sartorial style up to scratch, but also he
sometimes stayed at Stratfield Saye as the Duke's guest.

> Domestic enjoyment he never possessed, as his wife was intolerable to
> him (though he always kept on decent terms with her, at least ostensibly).

Kitty had the task in 1828, for Mr Rundle the jeweller, of correcting a
wax impression of the Duke's profile which was to go on a snuff-box. He
had become prime minister in January and Kitty was prouder of her hero
than ever before.

> The Hair grows rather up from the forehead, being naturally inclined to
> curl, it never lies flat and covers very little of the forehead, which is rather
> broad, open and beautiful. The nose is hardly large enough but from the
> Eye to the nostril. . . . it is too thick, it should be very fine indeed . . . the
> jaw from the ear to the chin requires to be rather more square.

Next year Kitty was distraught at the risk the Duke had run in his duel
with Lord Winchelsea at Battersea, and wrote accounts to her sons. In
the autumn a special guard of a dozen constabulary had to be mounted
to protect Stratfield Saye from farm worker agitators. One weekend the
Duke spent there he complained to Harriet that apart from his brother
Gerald (the parson) he knew no one else – 'The Duchess has certainly
the most extraordinary fancy in the selection of her acquaintances.' A
few months later the same thing happened. This time there was a large
family of Brownes who were probably on Kitty's hand-out payroll. Of

course, there was no reason why Kitty should not invite her friends to the Wellington home but her husband was prime minister and expected guests of, as the French would say, a certain '*niveau*', not bewhiskered Poles, and officers on half-pay.

Kitty's health was now causing her problems and from 1829 she spent much of her time in bed, writing letters to her sisters, friends and children. Her husband decided to ask her to be a joint guardian to the three unfortunate Long-Wellesley children. William Wellesley-Pole was the only son of William, Lord Maryborough, the Duke's elder brother. A very dissolute young man indeed, the Duke's nephew once his ADC, had squandered his wife's fortune, seduced the wife of a Guards officer, had eloped with her and abandoned his three young children who were made wards of Chancery with the Duke as guardian. The wretched near-crazy nephew unleashed a series of scurrilous pamphlets alleging that his uncle was totally unfit to be his children's guardian. He wrote that Harriet Arbuthnot was living with him at Apsley House (patently untrue), that the present Marchioness Welles-ley, when Mrs Patterson, had been his mistress (true but irrelevant), that her sister Lady Hervey had also been the Duke's mistress 'which had killed poor Sir Felton Hervey', with Lady Charlotte Greville, and with his Indian love Mrs Freese (whose son he educated with his own).

Wellington had to disengage from the responsibility with dignity if possible. At the beginning of 1829, he co-opted Sir William Courtenay to act with Kitty 'under the shield of my Protection', the Duke wrote. It was a master stroke and delighted Kitty for a variety of reasons. The Duke was asking a favour of her which was a sign of his esteem. She loved children and her two were now rarely at home. So she wrote, 'I with the greatest pleasure agree to that which you propose, and will do as you wish.'

For the next two years, the marriage took on a new lease of life. She and Sir William (with the Duke's advice) had to deal with the responsibility and correspondence connected with the guardianship. William, the father, although threatening a duel with his distinguished uncle, kept up the pressure, by enticing his son James away from Eton. With William, a difficult backward child, Kitty was a second loving mother 'Well, I will sap [swat] since the Duchess wants it.' In July 1830 Kitty was very ill at Apsley House and her husband brought the new King William IV and the queen on a special visit to see and cheer her up. She had neglected her health, which was being ruined by rheumatism and an internal complaint. She had two severe falls and was frequently bedridden.

Maria Edgeworth believed that the duchess was suffering from cancer, although it may have been cholera (of which Harriet Arbuthnot was to die a few years later). Kitty spent the last few months at Apsley House, her life slowly ebbing, visited every day by her husband, occasionally by her sons and by Maria Edgeworth. At the last moment she discovered her husband was wearing an armlet she had given him many years ago, 'She found it as she would have found it any time these twenty years had she cared to look for it'. (Mrs Stewart Mackenzie told this poignant little story later to the Arbuthnots). He also ruminated, 'It is a strange thing that two people can live together for half a lifetime and only understand one another at the very end.' Maria Edgeworth wrote 'There she lies fading away, still feeding, when she can feed on nothing else, on his glories, on the perfume of his incense.'

Just before her death Kitty quoted the words of an old French song.

> Oui, ma folie est de l'aimer
> Je l'aimerai toute ma vie
> Gronde moi, si c'est ton envie
> Mais ne crois pas me corriger
> Car ma folie est de l'aimer
> Je l'aimerai toute ma vie.
> So I will: I swore it.*

England has always been able to produce mobs at crucial moments in our history. By a particular irony Kitty died on 25 April. King William IV had dissolved parliament the day before. The Lord Mayor of London, obviously a fool, ordered illuminations in all windows in honour of parliament's dissolution – a most convoluted idea. The rampaging mob decided that Apsley House in mourning for the poor dead Duchess of Wellington was a prime target and wrecked every window and pulled up the Piccadilly railings outside with exquisite vandalism and timing. No wonder the Duke said to Harriet, 'The people are rotten to the Core. The people are gone mad.'

Although the Duke had manfully paid up Kitty's debts in 1828 and he had relieved her of all house bills since then, she had still managed to run up further debts in the last three years of the same amount – £10,000! Most of this went to supporting various Irish relatives. Kitty wrote to a

---

* Yes, my folly is to love him
  I will love him all my life
  Scold me, if you want to
  But do not think you can change me
  For my folly is to love him
  I will love him all my life.

General Allan, 'With all my heart and soul I have loved him [the Duke] straight on from the first time I knew him. (I was not then fifteen) to the present hour.'

There is little doubt that the last few years were as happy as any other period. But sentiment aside – endings should be happy – the truth was put by the Duke to another of his closest confidants, the gentle Fanny – Lady Salisbury.

> The Duchess was one of the most foolish women that ever existed, a sort of wise and uneducated folly, an obliquity in all her views of things, which it was impossible to remove. She was very vain. She thought herself the prettiest woman in the world (she had been pretty in her youth) and the cleverest. She used to buy a great many books and write her name in the title page but never read them. She always professed a wish to do everything to please me but if I desired anything might be done, the wish was complied with at the moment and it was always neglected afterwards.
>
> In her observations upon other women (and she was very censorious) there never was anything that showed observation or discrimination of character. The remarks she made upon one would have done equally well for half a dozen others. She spoilt my sons by making everything give way to them and teaching them to have too high ideas of their own consequence. She was in debt £10,000 at Stratfield Saye when she died and I discovered debts of another £10,000 or more. The debts preyed upon her mind, she was constantly wretched about them. She gave a great deal to a sister of hers who married a Mr Stewart -- a banking house that went broke.

Indian Summer

Chapter Twenty-Four

MY DEAR
MISS JENKINS –
THE SPIRITUALIST

The appearance of letters purporting to be from the Duke to a certain Miss J. at the end of the nineteenth century caused his biographers to doubt their provenance. Why should the Iron Duke write so many letters to a completely 'unknown' young woman?

There is now no doubt whatsoever that the Duke wrote a total of 390 letters over a period of seventeen years to a certain Miss Anna Maria Jenkins. The bulk of these letters were written in 1835 (78), 1836 (56), 1844 (55) and 1845 (32). They started in 1834 and ended about a year before the Duke's death in 1852. In September 1835 she had a tiff with the Duke and returned sixty letters which he promptly burned! Mrs Christine Terhune Herrick was responsible in 1889 for editing not only the letters but also Miss Jenkins's personal diary which had lain in a trunk in the attic of a country house thirty miles from New York.

She was a very beautiful young woman of twenty when she first wrote to the sixty-two-year-old Duke. Her parents were minor English gentry and she had been well educated although she and her sister were orphaned when they were young children. On her mother's death Anna Maria claimed to have seen a vision of the heaven her mother was entering! The elder sister married a doctor and went to live in America, leaving Anna Maria with a companion called Mrs Lachlan and a guardian who looked after the investments from her mother's will. She had no taste for the society the Duke moved in, but visited many of her school friends' country houses from time to time. She lived occasionally in lodgings or a rented house, but most of the Duke's missives were directed to 42, Charlotte Street, in Portland Place. A harpist, she was highly emotional, almost unbalanced on occasions. She was a religious zealot who had converted a murderer called Henry Cooke just before he went to the scaffold in 1830. During the seventeen years of their acquaintanceship the Duke and Miss Jenkins met on about a dozen occasions. There was a four-year gap from 1840 to 1844 when apparently the Duke wrote no letters, but he made up for it in 1844 when he sent her his picture, plus a letter a week.

During September 1834 the Duke showed Fanny, Lady Salisbury a Bible in a morocco case like an almanac, sent to him by a Miss J. The title page was marked in pencil St John, Chapter three verse five 'Except a man be born again, he cannot see the Kingdom of God.' She had called at Apsley House in April 1835 encouraged by a letter from the Duke. He then told Fanny of the conversion of Cooke the Murderer! In the summer he had called on Miss J. three times and told Fanny he was alarmed by her evident intention to marry him. Two years before his death Wellington complained to his favourite niece of his considerable daily mail, upwards of fifty letters, including 'the over-religious body from a numerous class of the writers to me. It is astonishing how anxious they are to save my soul!'

So why did the Duke for seventeen years write a total of nearly 400 letters to a young woman with whom he had nothing in common?

She was totally unworldly; they had no mutual friends; she was not interested in politics, foreign diplomacy, old campaigns or modern wars, nor in the theatre or the opera; and she could not or would not gossip in her letters (which the Duke expected from his female correspondents). On the other hand she was very beautiful, she made it clear that she wanted to marry the Duke; she also made it clear that she wanted to save his soul from damnation. The Duke was such a dedicated correspondent, that in some ways he felt compelled to answer if not all the letters that came to him, at least the majority of them. Perhaps after Harriet's death, even after Kitty's three years earlier, he felt the need of some spiritual help and guidance. Mrs Patterson was in his brother's care, unhappy but still unobtainable. Princess Lieven had left the country. Lady Charlotte Greville and Lady Jersey were excellent friends, but he was rarely at their 'fireside'. Fanny Salisbury was soon to die too (in 1839) and in that year of mourning he could only muster eight letters to his spiritual guide, for that is what Anna Maria set out to be.

Anna Maria's past included a mild love affair with a young man called Henry who fell far short of her high standards in spiritual matters. She gave him up and prayed for his salvation. Her life was to be devoted to good works and instructing village children at their school. She taught two gipsy boys the rudiments of Christianity, she read the Bible and every tract she could obtain, converted the murderer, wrote letters on religious topics to her friends, and adapted hymns for the harp. Her only confidante was Mrs Lachlan, a lady twice her age who lived with her. Her life was directed by over-ruling Providence – she often opened the Bible at random and shaped the course of her actions accordingly. Certain of her friends were labouring under the power of Satan, thus song and prayer was needed to bring them back into the fold. She herself had undergone 'persecution for righteousness sake.'

When she first wrote to the Duke she was unaware of the battle of Waterloo (after all she was only two at the time), and perhaps expensive young ladies' education did not include such terrible landmarks. Her first letter was written from Devonshire and was dated 15 January 1834. The Duke answered three days later and the various inkblots and mistaken date (1833 for 1834) encouraged her to think he was answering in a state of emotion. The Bible and note about St John's text was delivered to Apsley House by Miss J. on 24 April. At this stage the Duke could have called the whole business off. Four months later he took the initiative and wrote to her as Mrs Jenkins (after all most of his ladies were married woman).

On 27 August, out of curiosity, he suggested a meeting. Late in October he wrote rather pompously again in the third person 'Although the Duke is not in the habit of visiting young unmarried ladies with whom he is not acquainted, he will not decline to attend Miss J.' On 8 November he expressed his intention to call upon the lady on the 12th at the lodgings she shared with her chaperone Mrs Lachlan. Her diary has a full record of this momentous meeting, including . . .

> Since HE must have influenced the Duke of Wellington to love me above every other lady upon earth from the first moment he beheld me, I am not afraid, etc, etc . . . until he was compelled to exclaim 'Oh, *how* I *love* you' repeating the same over and over again with increasing energy.

Anna Maria, on divine instruction, was wearing 'my old *turned* dark green merino gown, *daily* worn – not permitting me to be decorated in any way likely to attract notice . . .' Mrs Lachlan was aiding her from the top of the stairs, saying 'Now if the Lord should send His arrow into his soul!' The Duke was standing by the fire and she was quite surprised to notice that he had 'such a beautiful silver head such as I have always from my childhood admired.' She put a large Bible on the table between them saying 'I will show you *my Treasure!*' The Duke took her hand, and she cried out, 'Ye MUST be born again' and raised her other hand emphatically. The Duke was struck dumb, until he was asked who caused him to feel the way he did about Miss J. To which there could be only one answer 'God Almighty.'

After a series of letters between them the next meeting took place on

23 December. Her diary quotes the Duke as saying of his feelings for her 'This must be for life' twice over. He then asked Anna Maria if she felt sufficient for him to be with him 'a whole life', to which she replied, 'If it be the will of God!' Two weeks later she wrote saying that his intentions must be strictly honourable and their meetings should be purely spiritual. The Duke agreed with her, and that they should part! Two days later he received a violent reply at which stage he could (and perhaps should) have desisted. But not a bit of it, an abject apology was sent. And so it went on. There were brief unsatisfactory meetings, many misunderstandings and spiritual exhortations. Sometimes she would not write to him 'because God would not let me.' In October 1835 she sent him a farewell hymn called 'The Shortness of Time and Frailty of Man':

> VAIN his AMBITION, NOISE and SHOW
> VAIN are the cares which rack his mind!
> He heaps up treasures MIXED with WOE
> And dies, and leaves them all behind!

Anna Maria signed most of her letters 'A Servant of Christ and a Child of God. A.J.'

The interesting point was that the Duke for most of the seventeen years was on the defensive, a campaigning art in which he excelled. Her efforts to promote his Everlasting Welfare were received with thanks. In her diary she asserted that she believed it was the will of God that she should become the next duchess, or to be more accurate,

> I was impressed throughout my correspondence with and knowledge of the Duke with a feeling that the end God had in view was my exaltation for His Glory or in other words to show forth His power . . . I attach so little importance to rank or worldly grandeur, that I should have considered I conferred as high an honour on the Duke in *bestowing my hand as he would in receiving it, of which he was well aware.*

Anna Maria admitted in her journal that the Duke's letters were always cautiously written. That was his nature. He wrote,

> I should not treat you as I should wish to be treated myself. The commands of all others which we ought to obey are those dictated to us by our social relations. What would be said, if I, a man of seventy years of age, nearly, *were to take in marriage a lady young enough to be my Grand-daughter?*

During a visit to Miss J. in 1836 the Duke was asked about his knee injured by a horse in a riding accident. He took that enquiry as an encouraging sign and moved his chair closer to hers. She recoiled 'due to Christianity' and in her next letter upbraided the old Duke for 'brushing up his chair.' Wellington now took deep umbrage and replied in the third person denying that he had been guilty of 'daring presumption.' The great Lord of Lords took a hand and decreed to his disciple that the Duke 'should not behold me again for nearly eight years.' The letters between them continued and she sent him little presents of pen-wipers and spectacle-wipers and lent the Duke books. Miss J. went on her visits to Ramsgate and Harrogate and on her return moved house to Hampstead, where the Duke visited her.

In the autumn of 1844 the Duke sent her a painting which he judged to be a good likeness. In the lady's diary she wrote,

> This was his own Picture in wax made by himself and was an impression conveying a striking resemblance. It is made upon one of his own cards cut in half on this is engraved 'Field Marshal the Duke of Wellington.' How this valuable Article is eventually to be disposed of, I wait upon the Lord of Lords who permitted it to be bestowed upon me, to point out.

Later on in her diary she planned, in a divine huff, to return it 'being made of sealing wax is of course of no value'!

The Duke wrote to Anna Maria about the losses in his family: his sister 'But I trust that by the Mercy of God! she is happy'; his brother 'His last moments were those of a good Christian in peace with all the world.'

Mrs Lachlan, her confidante, aided and abetted Anna Maria in her fantasies, which included letters addressed to the queen for the Duke to approve and remit! Their health problems came under scrutiny. Early in 1850 Miss Jenkins accidentally received a painful blow on her breast, a tumour followed and her 'affliction' was a topic during the next two years. Sir Robert Peel's death, publick duties, the queen's confinement, and good counsel were TOPICKS discussed. Wellington had one convenient let-out, 'The Duke is unfortunately for him not sufficiently informed to enable Him to write upon some of the Higher and more sacred Topicks of Miss J.'s.'

A typical tart exchange took place in the autumn of 1850 after the Duke had suffered another small injury. Anna Maria wrote,

> Notwithstanding my changed feelings I am deeply concerned to hear of your late accident. P.S. I do not give you my address, My Lord Duke, in order to elicit an answer, but merely to imply that should my Christian advice be required you may know *where* to find me.

The answer was predictable, 'The Duke of Wellington returns his thanks to Miss Jenkins for noticing the accident.'

Shortly after the Duke died, Anna Maria removed herself to America, lived with her sister, quarrelled with her, moved out and died an unhappy spinster.

Chapter Twenty-Five

MARY STANLEY, LADY WILTON 'CONSIDER ME YOUR BEST FRIEND'

The most unusual aspect of Wellington's long relationship with Lady Wilton, a beautiful but cold woman is that for some strange reason he kept, or failed to destroy, 223 letters received by him. In the final analysis Lady Wilton meant far less to the Beau than Mrs Patterson, Lady Charlotte Greville and Harriet Arbuthnot, all of whose letters were immediately destroyed.

Thomas Egerton, the 2nd Earl of Wilton, married Mary Stanley the daughter of the 12th Earl of Derby in 1821. Although 598 letters from the Duke to Lady Wilton have been preserved, covering the period October 1838 to April 1848, it is quite clear that the correspondence started considerably earlier, perhaps about 1834; and may have extended well beyond 1848 up until the Duke's death in 1852.

A letter to Lord Wilton dated 31 October 1837 contains the phrase 'It is a long time since I heard from her.' The last letter to her that has survived was dated April 1848 and there was no indication that the relationship was at an end. At this time gossip linked the Duke's name to Lady Georgiana Fane, to Mary Ann Jervis and, above all, to Angela Burdett-Coutts. It may be that Lady Wilton, a stickler for the proprieties, destroyed his letters after April out of pique.

To Fanny Lady Salisbury in the summer of 1834 the Duke talked about Lady Wilton, that 'she was a very sensible woman proved by her conduct, but that he never discovered the smallest spark of feeling in her.'

The lady in question was painted by A. E. Chalon RS in 1840 in formal ball-gown. She looks handsome, with thick black hair, strong eyebrows, a distinguished Roman nose, dimples and a slightly surprised look, or perhaps only quizzical. She was one of his major confidantes from the moment that young Fanny Lady Salisbury died in October 1839. Lady Frances Shelley, Lady Sarah Jersey, probably Lady Wellesley (Mrs Patterson) certainly Miss A. M. Jenkins, and Madame de Lieven (until her abrupt departure to Paris), all received weekly letters from the Duke.

The letters to Lady Mary were not at all skittish or coy in style as they often were with Harriet Arbuthnot and Lady Shelley. There was little of the intimate gossip about mutual acquaintances that characterised so many of his letters to his dearest friends, but there were some *bon mots* about leading personalities of the day.

'Lord Melbourne would prefer to sit in a Room with a Chime of Bells, ten Parrots and one Lady Westmorland to sitting in Cabinet with Mr Macauley.' 'It is said that Prince Albert is in love with Miss Pitt-Rivers.' 'I met Madame de Lieven yesterday (19 August 1840) in Storr & Mortimer's shop and had a curious conversation with Her which I will write down. She wanted to dine with me.' 'Lord Elgin has been here this morning, says the Hatred of the English Nation is quite extraordinary' (in Paris), and 'M. de Thiers (Louis Philippe's minister) has made about two millions of Francs by Jobbing in the Stocks.'

Only one of the Duke's letters is emotional and endeavours to clarify their relationship. It was dated 7 August 1839, a matter of weeks before Fanny Lady Salisbury's death.

I cannot express to you what I have felt upon taking leave of you. It is possible that if you had remained in or near England I should not have seen more of you for some Months. It is possible that you may return before the Winter. But I should not be separated from you by the sea. I should hear from you sometimes: of you frequently. I hope that you believe in the sincere *regard, affection and attachment that I feel for you, and that you consider me as your best friend.* If you don't, you do not do me justice.

I entreat you to write to me whenever you will have an opportunity, if only to tell me that you are well. I will write to you constantly to let you know how your Children are: and to communicate to you anything else that I may learn, calculated to interest you, that I can venture to entrust to a Continental Post Office, in each of which all letters are opened.

Whenever I shall hear of a safe opportunity I will write to you fully upon every subject . . .

The wide variety of subjects included the Cinque Ports feast at Dover for 3,000 people in the Duke's honour (1 September 1839), news of government reshuffles, the queen's proposed marriage, advice to the Wiltons then in Lisbon (24 October), visit of the Princes of Coburg to Dover, the Oxford Monument (the Duke was chancellor of Oxford), the Precedency Bill for Prince Albert, the royal wedding, visits to concerts, a visit by Lord John Russell, rumours of war and strikes in France, the military expedition to Syria, and possible European army command (1841) for the Duke!

Perhaps he was conscious that some of his letters dealing with domestic politics and European diplomacy might bore Lady Wilton because he wrote quite cordially on 30 January 1841,

unless you should feel a great Interest about publick Affairs I must bore you by my letters. But I hear of everything: everything is told to me or written to me: and I send you pretty nearly all that I receive, and tell you all that I hear. I hope it interests you.

All the Duke's letters contained fond references to Lady Wilton's children, which was naturally an important subject in her correspondence.

I saw them all on the day after I wrote to you as well and looking as well as possible. Poor Children! They were sorry to part from me, as I was to part from them (25 November 1839).

One child was called 'Naughty Catherine'!

Occasionally the Duke would mention her husband in his letters. 'Tell Lord Wilton that I dont care one Pin about the Duke of Monmouth's Precedent', and 'Sir James Graham was willing to appoint Lord Wilton Under Secretary in the Home Department the question was whether Lord Wilton would accept and Peel would agree.' The Wiltons, in common with most of the civilised English gentry, went on several European tours and the Duke could be relied upon to keep them fully abreast of the main events. But occasionally he would write to Lady Wilton on quite unexpected themes, demonstrating quite unconsciously his extraordinarily wide range of knowledge and interest.

Theology was a subject in which he appeared genuinely interested (possibly because Miss Anna Maria Jenkins was writing to him on most days).

The Schism in the Church of England and possible checks on the Schismaticks . . ., [and later] I recommend you to read Demonstration of the Truth of Christianity (by Alexander Keith). *It is the most interesting work upon any subject that I ever perused.* I sit up half the night reading it. I cannot quit it . . .

Other strange subjects included the Chinese opium trade.

The Radicals, Dissenters and Quakers have made the Opium Affair a matter of Conscience and think of treating it as they did the Slave Trade. They will not hear of War to maintain a Trade in Opium . . .

He wrote to Lady Wilton a thesis on the reason why he refused to go to see a large model of the field of battle at Waterloo made by a Captain William Siborn (1840). The Duke's reason was quite logical. The model could only hope to show the disposition of the adversaries at one particular moment. The ebb and flow of battle was so strong that the model could be seen as misleading.

Music had always been one of the Duke's passions. He went to see and hear Mademoiselle Rachel (Elisabeth Felix).

She is a great Actress: Her voice good; Her delivery and diction excellent: Her action easy and Natural – remarkably so for a French Woman. She is not Handsome: Her Eyes decidedly bad, Her features not good, Her face too fat. The whole appearance of Her Eyes and face that of Child who had been crying. Our actors admired her much. I can understand the French Enthusiasm for Her!

Lady Wilton wrote frequently to the Duke about his hunting and riding activities. The truth is that he needed to ride every day. He had been riding a horse all his life, not only on his campaigns which lasted at least twelve years, but for social purposes. Sometimes he took tosses which had a temporary effect for a day or so. When he was seventy-one Lady Wilton tried to discourage him, to which he answered,

I am sorry that you do not approve of my going out Hunting. I think it does me good. At all events I think that the vagabonds who are now doing so much Mischief presume a little in consequence of their belief that I am superannuated. They will not believe that I can make my saddle on my Horse's back my House, as heretofore, until they shall hear that I have been in at the Death of a fox or two! [And the following day] Saving your favour, I have been out with the Harriers this morning . . . Yesterday (31 December 1841) I went out with the Vine Hounds but we had no sport (near Stratfield Saye).

It was a long but unintimate relationship between them. At an early stage the Duke must have realised that Lady Mary wanted him as a friend, but a distant friend, who would keep her (perhaps her husband too) *au fait* with the corridors of power. He needed an interested audience, but in this case he was kept at a distance.

Chapter Twenty-Six

ANGELA BURDETT-COUTTS – THE PHILANTHROPIST

Angela Georgina Burdett-Coutts, youngest daughter of Sir Francis Burdett MP was born in 1814. The greatest influence in her life came from her governess, companion and friend Hannah Meredith, who was described as vivacious and most intelligent.

Angela was painted in 1828 when she was fourteen by Samuel John Stump. The portrait shows a dark haired, very intelligent young woman with a long strong Roman nose, a wide generous mouth and large serious eyes – not beautiful but distinctly handsome and rather solemn. Her father said of her that she had an exceptionally sweet disposition.

Just before the battle of Waterloo took place Harriet Mellon, a saucy actress secretly married Thomas Coutts, Angela's grandfather, a few days after his first wife, then senile, had scalded herself to death. Coutts died in 1822 and left his fortune entirely to Harriet, who in turn rather surprisingly on her death (by now she was the Duchess of St Albans) left the bulk of the fortune to Angela. Her father and her mother were astonished, although they also received handsome legacies.

So during 1837 a tall, thin pale-faced lady took over the lease of No. 1 Stratton Street, London. Via her grandfather, Thomas Coutts the banker, the young unmarried girl suddenly became famous – and rich. The *Morning Herald* estimated her fortune at just under £2 million. The house that she now lived in was a few yards away from the Duke's mansion at Apsley House.

For many years the young heiress was the target of a score or more of young and middle-aged adventurers interested only in her fortune. Queen Victoria noted in her diary some of them 'Spoke to Lord Melbourne, Lord Fitzalan's marriage to Miss Coutts being off.' A mad young Irish barrister, Richard Dunn pursued her for eighteen years. He followed her everywhere and bombarded her with proposals. After all £80,000 a year was in sight! Lord Broughton noted that 'she had a pleasing face, her figure though not full is good. Her voice is melodious, her expression sweet and engaging.' Louis Napoleon was said to have asked for her hand in marriage and William Gladstone and Benjamin Disraeli were part of her circle. Doubtless due to her companion, Hannah Meredith's influence, Angela became deeply religious, and through her faith, and guided by her father, she soon became known as the 'Queen of the Poor'. Her philanthropic activities started with funds for research in the natural sciences, geology, physics and archaeology. Michael Faraday, Wheatstone and Charles Babbage benefited from her undemanding generosity. She became friends with Charles Dickens, Florence Nightingale and the astronomer Sir James South. Her wide range of acquaintances included Rajah Brooke, Sir Henry Irving, Liszt and Marshal Soult.

The first recorded letter of a total of 842 from the Duke to Angela was dated 18 May.

> My dear Miss Angela, I am much flattered and obliged by your note which I received this night upon my return home (to Apsley House). I should be delighted to be presented to your Aunt and Cousin. I beg that you will make me acquainted with your wishes upon any subject at any time.

Angela lived in palatial style at No. 1 Stratton Street, attended by a Major Domo named Terry, and a caged parrot. For the first anniversary of Queen Victoria's coronation the Duke asked Angela and her father to a ball at Apsley House where the queen, and the king of Prussia were present. She was then twenty-five and the Duke aged seventy. The following month, July 1839, she sent the Duke a turtle, probably not for eating, and went to his house for a concert since she was as fond of music as he was. She then invited him to dinner. He sat for a portrait by her friend Richmond. 'Chalk or water colour, say which you choose'. On 9 September Angela, chaperoned by Hannah, now Mrs Brown, spent the night and two days with the Duke at Walmer Castle.

She asked for his help with some of her Coutts banking problems – after all it was now her bank. The Duke who had banked with Coutts all his life was delighted to help. He helped with her long list of charitable works and she often accepted his opinions, although Charles Dickens was her most helpful and consistent advisor on her charities.

They frequently gave each other presents. Angela received a Breguet watch which she treasured for the rest of her long life. The Duke received a purse which she had netted. Ideal for keeping coins 'so many old soldiers he met wanted something and he liked to gratify them'.

In his old age the Duke was increasingly concerned with health, not necessarily his own. He now had a pair of galoshes specially made for Angela – 'You must be kept dry when you go out into the wet streets'. He confided in her that he wore Bengal muslin next to his skin for warmth and rubbed himself with a special lotion of vinegar and rosewater to avoid colds (which predictably he still caught with frequency!). In his letters he used a phrase implying a telepathic link between them. 'Your mind and mine were again heading the same road.' Angela was a level-headed young woman and gave the Duke some practical advice, to which he was not accustomed. His statue which was to be erected on Constitution Hill was now exciting controversy about its size and style. She counselled him to keep out of the debate.

They advised each other on help for prostitutes 'those very young unfortunates who you saw on the steps, perhaps a Home for Fallen Woman?' 'Should Coutts Bank subscribe to the Irish Potato famine relief, or not?' They had a debate on 'skaiting', 'Women skait habitually in the countries in which the Ice is certain annually, and in England I have seen ladies skait beautifully.'

By now a touching innocent friendship had built up betwen the old man and his young friend. He had sent pressed flowers to her, geraniums and verbena and rose leaves. A small envelope exists with a tiny bow of his pure white hair tied with a few brown strands, presumably of Angela's thick hair. She had sent him an envelope full of 'the Duke of Wellington's favourite Poplins' filled with little bits of material, fawn shot with rose at 5s 9d, grey and deep purple at 4s 9d etc. She had written to him that it had been the happiest year (1846) of her life. To which the Duke answered on New Year's Day 'Nothing shall be omitted on my part as your friend to make this year as happy as the last.'

The crisis in their very happy relationship occurred in February 1847 when he was aged seventy-eight and Angela was but thirty-three. Her stepmother had been a duchess, perhaps she could also attain that rank? On 6 February he had written,

I am sensible of your kindness and confidence My dear Miss Angela and of the admirable good sense and goodness of heart which induced you to write me your letter of last night! You are right! There can be no secrets between us on such subjects!

On 7 February the wealthy young woman who had rejected a dozen or more suitors (usually fortune-seekers) herself proposed marriage to the elderly Duke. He was a wonderful safe father figure to her. He certainly was not interested in her wealth, much more in her keen mind. They shared a love of music and a common benevolence. She to her Ragged Schools, St Stephens Church and many others. He to the dozens of old soldiers and their wives (many spurious) who asked and nearly all received. She did not realise the elderly like their safe, ordered routine, that additional responsibility is unwelcome, and that staying alive and relatively well is a vital factor. His daily routine was fixed – time for his correspondence, time for meals, times for hunting, riding or visiting. It was a methodical regimented life that he set himself. The Duke had called on her at No. 1 Stratton Street and quietly listened to her proposal. He returned to Apsley House and wrote a charming, sensible and, above all, kind letter to his young friend.

My dearest Angela, I have passed every Moment of the Evening and Night since I quitted you in reflecting upon our conversation of yesterday. Every Word of which I have considered repeatedly. My first Duty towards you is that of Friend, Guardian, Protector. You are Young, My Dearest! You have before you the prospect of at least twenty years of Enjoyment of Happiness in life. I entreat you again in this way not to throw yourself away upon a Man old enough to be your Grandfather, who however strong, Hearty and Healthy at present, must and will certainly in time feel the Consequence and Infirmities of Age. You cannot know, but I do, the dismal consequence to you of this certainty. Hopeless for years during which you will still be in the prime of your life! I cannot too often and too urgently entreat you to consider this well, I urge it as your Friend, Guardian, Protector. But I must add, as I have frequently, that my own happiness depends upon it. My last days would be embittered by the reflections that your life was uncomfortable and hopeless!
God Bless you My Dearest,
Believe me Ever Yours   Wn.

Now it must be added that the Duke was also writing warm, lively and friendly letters at this time to Mary Stanley, Lady Wilton, also to 'My dear Miss Jenkins' the spiritualist lady, and probably to his old flame, now his sister-in-law, Marianne Wellesley. His attractive young friends

of the gay days in Brussels and Paris still saw him and wrote letters –
Dearest Georgie Lennox (now Lady de Ros) and Frances Lady Shelley.
Every day there must have been a letter for him at Walmer Castle or
Apsley House that recalled the halcyon days after Waterloo. One might
have thought that a rejected proposal would have severed this strange
relationship. Not a bit of it. Angela paid him a visit at Stratfield Saye and
he asked her to come again. He proposed building an apartment there
for her convenience. During the summer of 1847 the Beau, a little
stooped perhaps but with spotless clothes, sometimes bemedalled,
always debonair and polite despite his deafness, escorted her to
assemblies, concerts and balls.

Punch Magazine predictably carried a cartoon on the subject entitled
'Marriage of the Metals!' Scene – a Room in the Royal Institution.

> Professor Smith (reading the Morning Post) 'Very extraordinary! (To
> Professor Jones) Have you read this? No – well then, the *Post* says that the
> Duke of Wellington – the Iron Duke – is going to marry Miss Burdett-
> Coutts!'
> Professor Jones 'Nonsense! It can't be true!'
> Professor Smith 'But if it should be true, what would you think of such
> a match?'
> Professor Jones 'Think of it! Why with the Duke and the Heiress, I shall
> think it a most extraordinary union of Iron and Tin' [tin = money].

The diarist Charles Greville wrote in July,

> the Duke is astonishing the world by a strange intimacy he has struck up
> with Miss Coutts with whom he passes his life – and all sorts of reports
> have been rife of his intention to marry her. Such are the lamentable
> appearances of decay in his vigorous mind, which are the more to be
> regretted because he is in the most enviable circumstances, without any
> political responsibility, yet associated with public affairs and surrounded
> with every sort of respect and consideration on every side – at Court, in
> Parliament, in society and in the country.

Undeterred by all this gossip, the Duke squired Angela to the palace but
lost her in the crowd. 'I looked for you in the Drawing Room in vain. I
came away in despair.' Princess Lieven in self-inflicted exile in Paris
wrote to Lord Palmerston,

> Tell me if it is true that the Duke of Wellington is marrying Miss Coutts.
> I can hardly believe it, yet such extraordinary things happen in this world
> that I should never say anything was impossible.

In October and November of that year, Angela, who was a great traveller, was in France and the Duke missed her acutely.

> My dearest! For so I must call you – your constant recollection of and
> kindness to me, charm me, and I must express what I feel for you! We
> think aloud – and the thoughts of the one are imparted to the other, that
> is the charm of our existence.

The affectionate little interchange of presents continued. He sent her
bouquets and gloves from Stratfield Saye and Angela sent him fruit and
vegetables from her garden. Charles Dickens was peeved! He who had
for so long regarded Angela as his private confidante was most offended
by the dalliance with the old Duke. She was rarely at home to him and
the Duke's carriage was frequently outside her front door. He was
invited to dine there with his wife, but Angela had obviously forgotten
and was not at home. The rumours grew of an impending marriage.

But nothing had changed. The Duke had no intention of marriage. His
only expedition had been a failure, not only to him, to Kitty, but very
noticeably to the outside world.

The letters continued between them almost on a daily basis. On
charity the Duke penned his thoughts.

> Before I give I consider well whether I can afford it? What are the means
> actually at my disposition? What the actual or probable demands upon
> them? . . . Everybody wants!

They exchanged books – *Mrs Fry's Journal*; *La Martine*; 'Histoire des
Girondins' ('but awful horrors – your health might be serious affected');
a book of lectures by Dr Nicholas Wiseman on *Science and Revealed
Religion*.

The Duke was proud of the fact that he had been primarily
responsible for putting an end to duelling. He wrote to her about the
modern French theatre, about the château at Grosbois offered him by
King Louis XVIII, about drinking habits 'besides the Lower Classes in
this country drink Spirits; those in France, wine. This makes a great
difference in Manners, a social disposition.' The troubles in Spain were
due to the expulsion of the Jesuits there was 'no worthwhile education'
left.

They wrote about theology,

> So innate is the feeling of the existence of a Supreme being in the Mind
> of Man, wherever the Ceremonies of Divine Worship are performed with
> Decency and the truths of Christianity are propounded, crowds will flock
> and attend to them.

They exchanged views on church affairs; the high standard of the acting of the Comedie Française in Paris; chloroform in childbirth; on the death of Napoleon; the Irish problem; on entertaining the prince of Prussia; his preference for Jenny Lind's singing; his visit to the queen's 'accouchement' at Windsor.

Angela and the Duke continued their very civilised relationship. They went to Covent Garden and the theatre together and cared little for the rumours and gossip that fed on their many social visits together. She sent him handkerchiefs, and he tickets for her to attend the House of Lords.

The Duke was feeling his age, he wrote on 6 August 1848,

> But I am afraid that I shall never be able to prevail upon you to consider me as quite unfit for social purposes. Deaf, eighty years old and seeking for repose! The truth is that I am superannuated in reference to all that is required from me, publick as well as social, civil, military, political and private – everything must come to me.

Nine years before, in November 1839, he had had a stroke at Walmer and seizures earlier in the summer of 1835. It was a wonder that not only was he still alive and saying to Angela 'I am always on the Gallop.' Indeed in 1847 he had several epileptic fits; a result of cold or lack of food, due to his spartan regime.

The only subject on which he did not dwell – perhaps his favourite – was that of 'battles long ago'. Some of the Duke's old flames (when younger) had been not only fervent listeners but also would on occasion interrogate as well. Lady Shelley and Harriet Arbuthnot had that rare gift. But Wellington once paid Angela an unusual tribute 'Your latin is very correct. But you are better than a soldier. You have a clear correct judgement which with an excellent heart will always keep you right!' In the autumn of 1848 Angela called unannounced and received a crushing rebuke.

> The Queen's servants, the Adjutant, A Quarter-Master General, the Military Secretary, private secretary, my Aide de Camp, acquaintances and relatives are in the Habit of calling at all Hours . . . They would be greatly surprized to find me still dressing *and* a young lady in possession of my room. I did not think it possible that you would be guilty of such folly!

But the visits to Walmer happily continued. Subjects they wrote and talked about included the use of nicknames; expenditure of 'Millions Sterling' on these rail roads; Coutts' working hours; on mountaineering 'Fine views are very delightful certainly, but I don't relish the trouble, difficulty and risk attending the sight of them'. On private journals:

> Nothing can be so unfair as the publication of Private Journals. All such Impressions having been written down, ought to be corrected if doubt should be entertained of their original correctness.

The discovery of gold in California,

> It has driven mad the people in the United States and will not do them much good – it will divert their attention from all Industrious pursuits.

At the beginning of 1849 the London *Standard* 'reported that I was Dead. Thousands send me prescriptions!!' He was visited by a mad lady in a chaise, but he endeavoured to deter *his* young lady,

> I regret that my increasing years and occupations render me so unfit to attend upon a Young Lady! But I have frequently stated the same to you – I am not a Young Man!

One summer Angela took a house on Walmer Beach so that they could be close but observe the proprieties. Another summer she went to Ramsgate. He wrote so many loving letters to her that he was worried in case they went astray. 'I should not like to see any of them published which would be the wretched consequence of any of them falling into any hands but yours.'

When she was away he longed for the return 'of his companion whom I look at and caress who is happy and delighted and smiles on me in return!' He gave her much advice about her health – the old soldier knew all about keeping feet dry and warm.

The wide variety of interesting subjects for debate continued 'The little question 'Why?' is not easily answered, always brings people up very short and forces them to reflect.' He said of the execution of Marshal Ney, 'I did not consider it my duty to interfere.'

On private prayer and attending divine service; only when the queen visited Stratfield Saye did the Duke have family prayers.

He recommended Mackay's *Travels in the United States* and Francis Wyse's *America* as books for Miss Coutts to read. 'The Duke does not understand the Irish language but he knows Spanish and can read a Spanish Prayer Book; Castilian being a precise version.'

Memories of spearing a wild boar in France required a feat of horsemanship *and* management of the spear! Other topics included the Kaffir revolt in the Cape; the loss of the *Birkenhead* with hundreds of brave redcoats, the *coup d'etat* for Prince Louis Napoleon in Paris.

The queen frequently sent for the old Duke and relied on his sound advice. His visits to Windsor often meant deferring engagements with Miss Coutts, but she always had Charles Dickens to fall back on.

His deafness, despite a primitive hearing aid, made him irritable and perhaps frustrated that he was no longer a fit young man. The death of his old friend and companion Charles Arbuthnot on 16 August 1850 further depressed the Duke. His letters often alternated between the loving and the irascible but they always ended with the words 'God Bless you, Dearest, with much affection Wn,' which was his greatest accolade. When Angela was ill early in 1851 he was as tender and thoughtful as always.

I am very happy to learn that you are satisfied with the tickets for the House of Lords. To be sure! It does amuse me mightily at times to find a veteran eighty two years old, deaf with all! turned into a lover.

There were rumours in both families of a secret marriage and on his death she was treated almost as though she was his widow. Think of his warm letters, the winding staircase to his private rooms at Stratfield Saye and the inter-twined locks of their hair. It is an intriguing thought but there is no hint of marriage in their intimate correspondence and it would have been out of character for the Duke to take part in such a clandestine activity!

In May of that year he was responsible for the security of the Great Exhibition and paid many visits to it. On the night it opened Angela gave him a large birthday banquet with all his friends attending.

In the last two years of his life he was involved, unbelievably, with three more ladies. The second young Mary Lady Salisbury, 'My dear' Mrs Jones at Pantglas, and the curious affair of Lady Georgiana Fane.

The first time that the Duke danced in England after Waterloo was with Lady Georgiana Fane at a ball at Apethorpe, whilst cousin Harriet Fane danced with Georgiana's father. Fanny, Lady Salisbury in March 1834 commented on Lady Georgiana's never ceasing to pour her eloquence into the Duke's ear 'It won't do'. She used to go riding with the Duke to the Surrey zoological gardens and they both admired a young orang-utan wrapped in a flannel. The Duke talked about all the strange Indian animals he had encountered.

Three years later Fanny, Lady Salisbury was delighted to pull the Duke's leg as gossip announced his imminent marriage not only to Miss Jervis but also to Lady Georgiana Fane. The Duke was beside himself with laughter. But not for long! A few years later the persistent lady trapped him after a church service at St James, Piccadilly and caused a scene. On Waterloo Day in 1849 he wrote to all his more staid lady friends asking them to refrain from inviting Georgiana with them to Apsley House. To Angela Burdett-Coutts he wrote, 'I have refused to receive my lady and have requested Lady Charles (his daughter-in-law who lived at Apsley House) not to receive visitors. Allow me to ask this favour.'

> My dear Lady Charles (Sophia Pierrepont) I have long been under the necessity of declining to allow this house to be made a shew on the 18th of June. People however still persevere! and this morning I learned that Lady Georgiana Fane, knowing that I will not receive her visits, intends to apply to you to receive her! I shall be very much obliged to you if you will refuse to receive her *on this day* . . .

But even worse was to follow. Charles Greville recounts how the Duke was manoeuvered into a terrible pickle.

> The Duke of Wellington has got himself at 82 years of age into, if not a scrape, an embarrassment, with Lady Georgiana Fane who is half-cracked. It seems that he has for some years past carried on a sort of flirtation with her and a constant correspondence writing her what might be called love letters and woefully committing himself. He has now broke with her and she persecuted him to death she is troublesome and He is brutal and will not see her or have anything to do with her. She tries to get at him, which it seems she can only do as he comes out of Church (early service) at St James, and she made a scene here not long ago. She says all she wants is that he should behave *kindly* to her, which is just what he will not do.
>
> Meanwhile she has placed his letters in the hands of her solicitor, Mr Frere (an outrageous thing) who tells her they are sufficient to establish a case against him for a breach of promise of marriage. Nothing of this queer but lamentable affair seems to have got out, and for the credit of the Duke it is to be hoped it may not. It would be painful to see him an object of ridicule and contempt in the last days of his illustrious life. My mother told me the story. She had it from Lady Georgina Bathurst to whom Lady Georgiana Fane herself told it and showed her the Duke's letters wanting her to get the Duchess of Gloster to read them, who, however, declined to do so. He has always had one or more women whom he liked to talk to, but the strangest of all his fancies was this tiresome troublesome crazy old maid.

Margaret Charlotte Jones was a handsome young matron in her early twenties with three small children, Lilla, Louise and Albert, when she first met the Duke a year before his death. Her husband was an MP and she was the niece of Lord Campbell. She was a popular society lady, a well known hostess, gifted conversationalist, and travelled on the country house circuit from her home at Pantglas in Herefordshire. In her frequent absences the children were looked after by their governess Madame Laure Simon. During the summer they took lodgings in Biggin Street, Dover, where the Duke sometimes visited them.

This quite innocent relationship was cruelly reported by Mrs Effie Ruskin (supposedly an acquaintance of Mrs Jones) to her mother after the Duke's death:

> It is much better that he is dead for this Love Affair he had with Mrs Jones during his last season was very unbecoming. He always was in love with someone but had never made himself ridiculous till this one which was a source of great grief to his family and made him laughed at by every empty-headed fool in London ... At every party Mrs Jones and the 'Dook' were ushered in together. As she has never been known to blush since she came to town, I daresay she will feel no remorse at all for making the last years of so great a Hero contemptible, when perhaps she might have done him some lasting service.

Mrs Ruskin was in the same class as Charles Greville for malevolent 'Duke-watching'. She had one more anecdote to relate. 'Why is the Duke the rudest man in London?' 'Because he always comes into a room with his Hat On!' – a snide reference to the chatterbox Miss Hattons with whom Mrs Ruskin had seen the Beau 'flirting away tremendously' in 1850.

Angela Burdett-Coutts left England on 3 September for a four-month tour of Germany and France and their correspondence continued on a less intimate note. The Duke attended his last Waterloo banquet in 1852 where he put on a brave show with his splendid uniform with dozens of decorations and orders. In the summer he was as usual at Walmer. Angela's companion Mrs Brown was seriously ill and the proposed visit to Dover was postponed. On 14 September the Duke died peacefully.

Lord Douro, the new Duke, wrote to Angela that he was giving copies of Wellington's death mask 'to no other ladies but you – that is votre affaire.' She attended the funeral with the Wellesley ladies and later commissioned a marble work of the Duke's hands – those which had written her nearly a thousand letters.

Chapter Twenty-Seven

THE SECOND LADY SALISBURY

Hatfield House had always been a refuge since a young man called Mr A. Wesley, a cousin of the Cecils' rode to hounds with the indomitable dowager Lady Salisbury well before the end of the eighteenth century. When the Sepoy General returned home to a reluctant marriage, the Salisbury country house was Wellington's second home. His friend James, Lord Salisbury and his sweet beautiful wife Fanny had provided sanctuary for Wellington for twenty years, until she died in October 1839. James, now Lord Lieutenant of the County and a prosperous businessman, father of six motherless children, married for the second time at the age of fifty-six. His second bride, Mary Sackville-West was thirty-three years younger than the marquess. She was the second daughter of George John West, 5th Earl De La Warr and their marriage took place at Knole in 1847 (the year in which Wellington received an offer of marriage from Angela Burdett-Coutts).

The Beau had known the second Marchioness of Salisbury since she was a small girl. She came of a large family of six brothers and two sisters, and Lord Byron had christened her as the 'Fair Euryalus' in his *Childish Recollections*. Like Lady Shelley she was a country woman, who wore plain short stiff skirts, thick boots and her dresses were made of calico, spotted muslin and spring chintzes (a more elegant version of Kitty Pakenham). Unlike Kitty she was a very pretty girl with beautiful eyes, a French and German linguist, and the skill to be a superb hostess at Hatfield and Knowsley. The Salisbury balls were attended by four or five hundred people, and entertainment was her forte.

Lord De La Warr had soldiered with Wellington at Fuerte Guinaldo in the Iberian campaigns. But the links with the new bride went back to 1835 when she was a child of eleven,

I recollect your standing on my knee in the open carriage and your delight with the cheers of the mob and the horses of the yeomanry galloping about the carriage at Bourne and Cambridge.

Lady Mary was a harder more ambitious wife than the warm, beautiful first wife, Fanny Salisbury, but she was indubitably under the old Duke's spell. Not only were her first three children named after the Duke – Sackville Arthur born in 1848, Mary Arthur in 1850 and Arthur born in 1851; but she convalesced after each confinement at Walmer Castle. Every summer she and her offspring spent happy weeks there and the old Duke regarded them as his own grandchildren. 'Mary Arthur now has teeth', 'Sackville's digestion not up to scratch', 'Sackville has symptoms of measles'. He designed medals for them made up of shillings and ribbons, and allowed 'Your Babes' to romp where they wished. He devised a baby jumper machine for them to be suspended safely from the ceiling. The conqueror of Europe was such a genial lover of very small children.

In her old age in 1896, as Lady Derby, she reminisced to her family that she regarded the Duke as an intimate friend, and that she knew him well for twenty years until his death in 1852. She said that she owed more to him in forming her character than to anyone else. She never heard him say a severe or unkind word. He was very good and sympathetic to small children.

> It is to the Duke that I owe the best of the good I have learnt and in especial the forgiveness of injuries.

He came to see her when she was very unhappy at the death of her eldest brother and said to her 'I shall write to you every day, it may amuse you.' He kept his word and either saw her at the London house in Arlington Street, or at Walmer Castle, or else wrote to her everyday. In town they would take 'quarter-deck exercise every day with him in St James Park.'

The letters from the Duke to Lady Mary that have survived are for the last three years of his life from 1850–52. At that time his correspondents included Angela Burdett-Coutts, My dear Mrs Jones, Anna Maria Jenkins, his niece Lady Burghersh, Lady Shelley and Lady Jersey. In terms of the wide variety of subjects covered, the letters to Lady Salisbury must rank very high.

It was only to be expected that he would write about death. His own brothers and sister had faced the reaper, but the loss of Charles Arbuthnot was a bitter blow. Charles had been not only a great friend of nearly forty years duration, but he also possessed a natural gift for reconciliation. Over the years the Duke's forthright comments and brusqueness often needed someone to tidy up after him, and this Charles did uncommonly well. The old Duke wrote of him,

Poor fellow, I really believe that he would have died sixteen years ago when he lost his wife, if I had not gone on to him from Hatfield when I was apprised there of her death. I have kept him alive and in general good health and tolerable comfort ever since.

Charles Greville wrote in his diary 'Gosh (Arbuthnot's nickname) *fidus Achates*, the Duke's second self from whom he seems to have no secrets hid.'

There were many other deaths recorded by the old Beau. That of Sir Robert Peel, the Duke of Cambridge, the king of Hanover, King Louis Philippe, Sir Willoughby Gordon, Lord Alford and his sister-in-law Lady Mornington.

On the brighter side – and Wellington was rarely gloomy or depressed other than after the carnage of battle – he went to many marriages and christenings. He took much pleasure in being asked to give away in marriage the pretty young society ladies, usually the daughters or occasionally granddaughters of his equally old friends. Lord Lonsdale's daughter and two of Lady Pakenham's daughters, but 'the handsomest of the three was Miss Prudence Leslie' (known as Britannia.) One of his quips was 'I believe the mob took me for one of the Bridegrooms in my usual bridegiving dress!' Queen Victoria asked him to stand as godfather to Prince Arthur and he admitted to her 'I have an immoderate number of godchildren.'

His social life, despite his half-hearted protests, was still enough to daunt a much younger man. He still went to assemblies at Lady Wilton's, Lady Hardwicke's and Lady Jersey's. He went to *thé dansant* at Mrs Granville Harcourt's (but unexpectedly made no wry comments). He frequently took his comely, childless daughter-in-law Lady Douro to concerts and to the opera. He took Lady Jersey to the Royal Exhibition, which as the Queen's Ranger of the Parks was one of his responsibilities. He was asked to many balls, and recorded visits to that given by the queen and Duchess of Invernesss. He gave one himself at Apsley House for the Duchess of Cambridge and Princess Mary. He visited the Royal Academy and gave dinners there to Lady Douro and Lady Jersey. He went to the cattle show, to Madame Tussaud's, to a private play at the Duke of Devonshire's and a concert at the Duke of Beaufort's. Despite his increasing deafness, he appeared to enjoy himself considerably.

He was always now welcome at Windsor and he reported to Lady Mary his reception by the queen and Prince Albert. Little Prince Arthur received birthday presents, called Wellington the 'Duke', and gave him very tolerable military salutes. The small child gave him in return a nosegay and the royal parents presented him with a portrait of his royal godson. He attended the queen's fancy dress ball with Lady Douro, who was disguised in a wig.

Not only was he needed at the palace, but visiting royalty made a point of seeing the grand old military man. The queen 'of the French', the Duchesse d'Orleans, the Comte de Paris, the Duc de Nemours and Prince Frederic of the Netherlands all made a point of meeting him either in London or at Walmer Castle, conveniently close to the Channel ports. The Russian Grand Duchess Catherine and Prince George of Mecklenberg came to see him and he dined with them and Count Brunow.

Sometimes he confided some of his problems to Lady Mary. Sir Walter Scott had accused him of having caused his soldiers in the Peninsula to have women flogged.

> What makes it worse he was an intimate acquaintance and friend of mine and lived with me the whole time he was at Paris collecting these lies. He was of a class not a little numerous in the world of which the Individuals prefer Fiction to Fact upon military affairs and operations.

The Duke was still needed to make political and military recommendations. His old friend, Sir Harry Smith (and Lady Juanita Smith) had problems in the Cape and the Duke wrote a paper on the subject for Sir John Pakington. The queen asked his advice about a replacement C. in C. for India.

As Constable of the Tower he took military reviews of the Scotch Fusilier Guard in the Tower of London, and inspected the 30th Rifles at the barrack yards at Walmer. As ranger of the royal parks the safety and protection of people and buildings was his responsibility, and his letters to Lady Mary were full of references to them.

Painters and sculptors flocked to Walmer and despite his many grumbles the old man enjoyed their attentions. 'I considered what Hannibal and Caesar had done. They must have had a Painter and a Sculptor on the Establishment.' Like all old soldiers he had his ritual grumbles 'In short I am used for all purposes as usual!' As always, he had plenty of *bons mots*. Writing of the new submarine telegraph cable 'Electric Telegraph is certainly wonderful. I confess that I should not be surprised if I lived to fly in the air,' and 'Election results, a choice between Bribery and Ruffianism.' 'I detest the Railroads', and he was amused by 'the Bloomer discussions being somewhat of a Taylor;' but on reflection, he tended to disapprove of the new ladies fashion of bloomer underwear!

Personal gifts were exchanged. Lady Salisbury was given a pattern for a waistcoat 'better without buttons', a pedometer for the country lady to measure her daily walking mileage, a pin cushion and a piece of Irish Cambric. The Duke showed rather unexpected talents for poetic descriptions,

> never saw the Castle looking so well. The fields at the back of the beach were quite green, the sky without a cloud, the sea calm and blue, everything in tranquility. I walked on to the Tower above, and on the platform below, and reflected on what had occurred since these same scenes had been inhabited by you. It is certainly a most delightful residence.

One of his most touching letters to Lady Mary was written in the autumn of 1850.

> You are very kind to me my dear Lady Salisbury. I appreciate your confidence as it deserves and I trust I shall never abuse it. I am sensible of your kindness in manifesting it. You are aware how highly I appreciate it and how happy the manifestation of it makes me.

Preservation of health had always been an important factor to him – for himself, his troops and now for his friends. He produced some odd remedies. Rubber gloves for Lord De La Warr to keep colds at bay. Always rub one's skin with vinegar and water 'friction with vinegar' was important. He frequently suffered from appalling colds and fevers, and increasingly now from catarrh and rheumatism in the neck and shoulders,

> I certainly am a good doctor, at least for myself, [he claimed] but my deafness is terrible to myself as well as to everybody else. . . . My only remedy is temperance and keeping the skin in order by ablution and friction. I eat very little and never eat or drink anything that can disagree with my stomach. . . Consequence always well, never fatigued and can do anything!

At the age of eighty he was out with the Harriers, shooting pheasants at Stratfield Saye, riding twenty miles a day and walking in the parks with his pretty ladies. Most of his letters, including his last to Lady Mary on 13 September 1852, concluded,

> God bless you my dear Lady Salisbury, with my constant wishes for your children, believe me as ever. Yours most affec. Wa. P.S. The wind has changed to the West, but it is cold.

He died the next day.

Chapter Twenty-Eight

QUEEN VICTORIA – 'SEND FOR THE DUKE'

Just before the Congress of Aix La Chapelle, the Duke and Duchess of Kent visited the Duke of Wellington at Valenciennes. He was still commander-in-chief of the Allied army which was due to disband in November of 1818. He gave the recently married, but mature couple a splendid dinner and ball. The bride, née the dowager Princess of Leiningen, waltzed only a little because she was pregnant with the future Princess Victoria who was born eight months later. It was appropriate that Wellington was present at the London accouchement on 24 May of the next year when the Duchess was delivered of a healthy child, 'a pretty little Princess, as plump as a partridge.'

According to Charles Greville, King George IV, who disliked the Duchess of Kent, was always talking of taking her child from her. He would probably have done so, but for the Duke of Wellington. He saw the young child quite often – once at the royal lodge on 2 August 1826. 'The little Princess is a delightful child. She appeared to please the King . . .'

When the princess was eighteen a grand ball was given for her by her mother the Duchess of Kent. The Duke of Wellington was at Kensington Palace to greet her and it was noticeable that he treated her with particular deference. The princess danced with the Duke of Brunswick and five princes of various ages including Albert. When she succeeded to the throne in June 1837, society thought that she would send for the Duke to lead her government and Lady Salisbury staked 5 shillings on its happening. But it was her favourite Lord Melbourne who retained the premiership and the Duke wrote 'She is surrounded by Whigs and Whiglings male and female and nobody knows anything excepting gossip!' At her first Privy Council on the 21st which he attended, the Duke was full of praises 'that if she had been his own daughter he could not have desired to see her perform her part better.' Croker recalled that the Duke said 'she not merely filled her chair, she filled the room.'

She wanted to ride at a Hyde Park army review and the Duke's advice was sought. He thought that it was 'unsuitable for her to attend on horseback in company with men only.' Did he recall the heady days of 1815/16 when the beautiful spoils of war accompanied him as private ADCs on his grand reviews?

Charles Greville, as clerk to the Privy Council, commented,

> Everything is new and delightful to her. She is surrounded with the most exciting and interesting enjoyments: her occupations, her pleasures, her business, her Court, all present an unceasing round of gratifications. With all her prudence and discretion she has great animal spirits and enters into the magnificent novelties of her position with the zest and curiosity of a child.

Lady Salisbury noticed at the queen's coronation in June 1818 that the applause was so tremendous as the Duke touched the crown that 'Lord Melbourne coloured and grew pale again.' Wellington received the loudest cheers and looked embarrassed that they were for him and not for the queen.

When Lord Melbourne resigned in May 1839, the queen was truly heartbroken – she really thought her heart would break and besought him 'You will not forsake me'. Melbourne suggested that she should bring Wellington back in his place and on 8 May they had a twenty-minute interview. The Duke said that at his age of seventy and with increasing deafness she should send for Sir Robert Peel, a man of honour and integrity. The queen asked Peel to form a government but thought him a cold, unfeeling, disagreeable man! It must have been a great temptation for the Duke to have another few years serving his country and his queen.

At a Privy Council in November the queen,

> appeared to look out for me when she came into the Council Chamber and was satisfied when she saw that I was present. H.M. read Her Communication perfectly. She was as cool and collected as she had been upon all the former occasions that I had seen her in Publick.

In his letters to Mary Stanley, Lady Wilton, the Duke frequently mentions his visits to the queen and the growing romance with Prince Albert who, 'danced, waltzed, sang with the Queen. He has been greatly favoured! But all this is not marriage . . .'

Next February the queen was very angry with the Duke. She had had a difficult time with the so-called scandal of the wretched Lady Flora Hastings' illness (suspected pregnancy, and death in agony of a large tumour); the queen's bedchamber ladies (Peel wanted to change some of them); and the Sir John Conroy affair (the queen's mother's fraudulent business manager). The Duke was in the background of these royal problems giving, as ever, sound shrewd advice, which was not always acceptable to a strong-willed nineteen-year-old girl. The queen attempted to have a Bill steered through parliament for Prince Albert's naturalization. She wanted him to be given rank and therefore precedence immediately after herself for the whole of his lifetime. The Duke and many other peers objected and the Bill was defeated comfortably.

The queen said she would never look at the Duke again. She would not invite him to the Chapel Royal in St James for her marriage. 'I was perfectly frantic' she wrote in her diary 'this wicked old foolish Duke, these confounded Tories. . . . I cried with rage.' She called him 'That Old Rebel'. He took it all in his stride and said almost proudly 'I hear that our Gracious is very much out of Temper.' Greville told Lord Melbourne, knowing that he was still the queen's favourite minister, 'She will get into a great scrape. The people of England will not endure that she should treat the Duke with no respect.' Shortly afterwards the Duke dined at the palace and Greville reported 'She has endeavoured to repair her former address by every sort of attention and graciousness to which he is by no means insensible' (March 1840).

In the spring of 1840, after the marriage, Prince Albert came to Wellington's concerts and went shooting with him. In August the Duke was reporting to his main confidante Lady Wilton that,

> H.M. was certainly five months gone with child – God knows! I told you I believe that I thought she was grown taller and that she looked more like a Woman than she had appeared to be when I had seen her before.

Four days later he went to Windsor and announced,

> I never was so well received. I sat next to the Queen at Dinner. She drank wine repeatedly with me. In short, if I was not a Milksop I should become her Bottle Companion. It is impossible to be in better Humour than she was with me. Prince Albert and King Leopold visited me in my room yesterday. . . .

So all was forgiven.

He was now in great favour and represented the queen's father-in-law at the Princess Royal's christening in December 1840. 'I must be in favour to be thought of as a Beau Pere' and several years later he represented Prince Charles of Leiningen at the infant Prince Alfred's christening on 6 August 1844, her fourth child and second son. The Duke stood behind the queen holding up the sword of State.

The Duke was at Woburn Abbey in July 1841 and rode in the queen's suite 'on Her Airing to visit the Evergreen Drives'.

The Duke was mobbed by the loyal and noisy crowd.

> I was literally hunted, run hard through the Park by people in carriages, on horseback and on foot! The Queen appears to have been in good humour with everything. She has been remarkably civil to me. The first night we sat round a table while H.M. was looking over the pictures in a book. H.M. did the same last night.

During September and October he was at Windsor to see the queen and Prince Albert. 'H.M. was souffrante and they were apprehensive that she would be prematurely confined.' The Duke went out with Prince Albert with his Harriers (aged seventy-two). To Lady Wilton he reported, 'A Prince at 12 minutes before eleven. He is as red as a lobster!'

In November 1842, the queen asked if she could borrow Walmer Castle and she took the young Prince of Wales with her. The crowds were immense,

> continual cheers, wreaths, bonfires, triumphal arches, peals of church bells and cannons, and shouts to see the royal infant.

The Duke met the royal party in Dover, rode before the queen's carriage into Sandwich and reached his seaside castle ten minutes before HM did.

> Her Postillions (her own) drove Her very badly into the Gate of the Tower. She stuck in it and was obliged to get out of the Carriage – I believe that the Children were carried over the bridge! [The Duke described – almost with glee – the total confusion] Abigails, Maids, Nurses, of all Ages and descriptions running about . . .

The queen asked the Duke to dine and sleep there but he declined!

The next year in midsummer in a gale and strong winds, the Duke went to Southampton to meet the queen to escort her from the railway station to the docks, on board the admiral's bridge to the royal yacht. The queen planned to sail across the Channel to meet King Louis Philippe at Eu castle via Weymouth, Plymouth and Brighton. Two weeks later on 13 September the Duke boarded the *Ariel* steam packet off the south foreland to meet his sovereign on the new royal yacht called the *Victoria and Albert* where he was well received. He stayed on board for four hours and predictably, 'Her Majesty saw me get a complete Ducking on the Bottom of the ladder of the Yacht'. On his arrival on shore he was soaked by several more breakers, but was none the worse for it.

At a Windsor Park review in June 1844 for the Emperor Nicholas of Russia, since the queen was heavily pregnant, the Duke ordered the artillery *not* to fire the royal salute until the queen had left. However the gunners fired the salute at the wrong moment. The queen was very amused but the Duke stormed at the artillery and in a rage ordered them back to barracks.

Undeterred by her experience at Walmer Castle, the queen was determined to pay the Duke a visit at Stratfield Saye. By this time she was very fond of her distinguished old warrior, but she did not realise, as he did, that the Duke's country seat was very modest indeed compared to Walmer and Hatfield. His housekeeper Mrs Apostles, who had been there since the Duke bought Stratfield Saye, wept bitterly at this unexpected (and unwanted) honour. She told him, 'My Lord, Your House is a very Comfortable Residence for yourself, your Family and your Friends, but it is *not* for the reception of the Sovereign and Her Court,' to which his lordship agreed 'Very true! But HM coming is decided and what cannot be prevented must be borne!'

The Duke's expertise in administration was demonstrated again. He was the perfect host, showed her to her room, fetched her for dinner, helped her to tarts and pudding, talked to her rather loudly after dinner on the sofa, and escorted her to her bedroom with five lighted candles. Prince Albert sang duets, played tennis and billiards indifferently. The queen asked him not to go shooting with her consort a second day in the rain, so he obeyed and 'stayed at Home. I think that the Result of this visit will be that the Prince will have a Tennis Court at Windsor which will be a vast relief to the habituées of the Castle!' Then there was a brouhaha about the Duke's 40-ton bronze statue. The queen and Prince Albert objected not to the sight, but to the site adjacent to the palace. Letters were politely exchanged and the statue, christened the Archduke, stayed where it was for another thirty-six years.

At the end of the next year the queen sent a message to the Duke begging him to remain as army commander after Peel's resignation. 'The Queen appeals to the Duke's so often proved loyalty and attachment to her person in asking him to give her this assurance.' Wellington after many weeks of negotiations persuaded Peel to resume government, which was what the queen, Wellington and Peel all wanted anyway. But their party fell again in the summer of 1846 and the Duke at the ripe old age of seventy-seven decided to leave politics and army command.

The queen stood godmother in May 1847 to his grandchild, 'Lady

Arthur's little girl, Victoria Alexandrina a very pretty little child'. A few years later, the queen's seventh child and third son was born on the Duke's eighty-first birthday. It was appropriate for the Duke to stand as godfather and see the child baptised as Prince Arthur.

> *Queen Victoria's child Prince Arthur*
> by WM. THACKERAY
> The Royal Prince unto
> the Gallant Duke did say
> 'Dear Duke, my little son and you
> was born the self-same day.
> The Lady of the land
> My wife and Sovring dear
> It is by her horgust command
> I wait upon you here.
> That lady is as well
> As can expected be
> And to your Grace she bids me tell
> This gracious message free
> That offspring of our race
> When yesterday you see
> To show our honour for your Grace
> Prince Arthur he shall be.
> You fought with Bonypart
> And likewise Tippoo Saib
> I name you then with all my heart
> The Godsire of this babe.'

The queen wrote of the Duke in 1850, 'How Powerful and how clear the mind of this wonderful man is, and how honest, loyal and kind he is to us both.'

The year before he died, the prime minister, Lord John Russell, resigned and the queen could find no one suitable to take his place. So Wellington was asked to visit her and give his advice.

'Is your Majesty dissatisfied with your Ministers?'

'No.'

'Then you had better keep them.'

So Russell stayed on for another year until Lord Palmerston brought him down.

As noted, the Duke had been made ranger for the royal parks and the planning for the Great Exhibition in Hyde Park brought him many headaches, including squatters, Arab encampments, dangerous foreigners and protection to Buckingham Palace, the Houses of Parliament and the Glass Crystal Palace itself. One story has it that the queen asked for his advice on the sparrows nesting inside the new Glass Palace.

'Send for the Duke.'

'Try sparrow-hawks, Ma'am' – and that problem was solved. On his birthday, 1 May 1851, he toured the exhibition, arm-in-arm with Henry Paget, Lord Anglesey. The queen wrote in her diary, 'What a touching sight.'

On the Duke's death on 16 September 1852 the queen wrote to his younger son, Lord Charles Wellesley.

The Queen cannot let any one but herself express to Lord Charles Wellesley her deep grief, her unfeigned sorrow at the immense loss the whole Nation and herself have experienced in the death of his dear, revered and great Father! The Queen is so stunned by the awful suddenness of this sad event that she cannot believe in the reality of it and cannot realise the possibility that the Duke of Wellington, the greatest Man this Country ever produced, is no more! To the Country his loss is irreparable but not less so to the Crown – who possessed in him the most devoted loyal and faithful servant and one of his staunchest supporters! To the Queen personally he has ever been a kind and true friend and a most valuable Adviser. It is dreadful to think that all this is gone!

Chapter Twenty-Nine

EPILOGUE

Once the Duke said to Harriet Arbuthnot, 'No woman ever loved me, never in my whole life.' He very rarely talked nonsense but that statement is absurd. The truth is that the Duke was such a strong independent character that in his view he did not need or require love from anyone else. After the deaths in action of many of his close and intimate friends, he would be in great distress, might perhaps weep for a moment, but like an indomitable gun-dog, would shake himself and get on with living. Living was a challenge – the enemy on the other side of the hill, a political problem, the challenge of a beautiful woman – and this book has identified many ladies with whom the Duke had a significant relationship.

The evidence is that although he felt the loss of Harriet Arbuthnot acutely, and also that of Fanny, Lady Salisbury, and indeed went into formal mourning for both of them, his heart was not deeply involved. The loss of friendship, the fireside warmth and the near-matrimonial relationship were blows. But the Duke had been absorbing bitter blows all his life from the moment his mother made it obvious on many occasions that he was a distinct disappointment to her, until the last moment when Charles Arbuthnot passed away in Walmer Castle.

The many years of campaigning in India and the Peninsula had blunted whatever deep sensitive emotions he may have had for the opposite sex. And the evidence points only to one woman that he *truly* loved – Mary Anne Patterson, née Caton.

The Duke was the most experienced military campaigner in Europe and he would never allow himself to be pushed into a corner. Possible avenues of advance and retreat were essential for the survival of himself and his army. Inevitably, he would bring the same strategies into the hectic social life into which he was thrown from 1814 onwards at the age of forty-five! Although he complained about his inadequate marriage with Kitty to his close friends Mrs Arbuthnot and Lady Shelley, the evidence is that he thoroughly enjoyed a situation whereby he considered himself totally free to make his own life outside Stratfield Saye.

During the last thirty-eight years of his life, from 1814 onwards he never had less than three or four ladies to whom he was addressing himself as a close personal friend – *at the same time*. Moreover in the background were the reliable ladies at whose firesides he knew he would always receive a warm welcome – Lady Charlotte Greville, Lady Frances Shelley and Lady Sarah Jersey.

After Kitty's death the candidates to become the second duchess increased dramatically, but there was not the slightest chance that the Duke wished to 'surrender' his independence. There were a dozen ladies who pressed their claims, but the hermit crab was lucky – there were three shelters for him – at Stratfield Saye, Walmer Castle and Apsley House. Despite rumours and gossip the old campaigner was taking no chances at all, or at least not in the matrimonial stakes.

Sir Robert Peel, who had a high regard for the Duke, wrote to his wife on 10 November 1830:

> No man has any influence with him, he is led by women: the foolish ones envelop him with incense, and he has fallen a victim to this weakness and to his own vanity.

He might have been 'happier', if that can be quantified, with Mrs Patterson, Lady Charlotte Greville or Mrs Arbuthnot, if the dice had been shaken in a different way. But it is most unlikely. He did not want to be tied down to one domestic hearth. All his life he was on horseback, skirmishing, feinting, before the occasional set-piece battle. His life was one of restless movement. Even in his eighties the movement was continued with people of all ages from royalty to tiny tots visiting him, and he in turn on the move for a day or so to Windsor or Hatfield or Dover before retreating to one of his fortresses.

Thomas Raikes' diary described the Duke's life at Walmer in 1843. He rose at six in the morning, walked on the platform and ramparts, returned to dress and shave himself (which took a long time). He was remarkably neat, always wearing a white waistcoat and trousers under which he wore a good 'guard of fleecy hosiery' against the cold. He put on a blue riding coat for his morning ride. At ten o'clock he ate a good breakfast, with messes of rusks and bread in his tea, never meat or eggs. He was talkative at breakfast discussing plans for the day. From about eleven until two he would be in his study examining his huge mail, writing many letters himself and dictating to Algy Greville the gist of answers to others including charitable gifts. At 2.00 p.m. he would get on his horse and ride on the Downs or gallop into Dover on Cinque Ports business as the warden. On his return he would walk again around the castle ramparts until it was time to dress for dinner at 7.00 p.m. Having had no meal for nine hours he would make a modest meal of meat, rice (from Indian days) and vegetables into a 'mess which fills the plate'. In his old age he drank little wine, but drank two decanters of chilled water during the evening before going to bed at about 11.00 p.m. He needed little sleep and usually much less than the conventional seven hours.

When there were men only for a meal he would dress in boots, but with ladies present he would wear shoes, silk stockings and possibly wear his Star and Garter in the evening. Raikes commented that he was exceedingly polite to all and particularly attentive to women. He was '*la vieille coeur personnifiée*'. Aged seventy-four when Raikes wrote,

the Duke was active, hair quite white but not scanty, very deaf in the left ear – by himself he stooped very much, and his head drooped on his breast, but when interested his eye brightened and he cupped his right ear to catch the sound. When he examined his mail in the morning there were momentary fits of anger and excitement . . .

Benjamin Robert Haydon, the painter, described in 1839 the Conqueror of Napoleon . . .

> his mind is unimpaired, his conversation powerful, humerous, witty, argumentative, sound morals. 'Twas a noble head. I saw nothing of that peculiar expression of mouth the sculptors gave him, bordering on simpering. His colour was beautiful and fleshy, his lips compressed and energetic. He looked like an eagle of the Gods, who put on human shape and had got silvery with age and service. Riding had made him rosy and dozy and his colour was fresh . . .

And Byron wrote, 'Proud Wellington with eagle beak, so curled that nose, the hook whereon he suspends the world.' Byron had little respect for authority. The Beau was an aristocrat to the marrow of his bones, unflinchingly honest, unaffected and loyal with a high sense of duty – all anathema to Lord Byron.

One visitor to London in 1848 was amazed to 'see well-bred ladies stretch out their hands to touch the hero as he passed down the stairs',

> like a silver penny at a royal ball – the very essence of spotless neatness with his blue coat, red ribbon (Spanish Golden Fleece) and splendid diamond order and his silver hair most carefully brushed – a perfect picture, his benevolent expression has all the *iron* worked out of it. His face is as fresh as a young man's. His large forehead has but few wrinkles. He does not show the wear and tear of time and thought.

Charles Greville in his diaries wrote five full pages on the Duke's character, and after his resignation as premier in 1830 a further four pages on his political merits and demerits. The biographical notice in *The Times* on the Duke was composed by Mr Delane and the feature article by Mr Reeve. Both notices were submitted in the first place to Greville for his views and comments before printing. One of the key phrases that Grevillle used was 'The Duke was a good-natured *but not an amiable man, he had no tenderness in his disposition*'.

Thomas Carlyle's imaginative description of the old Beau at Lady Ashburton's ball in 1850 is the most appropriate for the end of this Epilogue.

> Rhapsodies! Truly a beautiful old man – I had never seen till now how beautiful and what an expression of graceful simplicity, veracity and nobleness there is about the old hero when you see him close at hand. His very size had hitherto deceived me. He is a shortish, slightish figure about five feet eight, of good breadth however and all muscle and bone. His legs I think must be the short part of him, for certainly on horseback I have

always taken him to be tall. Eyes beautiful light blue, full of mild valour, with infinitely more faculty and geniality than I had fancied before. The face, wholly gentle, wise, valiant and venerable. The voice too as I again heard is 'aquiline clear' perfectly equable, uncracked that is, and perhaps almost musical but essentially tenor or almost treble voice – eighty-two I understand.

He glided slowly along, slightly saluting this and that other, clear, clean, fresh on this June evening itself, till the silver buckle of his stock vanished into the door of the next room and I saw him no more.

BIBLIOGRAPHY – MAIN SOURCES

The Journal of Mrs Arbuthnot (1950)   Francis Bamford & Duke of Wellington
The Game of Hearts, Harriette Wilson & Her Memoirs (1957)   Lesley Blanche
Comtesse de Boigne Memoires (1907)   Ch. Le Boigne
Correspondence of Lady Burghersh with the Duke of Wellington (1903)   Lady Rose Weigall
The Capel Letters 1814–17 (1955)   Marquess of Anglesey
Thomas Creevey Papers (1904)   Sir H. Maxwell
John Wilson Croker Papers 1808–1857 (1967)   Ed. by B. Pool
The Diaries of Madame D'Arblay 1854
Life of Georgiana Lennox Lady de Ros (1893)   Mrs J.R. Swinton
Memoirs of George Elers 1777–1842   Monson & Leveson Gower
La Chanteuse de l'Empereur (La Grassini) (1949)   R. Jeanne
The Greville Memoirs 1817–60 (1938)   L. Strachey & R. Fulford
Reminiscences of Captain Gronow (1964)   John Raymond
The Duke (1931)   Phillip Guedalla
B.R. Haydon Correspondence and *Table Talk 1876*
Warriors in Undress (1925)   F.J. Huddleston
Miss J., letters from the Duke of Wellington (1924)   C.T. Herrick
My dear Mrs Jones, letters from the Duke of Wellington (1954)   Ed. Mrs Davies-Evans
Letters of Lady Sarah Lennox; Ilchester & Stavordale (1901)
Life of Wellington (1899)   Sir Herbert Maxwell
The Years of the Sword (1969)   Elizabeth Longford
Pillar of State (1972)   Elizabeth Longford
Granville, Correspondence (1916)   G. Leveson Gower
Diary of Philip von Neumann 1819–50 (1928)   E.B. Chancellor
Princess Lieven Letters 1812–34 (1902)   L.G. Robinson
The Gascoyne Heiress, Life & diaries of Lady Frances Salisbury 1802–39 (1968)   Carola Oman
Life of Angela Burdett-Coutts (1953)   Clara Patterson
Lord William Russell correspondence (1972)   G. Blakiston
Salisbury, Letters of the Duke of Wellington to Mary, Marchioness of Salisbury 1850–52 (1927)   Lady Burghclere

Diary of Frances Lady Shelley 1787 (1912)   R. Edgcumbe
Conversations with the Duke of Wellington 1831–51 (1947)   Philip Henry Stanhope
Madame de Staël, Correspondence with the Duke of Wellington (1962)   Victor de Pange
The Man Wellington (1937)   Muriel Wellesley
Wellington in Civil Life (1939)   Muriel Wellesley
Wedderburn-Webster Trial (1816)
Thomas Raikes Journal 1831–47 (1856)

CREDITS

The index was compiled by Gillian Delaforce.

The publishers would like to acknowledge the following for the use of the illustrations: Mary Evans Picture Library: The young Arthur Wellesley; Harriette Wilson and the Duke of Wellington; the Duchess of Wellington; Madame de Staël; Guiseppina Grassini; Duke of Wellington; the Marchioness of Wellesley; Harriet Arbuthnot; the Countess of Jersey; the Countess of Wilton. The Mansell Collection: Lady Caroline Lamb; Madame Récamier; Baroness Burdett-Coutts. Lady Charlotte Greville from Goodwood House by Courtesy of the Trustees. Lady Salisbury, National Portrait Gallery, London, reproduction by courtesy of the Marquess of Salisbury. Princess Lieven, the Tate Gallery, London.

Please note that where material appears within square brackets within the quoted matter, these are the author's insertions.

INDEX

Notes W = Wellington; page numbers in bold indicate main biographical details.